rand Portage
lational Monument

MAJOR HISTORIC SITES
IN MINNESOTA

★ MAJOR HISTORIC SITES

☆ ASSOCIATED HISTORIC SITES

— — — ★ TWIN CITIES SITES

Chapel of St. Paul
Falls of St. Anthony
Fort Snelling
Minnehaha Falls
Minnehaha Depot
Indian Mounds Park
Minnesota Capitols
Old Mendota
Ramsey House

Carver's Cave
Stone Arch Bridge

Publications of the

MINNESOTA HISTORICAL SOCIETY

RUSSELL W. FRIDLEY
Editor and Director

JUNE DRENNING HOLMQUIST
Managing Editor

COMPLETELY REVISED
SECOND EDITION

Minnesota's
MAJOR HISTORIC SITES
A Guide

By June Drenning Holmquist and Jean A. Brookins

MINNESOTA HISTORICAL SOCIETY   •   ST. PAUL   •   1972

⬙ Preface

THE FIRST EDITION of this book was published in 1963 in response to numerous requests for brief, accurate information on Minnesota's historic places. Readers' reactions were indeed gratifying, and after the book went out of print, the Minnesota Historical Society received continuing requests for a second edition. Because of the first guide's wide acceptance and because a great many exciting things have happened in the field of historic preservation since 1963, the society in 1970 asked the authors to revise and update *Minnesota's Major Historic Sites*.

The result is virtually a new book. A larger page size has been adopted enabling us to add many new illustrations. The text is grouped into four geographical divisions — the Twin Cities, Central, Southern, and Northern Minnesota. Each section is introduced by a revised map locating the places discussed in the pages that follow. The text and illustrations explain the significance of each site, tell how to reach it, and describe what can be seen there. In this new edition, forty-five major sites are treated at some length, fourteen associated places are more briefly described, and at least twenty other points of historic interest are mentioned. Six new sites (pages 51, 79, 84, 98, 101, 103) and two associated places (pages 40, 47) have been added; their presence reflects the phenomenal growth in historic preservation and interpretation that has occurred.

The section devoted to Southern Minnesota is perhaps the most greatly changed. Here the chapter formerly entitled "Sioux Uprising Sites" has been rewritten to focus on the Upper and Lower Sioux agencies and Fort Ridgely, and the story of the Dakota Indians in Minnesota has been expanded and broadened to give what we think is a more accurate view of their past in this portion of the state.

We have also added a "Selected Bibliography" for those readers whose appetites are whetted for more detailed information. Far from being a complete collection of source materials, the list contains only published books and articles and does not include the voluminous and important manuscripts in the Minnesota Historical Society from which we gleaned considerable information. Among the manuscript collections extensively used (and often representing months of research time) were the papers of W. H. C. Folsom, the two Charles A. Lindberghs, Alexander Ramsey, and Henry H. Sibley, plus those compiled during the 1930s and 1940s by the Works Progress Administration in Minnesota.

In addition, all of the material throughout this text has been carefully scrutinized, rechecked, and often rewritten in the light of fresh information and research. Mistakes pointed out to us by kind readers have, we hope, been corrected. The status of several sites changed during the past decade, and new information updating the original text to 1972 has been diligently sought and incorporated. For whatever errors that persist or have been unknowingly added to the second edition, the authors are, of course, responsible.

The process of gathering information was made easier by staff members of the historic sites department of the Minnesota Historical Society, a department that did not exist in 1963. What the authors undertook in 1958 and completed four years later — a survey of historic sites in Minnesota — is now updated annually by the historic sites department, which also operates and interprets more than a dozen historic sites for the public's enjoyment and education. For their co-operation and assistance in the preparation of this edition the authors are grateful to Donn M. Coddington, supervisor of historic sites; Nancy Eubank, interpretation supervisor; John F. Grossman, historian for Fort Snelling; Loren C. Johnson, director of restoration; Janis K. Obst, curator of historic houses; and other members of the department who contributed bits and pieces of sometimes elusive data.

We are indebted, too, to Minnesota Historical Society archaeologists Alan R. Woolworth, David W. Nystuen, and Gordon A. Lothson, who patiently explained the technicalities of their specialized field; to John H. Martin and Milton Krona in the Minnesota division of state parks and recreation for cheerfully supplying up-to-date answers to our many inquiries; to Professor Elden Johnson, state archaeologist, who provided expert advice and guidance on the state's prehistory, thus saving us from numerous *faux pas*.

Once again we acknowledge our indebtedness to the society's director, Russell W. Fridley, whose counsel and encouragement never failed; to Lucile M. Kane, manuscripts curator, and James Taylor Dunn, recently retired chief librarian, for their continued interest and for sharing their knowledge of the Twin Cities and the St. Croix River Valley; and to the staffs of the society's audio-visual and manuscripts departments for making segments of their vast collections available to us. Other present or former co-workers who offered helpful suggestions are Rhoda R. Gilman, Helen M. White, Viki L. Sand, and Ralph K. Shaver. Special thanks go to Dorothy P. Kidder and Virginia L. Rahm for research assistance and proofreading chores. And to Phyllis N. Sandstrom, the publications department's extraordinary typist, we offer bouquets and gratitude for producing successive versions of the manuscript without complaint and with great speed.

Most of the present-day photographs in this second edition are the work of two fellow Minnesota Historical Society staff members: Alan Ominsky, production supervisor in the publications department, who also created the book's new design and was responsible for the maps, and Eugene D. Becker, the society's chief photographer. We want to record our debt also to several members of the historic sites staff for allowing us to use their photographs — Nancy Eubank, Loren C. Johnson, Alan R. Woolworth, and David W. Nystuen, who wins the prize for dedicated effort and the longest walk with his photo of Minnesota Point Lighthouse. We are grateful to Gordon A. Lothson for his valuable advice and for his photographic studies of the Jeffers Petroglyphs. Unless otherwise credited, all of the photographs in this book may be found in the society's picture collection.

And to the many people throughout Minnesota who contributed by letter and conversation to the mass of information necessary for this book, we again say thank you. We sincerely hope this second edition will lead you and other Minnesotans to a greater enjoyment and understanding of the state's historic heritage.

St. Paul, Minnesota
June 27, 1972

June Drenning Holmquist
Jean A. Brookins

Introduction

IT COMES as no great surprise that in an age of upheaval such as this country has experienced during recent years Americans are increasingly aware of and interested in the past. Sweeping changes in the nation's social fabric have forced most Americans to re-evaluate or reinterpret the values, institutions, and priorities established by earlier generations. With large segments of the population constantly on the move, community and family ties are strained if not broken. Society is fragmented by specialization, dehumanized by technology, and individuals in alarming numbers feel a loss of identity and a lack of continuity in their lives. Even the natural environment is threatened with irreversible change. In the hope that it will inject some meaning into uncertainty, people reach backward into history to establish their own links with the past. Nostalgia for the "good old days" is increasingly apparent. Young men and women, rejecting the materialistic culture they were born into, seek to experience the basic life style of their forebears. Symbolically, Americans in larger numbers than ever before are not only visiting the landmarks of the nation's heritage, but are eager to become personally acquainted with the histories of their towns, their counties, and their states — no matter how short the period of their residency.

Today many visitors to historic sites are searching for answers to the eternal questions of Who am I? Where did I come from? For them the historic spots tangibly recall the aura of a vanished past. They show how people lived, worked, played, or died, and they help young and old alike, as few books can, to visualize the past from which we have all emerged. The site may be a rocky prairie like the Jeffers Petroglyphs in southern Minnesota revealing the art of a forgotten people. It may evoke the personality of a man, as does the gracious mansion built in the heart of the Minnesota wilderness by Henry H. Sibley, the fur trader who became the state's first elected governor. It may be the lakeside farm on which Peter Gideon developed the Wealthy apple or an underground mine on one of the iron ranges which substantially influenced the economic growth of the state. Whatever its character, the historic site often suggests a world long vanished. It may, however, bring to life a world that has only recently passed from the scene — a world that is, nevertheless, as remote to our children as that of the mound builders seemed to our grandfathers.

Like the first edition published in 1963, this book has been prepared for the growing thousands who seek a deeper understanding of their heritage in the places where history happened. When the authors tackled the task of revising the 1963 edition, they quickly found that the historic sites scene in Minnesota had changed dramatically in the nine years since the first work appeared. So much had happened, in fact, that what started out as a simple revision became a new book. Some of the background events that made necessary this extensive revision and the addition of six major sites not included in the 1963 version may be of interest.

From 1958 to 1962 Mrs. Holmquist and Mrs. Brookins conducted the first state-wide survey of historic sites since the Works Progress Administration's work in the 1930s. The findings of their survey were of considerable consequence. One result, of course, was the first complete and authentic guide to the state's most important historic sites — the first edition of this book. But the survey was perhaps even more valuable as the basis on which to initiate a program of historic sites preservation in Minnesota. It pinpointed the weaknesses and strengths in the preservation picture of the state. It provided factual evidence about which sites were irretrievably lost, which of those that remained had potential as public sites, and which were threatened with destruction. It also made quite clear the shortcomings in the limited programs of historic interpretation in the early 1960s.

In 1963, the very year the first edition of this book appeared, forward-looking people in the Minnesota legislature passed a landmark bill relating to historic places in the state. This unique bill, called the Minnesota Omnibus Natural Resources and Recreation Act, was important for two reasons: (1) it recognized historic sites as a valued natural resource in Minnesota, and (2) it opened a significant source of funds to support the state's long-range program of historic preservation, restoration, and interpretation. Three years later the United States Congress passed the National Historic Preservation Act, which lent substantial strength to the emerging historic preservation plans of the states.

These two bills, plus later legislation, have made possible several encouraging accomplishments in Minnesota. The first was a follow-up survey of historic sites which expanded on that conducted earlier by the authors. The findings of the survey were published in 1963 by the Minnesota Outdoor Recreation Resources Commission in a report entitled *An Historic Sites Program for Minnesota*. In it, seventy-nine historic sites selected by the Minnesota Historical Society were identified, located, appraised, and described. This list, which is updated and revised annually, now comprises the official State Registry of Historic Sites and Places. The most recent inventory, completed in 1971, contains 177 entries representing fifteen major themes in the state's history. A similar catalog of sites, known as the National Register of Historic Places, is administered by the National Park Service. Sites entered in these two lists have limited protection augmenting their chances for survival against thoughtless destruction. For example, public works projects that could negatively affect the historic character of sites owned by the state or by municipalities must have the approval of the Minnesota Historical Society before they are initiated.

In 1969 the state legislature assigned additional responsibilities to the Minnesota Historical Society, the institution which now co-ordinates all state activities in the field of historic preservation. Many of the major historic sites owned by the state and formerly managed primarily by the Department of Natural Resources are now administered by the society. Development and maintenance of historic markers are now part of the program of the society's historic sites division, which is also responsible for administering federal funds and distributing grants-in-aid for historic preservation in the state.

A significant increase in state funds and a modest increase in federal monies have brought new vigor to institutions and organizations involved in the acquisition, development, and restoration of historic places in Minnesota. Several major sites have been acquired by the state since 1963, when Minnesota's preservation program looked forward to motivating a state-wide effort to save for interpretive purposes most of the seventy-nine places identified in the survey report. Among them are the Marine Millsite at Marine on St. Croix; the Grand Mound in Koochiching County; the Morrison and Stumne mound groups in Otter Tail and Pine counties; the W. H. C. Folsom House in Taylors Falls; Dr. W.

W. Mayo's home in Le Sueur; and the Lower Sioux Agency near Redwood Falls.

Local and regional agencies, some with the assistance of state grants-in-aid, have rescued such sites as the covered bridge at Zumbrota, a former opera house in Lake Benton, the E. St. Julien Cox House in St. Peter, and the Sinclair Lewis Boyhood Home in Sauk Centre. On the endangered list ten years ago, the Lewis House was purchased, restored, and opened to the public by the Sinclair Lewis Foundation; it is now an award-winning example of what a group of dedicated, organized citizens can accomplish with adequate support and professional guidance. One type of structure that has fared better than most in the fight for survival is the community depot. Preserved early railroad stations in Duluth, St. Louis Park, Askov, Hinckley, Minneapolis, and Moorhead will serve to remind future generations of a transportation system that is quickly passing from the scene.

But the hard economic facts of historic sites preservation have dictated a major revision in the state's original program. The hope of preserving most of Minnesota's best historic sites simply cannot materialize. With the wisdom of ten years' experience, we have had to become more realistic about what the preservation of a public site entails. In many ways, the initial salvaging of a site is the easiest phase in a lengthy process. It is the ongoing maintenance, interpretation, and operation of the historic site that is enormously expensive. For this reason, the idea that a large number of sites could be utilized as interpretive laboratories for the teaching of history has also been abandoned. In the 1970s the long list of possible places to be developed will be narrowed to focus on only those of the highest quality and potential.

It may be that future decisions on whether to develop a historic site will rest ultimately on its ability to illustrate a theme crucial to the state's history. Currently, the state registry includes sites representing fifteen such themes — aboriginal cultures (prehistoric and historic), agriculture, architecture, commerce, education, immigration, industry, literature and the arts, medicine, military, natural history, politics, religion, and transportation.

The sites described in this book represent fourteen of these themes, although some assignments are arbitrary. More often than not, a historic place reflects more than one theme. Old Mendota, for example, can be assigned to five themes: the fur trade (commerce), the influx of settlers (immigration), the establishment of St. Peter's Catholic Church (religion), and the frontier home of Henry H. Sibley (architecture, commerce, and politics).

The story of a first-rate historic site is inevitably many faceted, encompassing the diverse lives of the people inhabiting it and broadening in wider ripples to reflect a region, a nation, a time in history. At Old Fort Snelling the interpretive program, which was begun by the Minnesota Historical Society in 1966 and which is the most extensive in the state, is a prime case in point. The original fort existed as some seventeen structures standing on a ten-acre plot and enclosed by a stone wall. When its restoration is completed in 1977, Old Fort Snelling will look physically as it did about 1825, a fine example of a restored frontier post. But what of the 250 military men who garrisoned the fort? What of the women and children who lived there and the civilians who worked as sutler, school teacher, or preacher? Their stories, too, are told at Old Fort Snelling, where the activities they undertook are performed by modern-day frontiersmen. While restoration efforts continue, visitors to the fort become acquainted, via authentically costumed personnel, with the soldiers, cooks, laundresses, candlemakers, bakers, and blacksmiths who peopled the post. A fife and drum corps performs the music played a hundred and fifty years ago. Muskets and cannon are fired, filling the air with the same acrid smoke familiar to the drilling soldiers of the 1820s. Visitors will also learn that the United States government built this northwesternmost fort at the junction of two major rivers to control the fur trade, whose profits were sought by both the Americans and the British, and to keep an eye on the belligerent activities of the Chippewa and Dakota Indians, who were invited to meet with the United States Indian agent living near the fort's walls. The presence of the fort also encouraged adventurous frontiersmen and entrepreneurs to settle in the area. Thus various themes of Minnesota's history merge in the story of Fort Snelling.

Similar though perhaps less ambitious interpretive programs have been initiated by the society at thirteen other major sites described in this book. Because of limited space, these stories cannot be told in their entirety. Rather these chapters should serve primarily to give an overview of the state's history and to pique the readers' curiosity about the motivations and personalities of the men and women associated with the sites, about eras long past, and about the relationships of these places to today's world.

As the state's program matures, new ideas in preservation and interpretation are being pursued. In 1971 the state legislature established twenty-one historic districts in an effort to preserve certain areas of unusual historic or architectural value which represent elements of the state's social, cultural, economic, religious, political, and aesthetic heritage. Control over the protection and perpetuation of the districts was assigned to local boards or commissions to be named by the governing bodies of the subdivision of the state in which the historic district is located. By implementing this legislation, such areas as the birthplace of Minneapolis — located within the new Falls of St. Anthony Historic District — may yet recapture some of their historic character and atmosphere.

In the field of interpretation, the Minnesota Historical Society is developing a plan for regional interpretive centers, wherein the story of a site is expanded to weave together several major themes relating to the place or personalities concerned. At the Lower Sioux Agency, for example, visitors will learn not only what took place on the Dakota reservation from 1854 to 1862, but will also be informed about the history of the Dakota Indians in Minnesota from the time of their first contact with white men to the present day. (The Lower Agency interpretive center also is indicative of the tardy attention finally being paid to the state's pluralistic cultures, those of the Dakota Indians at the agency and of the Chippewa at the Mille Lacs Indian Museum.) In the same manner, the prehistory of Minnesota will be explained and illustrated in regional centers proposed by state archaeologist Elden Johnson. One such center has already been erected by the Minnesota Department of Natural Resources at Big Stone Lake State Park near the western border. A second is under construction at Mille Lacs-Kathio State Park in central Minnesota. It has been proposed that others be built near the Jeffers Petroglyphs in the southern part of the state and in the Red River Valley region.

DESPITE OBVIOUS ACHIEVEMENTS, the total picture of historic preservation in Minnesota has its darker side. There remain sites of major importance that have not been assured a place in the future program. What will become, for instance, of the St. Paul homes once occupied by James J. Hill, Frank B. Kellogg, and F. Scott Fitzgerald? We can be grateful that the historic elements of the magnificent state capitol in St. Paul have been placed under the guardianship of the Minnesota Historical Society, which conducts a tour program to enrich visitors' understanding of this beautiful and complex structure designed by Cass Gilbert. But how can we stop the accelerated destruction of other public and business landmarks throughout the state whose protection is most often left to local preservationists? We are now in an era when some of Minnesota's best courthouse architecture is being threatened. Many of these stately old structures will continue to fade from the landscape until contemporary or adaptive uses are found to justify their existence, or until their preservation is supported by the government.

Perhaps there are lessons to be learned from recent events in Winona County, where a thirteen-year controversy over the future of the eighty-four-year-old courthouse was finally resolved. An increasingly vocal group of local preservationists gathered force in a community divided into those supporting a plan for remodeling the building and those backing a proposal to replace the structure with a new courthouse. The question was put to a vote of the people in 1971 in a county-wide referendum, and more than 60 per cent of the voters approved a remodeling plan. The action of these citizens — young and old joined together — is a heartening reversal of a widespread American tendency to discard old architectural treasures as casually as if they were among the plastic products of our throw-away culture.

The program for historic preservation in Minnesota is aimed at the effective preservation, restoration, and interpretation of all the major themes in the state's history as revealed in public historic sites. To achieve that goal, the program in the future will move on two parallel tracks: (1) a state-administered, core program to develop the preservation and broad interpretation of sites of major historic importance, and (2) a less defined effort at the local level and in the private sector in which zoning laws, historic districts, and other controls will be employed to preserve what can be called the "historic environment" of a community.

THE FORTY-FIVE MAJOR HISTORIC SITES presented in this book were selected because they help fulfill the aims of this program and because they meet the following exacting and often overlapping criteria:

(1) SIGNIFICANCE — Although its application is unavoidably somewhat subjective, this is the factor to which greatest weight was given by the society's staff. To be included, a site or building must possess beyond question historical associations of lasting significance to the state, region, or nation. Places of importance to smaller areas, such as counties or communities, or to families were excluded. If they remained relatively unchanged, structures associated with major personalities and events in the development of Minnesota were given careful attention. While archaeological sites are less intensively dealt with than historic sites, several archaeological areas of true significance that met the other requirements have been included.

(2) INTEGRITY — Tangible evidence of factors that gave a site its importance must remain. If a structure, it must be on its original location and it must retain large portions of its original character, including authentic atmosphere. Changing uses (from private residence to gas station, for example) or removal from their original sites disqualified many structures. The architectural significance of a building was not considered as such. It is felt that this topic deserves a separate study. Architectural details are, however, discussed in the text where pertinent to the building's historic values. Museums were not construed as bona fide historic sites and were included only when the site itself was of major importance — such as the Mille Lacs Indian Museum which constitutes an integral part of the site's interpretive features. Physical setting was also given weight in determining the sites that were chosen. Did enough survive to make a visit meaningful? Some sites — like Fort Beauharnois, whose location on Lake Pepin has never been precisely identified — were included because of their significance and the evocative value of their settings.

(3) IDENTIFICATION AND INTERPRETATION — Certain sites which would have qualified for their significance had to be disqualified because they lacked identifying markers. In general, a site having a few tangible remains must be identified to merit inclusion. Thus the birthplace of Minnesota and the "boom site," both at Stillwater, Carver's Cave in St. Paul, and the Browns Valley Man site in Traverse County all warranted comment because they carry identifying markers. The site of Joseph Renville's early fur trade post on Lac qui Parle Lake, although mentioned in the text, could not be considered a major site because it lacked an interpretive marker and it is not easily located.

(4) ACCESSIBILITY — The site must be open or accessible to the public. If it is privately owned, the owner must be willing to admit the public at least on a limited basis. Several significant sites that had to be excluded from the first edition because they were inaccessible now appear in this book — the Folsom House, the Sinclair Lewis House, and Mayowood, for example.

NO PUBLICATION of this kind could be compiled without recognition of those organizations and individuals responsible for the preservation of the places portrayed. The Minnesota division of state parks and recreation is the public agency which has preserved the greatest number of important historic sites. Minnesota's park system was born in 1889 when Camp Release, one of the places associated with the Sioux War of 1862, was purchased by the state. The creation of Itasca State Park in 1891, however, firmly established the principle that the state should acquire and maintain parks. The movement at Itasca was led by a committee of the Minnesota Historical Society headed by Jacob V. Brower, whose vision of what Itasca Park could mean to the state and nation caused him to persevere in the face of many discouragments. Thus, the desire to preserve historic sites may be said to have provided the initial impetus for a state park system in Minnesota. Now more than thirty parks, waysides, and monuments exist largely because of their historic significance.

During the past decade, Minnesota's legislatures — always pressed for funds — have wisely risen above immediate considerations of economy to safeguard remnants of the state's heritage by providing increased funds for preservation and a program of archaeological study.

Many other groups have shared in the preservation effort over the years. The now defunct Minnesota Valley Historical Association marked battlefields associated with the Sioux War of 1862 while memories of that bloody conflict remained vivid; the Minnesota Daughters of the American Revolution rescued decaying Old Mendota, providing a pioneering stimulus to save other historic places in the state; the Minnesota Knights of Columbus reconstructed in part Fort St. Charles located in the upper reaches of the Northwest Angle; the Minnesota Highway Department erected numerous markers that provide "roadside history" for millions of motorists who travel the state's trunk highways each year; and the Works Progress Administration assembled valuable research materials in the 1930s which greatly enriched available information on Minnesota's historic places.

The steadily growing programs of Minnesota's county historical societies must also be applauded. Their responsibilities for the preservation of local history will become increasingly critical within the long-range program that will co-ordinate efforts in preservation and interpretation at all levels — federal, state, and local.

Indeed, much has been accomplished during the past ten years. Problems have been identified, a state-wide consciousness of preservation needs has been quickened, a number of threatened major historic places have been salvaged, and interpretive programs have been launched. The decade of the 1960s may well be remembered for its attention to historic preservation. May this momentum continue in the 1970s!

ST. PAUL, MINNESOTA   *Russell W. Fridley*
May 30, 1972

Contents

MAPS

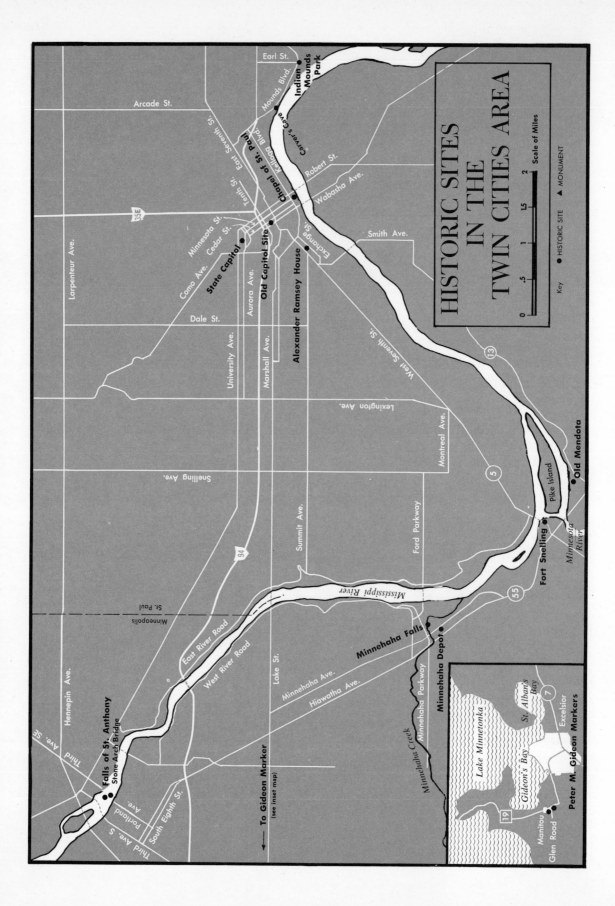

HISTORIC SITES
IN THE
TWIN CITIES AREA

Key   • HISTORIC SITE   ▲ MONUMENT

Scale of Miles

0   .5   1   1.5   2

Earl St.
Indian Mounds Park
Mounds Blvd.
Carver's Cave
Arcade St.
Robert St.
Wabasha Ave.
Chapel of St. Paul
East Seventh St.
Kellogg Blvd.
Tenth St.
35E
Smith Ave.
Minnesota St.
Cedar St.
Como Ave.
Exchange St.
State Capitol
Old Capitol Site
Aurora Ave.
Alexander Ramsey House
Larpenteur Ave.
Dale St.
University Ave.
Marshall Ave.
West Seventh St.
13
Lexington Ave.
Montreal Ave.
Old Mendota
Snelling Ave.
Summit Ave.
5
Pike Island
94
Ford Parkway
Minnesota River
Fort Snelling
55
Mississippi River
East River Road
West River Road
Minneapolis
St. Paul
Minnehaha Falls
Minnehaha Depot
Lake St.
Minnehaha Ave.
Minnehaha Parkway
To Gideon Marker
(see inset map)
Hiawatha Ave.
Hennepin Ave.
Falls of St. Anthony
Stone Arch Bridge
Third Ave. SE
Third Ave. S
Portland Ave.
South Eighth St.

Lake Minnetonka
St. Alban's Bay
Gideon's Bay
Excelsior
7
Minnehaha Creek
19
Manitou
Glen Road
Peter M. Gideon Markers

Historic Fort Snelling

Located in Fort Snelling State Park on the south side of the Twin Cities. Accessible from state highways nos. 5 and 55; the route is well marked.

FORT SNELLING, the state's first military post, is the historic site most intimately associated with Minnesota's beginnings. Before its establishment in 1819, the Minnesota country was a wilderness inhabited by scattered fur traders and the Dakota (Sioux) and Chippewa (Ojibway) Indians. Located at the strategic junction of the Minnesota and Mississippi rivers, Fort Snelling was part of a comprehensive system of forts proposed by the United States war department after the War of 1812 to block British infiltration and use of key waterways in the Northwest. Such posts, strongly garrisoned, would, it was hoped, counteract British influence among the Indians and protect and encourage the American fur trade. Because a proposed post on the Yellowstone River was not established, Minnesota's first fort became even more important as the nation's northwestern-most military outpost from 1819 to 1849 (when Fort Ripley was built). Although Fort Snelling was never attacked, it stood as an effective symbol of American authority over the vast region peopled by Indians and fur traders. For nearly thirty years it paved the way for white settlement of lands extending from Fort Crawford (at present-day Prairie du Chien, Wisconsin) northward to the British border and westward to the Pacific Ocean. The old fort area, preserved today within Fort Snelling State Park, is a National Historic Landmark and has been designated by the legislature as Old Fort Snelling Historic District. A multimillion-dollar program to restore and reconstruct the post to its original appearance was well under way in 1972. Three structures built by 1824 — the round and hexagonal towers and the commandant's quarters — still stand; they are the oldest existing buildings in Minnesota. The officers' quarters, which is also considered an original structure, was rebuilt in 1846.

The United States government showed interest in establishing a post in Minnesota soon after it acquired most of the area in the Louisiana Purchase. In 1805 the war department dispatched Lieutenant Zebulon M. Pike (later famous as the discoverer of Pikes Peak) to explore the upper Mississippi. The young army officer was instructed to select a site for a future military post. He held a council with the Dakota on the island in the Mississippi opposite Mendota which now bears his name. For $200 worth of rum and gifts plus a promise of an additional $2,000, Pike purchased from them tracts of land that included the commanding hundred-foot bluff where Fort Snelling now stands. Twelve years went by, however, before the government took the next step. Then Major Stephen H. Long was sent to survey the lands Pike had bought. He suggested

1

FORT SNELLING *in 1851 is depicted in almost photographic detail in this oil by Seth Eastman which hangs in the nation's Capitol in Washington.*

the exact site on which Fort Snelling was later built, and the war department made plans to erect a fort near the junction of the Mississippi and Minnesota rivers.

In August, 1819, Lieutenant Colonel Henry Leavenworth, commanding troops of the Fifth Infantry, arrived at the junction of the two rivers with orders to build a permanent military post. With him came Indian agent Thomas Forsyth, whose mission was to inform the Indians of the prospective fort and the benefits it would bring them and to distribute $2,000 worth of goods and trinkets which Pike had promised fourteen years earlier. The garrison of over two hundred soldiers spent its first winter in miserable log huts at Cantonment New Hope, located on low ground opposite the present fort near what is now Mendota. Plagued by scurvy and other diseases which caused the death of many men, the troops moved in the summer of 1820 across the river to Camp Coldwater, so named from a clear, cold spring that still exists along the Mississippi about half a mile upstream from the present fort.

Leavenworth selected as the site for the permanent post a rise of ground some two thousand feet up the Mississippi from the bluff overlooking the junction of the two rivers. When he was relieved of his command by Colonel Josiah Snelling in August, 1820, he had not yet begun to build. Snelling rejected Leavenworth's site, deciding that the fort would be built of stone (not wood as Leavenworth planned) on the extreme point of land between the two rivers earlier chosen by Stephen Long. Construction began immediately, and one month after Snelling's arrival — on September 10, 1820 — he laid the cornerstone of the post which was at first called Fort St. Anthony.

During the next four years, the resolute commandant put his sometimes reluctant troops to work quarrying limestone from the nearby bluffs and sawing logs at a mill erected at the Falls of St. Anthony. For this extra duty, the soldiers received fifteen cents a day in addition to their regular pay of about six dollars per month. By the end of 1825 Snelling had supervised the building of seventeen structures and a diamond-shaped parade ground enclosed by a twelve-foot stone wall. He had served as both architect and construction superintendent, ably assisted by Lieutenant Robert A. McCabe, whose work brought him a promotion. Early in 1825 on the recommendation of General Winfield

Scott, who had inspected the fort for the war department, the name of the post was changed to Fort Snelling "as a just compliment to the meritorious officer under whom it has been erected."

The pioneer fort was responsible for a large number of Minnesota "firsts." Within its walls the area's first school was opened in 1823, and its first Protestant congregation organized in 1835. There the first hospital in the state was to be found as well as the first circulating library. Minnesota's first brass band played at the old fort, and its first theatrical productions were given by the soldiers there. To it in 1823 went the "Virginia," the first steamboat to reach Minnesota. In the shadow of its walls gathered the first frontiersmen who founded St. Paul and Minneapolis. Soldiers at the post were the first to keep daily weather records for Minnesota and to make use of the water power of the Falls of St. Anthony. In 1837 the fort was the scene of the signing of a treaty by which the Chippewa ceded to the United States possession of the lands between the Mississippi and St. Croix rivers — the first tract in Minnesota to be opened to white settlement. The following year Franklin Steele, the post sutler, won a race with officers from the fort to build the first claim shanty on the east bank of the Mississippi at the falls. Steele's settlement was called St. Anthony; later it became part of Minneapolis.

As an outpost of western civilization in a vast wilderness, Fort Snelling provided hospitable quarters for many explorers, missionaries, and other travelers. According to the accounts left by these visitors, the fort, along with the Falls of St. Anthony and Minnehaha Falls, was a major tourist attraction for some forty years after 1823. Helping to popularize its striking scenic features were the sketches, oils, and water colors done by such noted artists as Henry Lewis, George Catlin, J. C. Wild, and Charles Deas.

Two soldiers also left a valuable legacy of paintings of Fort Snelling and

JOSIAH SNELLING, *a veteran army officer, designed and built Fort St. Anthony and served as its first commandant from 1820 to 1827. The frontier post was renamed to honor Snelling in 1825.*

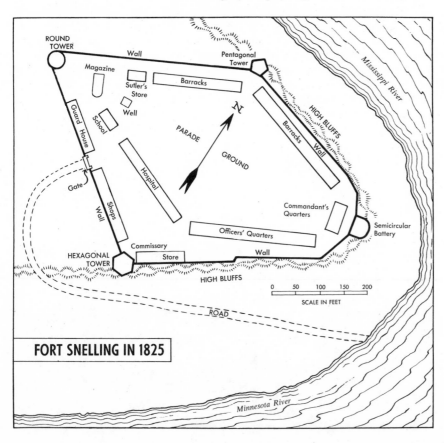

FORT SNELLING IN 1825

THE IRREGULAR SHAPE *of the fort, shown on the map at left, was chosen by Snelling to adapt it to the ground on which it was built. By 1825 seventeen structures, the wall, and the roadway had been built.*

A VIEW *of the fort from atop the round tower shows the interior as it appeared in 1852.* Harper's New Monthly Magazine, *July, 1853.*

A PHOTOGRAPH *(below) taken in 1863 provided detailed, accurate data for the reconstruction of the schoolhouse (g) and the sutler's store (f). Also shown are the round tower (p), the guardhouse (m), and several wooden structures built during the Civil War and later removed. Courtesy National Archives.*

its environs. Seth Eastman, a talented artist who was commanding officer of the post at four different times between 1841 and 1848, astutely realized that he stood at a crossroads in time. In his numerous oils and water colors he portrayed not only landscapes but recorded the customs of the Dakota and Chippewa Indians. Sergeant Edward K. Thomas, who was considered an artist of some merit during his tour of duty at the post in 1849–51, left behind at least three known panoramic views of Fort Snelling.

Other men who later became prominent national figures were associated with the fort. Zachary Taylor, a future president of the United States, commanded the pioneer post in 1828–29. Martin Scott, a notable marksman and eccentric who, like Taylor, distinguished himself in the Mexican War, had eleven years' service at the fort between 1821 and 1841. Officers who later became leaders in the Civil War included Edward R. S. Canby, Thomas W. Sherman, and Winfield Scott Hancock in the Union Army, and Simon Bolivar Buckner in the Confederate Army. Dred Scott, the slave whose case before the United States Supreme Court aroused the nation in the 1850s, was taken to Fort Snelling

by the post doctor in 1836. After his master's death, Scott began court proceedings to obtain his freedom on the ground that he had resided at Fort Snelling in free territory.

Assignment to Fort Snelling meant hard work for the soldiers, especially during its early years. Colonel Snelling, red-haired and middle-aged, was a tough-minded disciplinarian. A veteran of the War of 1812, he was a practical man who valued highly his soldiers' capacity for work but neglected the drills and smart appearances usually associated with army life. Rank and file of the garrison were kept busy maintaining or constructing buildings and roads; nurturing large vegetable gardens to supplement the diet of soup, bread, meat, and game; caring for livestock; collecting wood as fuel for the harsh winters; and standing guard. For entertainment, soldiers fished, hunted, turned to the much-used library of some four hundred books and periodicals, and attended the weekly theatricals. Dances and teas offered opportunities to meet the ladies of the fort. Artifacts retrieved in later archaeological investigations indicate that the men found relaxation in chess, dominoes, and letter writing, while the children played with marbles or dolls and the ladies sewed. What the artifacts fail to reveal is the sharply defined social gap that separated the officers and their wives from the enlisted men and their families.

Outside the fort walls a civilian population collected. By the late 1830s it numbered over 150 traders, mixbloods, refugees from Lord Selkirk's Red River Colony, and a few slaves and retired soldiers. As squatters on the military reserve, the residence of this motley group was illegal; and they were all forced to leave in 1840 after several of them were found guilty of selling liquor to soldiers and Indians. Earlier, in 1835, the fort's commandant had banned from the "Indian country" an unsavory whisky seller named Pierre "Pig's Eye" Parrant. In 1838 Parrant established his "liquid dispensaries" downriver near the site of a later settlement which at first took his name and then became St. Paul. Some refugees from the fort area also settled near the Falls of St. Anthony; still others moved across the river to Mendota. There the American Fur Company's trading post was operated by chief agent Henry H. Sibley, later Minnesota's first territorial representative in Congress and first governor of the state. Another civilian settlement close to Fort Snelling was the domain of Indian agent Lawrence Taliaferro. The several buildings of the agency had been constructed by soldiers about a quarter-mile west of the fort. With the post commandant and Sibley, Taliaferro represented the third voice of authority over the inhabitants of this wilderness.

As white settlement pushed westward and additional forts sprang up along new frontiers, the tiny communities near Fort Snelling grew to self-sufficiency and the post's importance diminished. In 1857 Franklin Steele quietly purchased the entire military reservation of six thousand acres, paying a third of the $90,000 price and planning to found the City of Fort Snelling. The following year troops were withdrawn, but before Steele's project could begin, the Civil War broke out and the state government reactivated the fort as a depot for collecting volunteer troops. (Ownership of Fort Snelling was formally transferred from Steele back to the government in 1871.) The post played its role, too, in the

LEAST ALTERED *of the fort's original buildings was the hexagonal tower, shown here after restoration work was completed.*

THE ROUND TOWER *retained its original appearance in the 1861 photograph below (left). Gutted by fire in 1869, it was rebuilt with the battlements and windows shown in a photograph from the early 1900s (right).*

Sioux Uprising of 1862. After that brief rebellion ended the Minnesota River flats below the post were for a time the site of a Dakota prison camp.

Even as troops gathered at Fort Snelling to train for service in the Union Army, the deterioration of the old post necessitated some renovations. At the same time, a vast increase in the number of soldiers stationed there demanded the construction of additional barracks and other buildings outside the walls, the beginning of an expansion that by 1900 stretched for about a mile southwest of the old fort itself. After the Civil War, the appearance of the post was further altered as a result of drastic changes in army policy. In 1881 Fort Snelling became the headquarters for the Department of Dakota, and more buildings as well as bridges and roads were built. Sections of the original walls cracked and crumbled in the 1870s and 1880s; during the latter decade the semicircular battery, the pentagonal tower, and portions of the walls were torn down. In succeeding years a street carried heavy traffic through the parade ground. The cities which the bastion had once overshadowed were engulfing the site, and it seemed for a time that the remnants of the old frontier post would not long survive.

While decay and the hands of men were erasing the outlines of Snelling's fort, thoughtful people spoke out as early as 1895 for its preservation. Not until the 1930s, however, did efforts to save what remained of the frontier post produce any tangible results. By then only a few of the fort's original features were left — the round tower, hexagonal tower, officers' quarters, commandant's quarters, and the old roadway leading from the river to the post's entrance. Working together, the Works Progress Administration, the United States Army, and other organizations renovated the round tower and made it a museum. The Minnesota Historical Society installed exhibits, and the post command furnished a custodian to keep it open to the public. This arrangement lasted until 1946 when Fort Snelling was turned over to the Veterans Administration and its career as an army post came to an end. The round tower museum, too, was closed.

Early in 1956, the old fort's survival was again threatened, this time by the state highway department's plans to construct a freeway through the site. Opposition to the plans was immediate, and Governor Orville L. Freeman,

FOUR PHOTOGRAPHS *of the fort taken in 1971 chart the progress made in its reconstruction. Below, the powder magazine and guardhouse flank the round tower. Opposite (top) uniformed guides chat with visitors in front of the schoolhouse and well house; (center) reproductions of nineteenth-century wares are sold at the sutler's store; (bottom) wooden pickets once again guard the top of the wall adjacent to the round tower.*

acting as mediator, successfully proposed to route the freeway through a 450-foot tunnel beneath the fort. In 1958 the Minnesota Statehood Centennial Commission granted the state historical society $25,000 for an archaeological investigation of the walled area of the post. The project got under way in September, 1957, and some sixteen months later the foundations of seven more original buildings had been uncovered. The Minnesota legislature moved in 1961 to preserve the site and the visible remains of the old post by creating Fort Snelling State Park, an area of 2,500 acres that also includes the confluence of the rivers, Pike Island, and the site of Cantonment New Hope.

Five years later the legislature endorsed a ten-year program of restoration and reconstruction of old Fort Snelling supported by state and federal funds and private contributions. After a year of research by a historian, an archaeologist, and a coordinator from the Minnesota Historical Society, restoration work began in 1966.

Restoration and reconstruction of the buildings was based on information gathered from army records, private letters, paintings, photographs, and archaeological evidence. Photogrammetry helped determine the original measurements of some structures and ground levels. The rebuilding process required the training of local craftsmen in the use of such obsolete tools as the adz and broadax and in the standard building practices of the early nineteenth century described in handbooks of the period. Hand-wrought rosehead nails and hardware were reproduced on the premises by a blacksmith. All the window glass was manufactured by hand in West Virginia. A supply of limestone, vital to authentic reconstruction, was located on riverbank property owned by the City of St. Paul and Webb Publishing Company who provided quarrying rights without cost to the project.

At the time of the fort's 150th anniversary in 1970, two of the four original buildings — the round tower and the hexagonal tower — had been restored. Undoubtedly the most widely known of the fort's structures, the round tower was built to command the western approach to the post from the prairies. Cannon were placed on platforms atop the roof, and muskets could be fired from loopholes placed strategically in the lower walls. During its 150-year history the tower served successively as a storage area, prison, offices, family residence, beauty shop, and museum, and it was modified numerous times. In 1862 the parapet was raised and a conical roof installed. After a fire in 1869, it was remodeled with battlements or embrasures at the top and enlarged windows. It was in this condition that the vine-covered round tower became best known as a Minnesota landmark.

The hexagonal tower had been little changed through the years and required primarily a new roof and floors to regain its original appearance. With five of its six sides extending beyond the wall, the tower was built to house twelve-pound cannons — the largest guns at the fort — which from the top level could protect about half the area surrounding the post. Loopholes in the walls at lower levels provided additional security.

Two other original buildings, the commandant's quarters and the officers' quarters, have been greatly altered and will require major restoration. The commandant's quarters, considered by some to be the oldest home in the state, was first constructed as a one-story stone building with a basement. Facing the parade ground, the top level had two large rooms, two bedrooms, and a central hall. The basement housed the kitchens and offices. Altered as early as 1833, the commandant's house had received a columned portico by 1861 and a mansard roof by 1873. The present second story was added in 1904, when the exterior was stuccoed.

The officers' quarters were originally built of wood and, like the commandant's house, consisted of one story fronting on the parade ground and a basement opening onto the lower level at the rear. Snelling described the structure in 1824 as comprising fourteen apartments, each with a living room and a bedroom on the first floor and a kitchen and pantry in the basement. In 1846 the wooden building was razed and replaced by stone quarters over the original basement. About 1904 an addition of one and a half stories was built, a piazza was added, and the exterior was stuccoed.

Along with the round and hexagonal towers, other structures reconstructed by 1975 were the powder magazine, sutler's store, schoolhouse (also used as a chapel), well house, guardhouse, pentagonal tower, shops, semicircular battery, two barracks, commissary, and the surrounding stone walls. Still to be reconstructed are the hospital and the gatehouse. When the project is completed in 1977, Historic Fort Snelling will once again crown the high bluffs overlooking the Minnesota and Mississippi rivers, providing a unique glimpse into the state's past and serving as a contrast to the fast-moving world of the twentieth century that surrounds it.

During the summer months, the fort takes on an especially colorful atmosphere when authentically costumed guides demonstrate the crafts and military practices of the post's early days. In the sutler's store, reproductions of nineteenth-century merchandise are for sale. Fort Snelling is open to the public daily from May through October. There is an admission charge. Tours for school groups are available in May, September, and October by appointment with the Minnesota Historical Society.

Old Mendota

Located on the Mississippi River a short distance south of St. Paul. Accessible from Interstate highway no. 35E and state highways nos. 100 and 13.

MENDOTA, meaning "meeting of waters" in the language of the Dakota, is the oldest permanent white settlement in Minnesota. It is also the site of the oldest private residence in the state built in 1835–36 by Henry Hastings Sibley, who has been described as "the most prominent figure in Minnesota history." Next door to the Sibley house is the stone home erected in 1839–40 by Jean Baptiste Faribault, a pioneer fur trader, and nearby is the brick house built in 1854 by Hypolite Du Puis, Sibley's secretary. Not far away stands St. Peter's Catholic Church, constructed in 1853 and now the oldest church building in continuous use in the state. Behind the village is Pilot Knob, where the Dakota gathered in 1851 to sign the important Treaty of Mendota. The Sibley and Faribault homes have been restored and are operated as museums by the Sibley House Association of the Minnesota Daughters of the American Revolution. The Du Puis house, also owned by the DAR, is now a tearoom. The Sibley and Faribault houses are open to the public from May 1 to November 1. There is an admission charge. Guided tours are offered.

Because of its strategic location at the junction of the two rivers, Mendota was frequented by fur traders as early as 1779 and possibly even earlier. Permanent trading camps were established there in the 1820s, and within a short time Mendota became one of the most important centers of the Minnesota fur trade.

Before the use of the name "Mendota" became general in the 1840s, the settlement was known variously as "The Entry" (of the St. Peter's or Minnesota River), "St. Peter's," or "New Hope." The latter was derived from Cantonment New Hope, a makeshift encampment on low ground near the east end of the present-day Mendota Bridge, which was occupied in 1819 by soldiers of the Fifth Infantry sent to build Fort Snelling. After Cantonment New Hope was evacuated in 1820, some of its wooden huts were used by Minnesota's first United States Indian agent, Lawrence Taliaferro, who maintained his agency there until new buildings were erected outside the fort's walls. The camp at Mendota was not entirely vacated until 1824, when many of the stone buildings at Fort Snelling were completed. (In 1963 the site of Cantonment New Hope was located by archaeological excavation; it is protected, though not marked, within Fort Snelling State Park.)

Old Mendota thrived on the economic activities directly related to its close associations with Fort Snelling and the fur trade. Employees of the American

9

Fur Company erected several buildings, including a large stone warehouse in 1836. In it Sibley operated a store that has been noted as "the beginning of the great commercial interests of the state." During those early days, wrote a historian, "Mendota was the only place where tea, flour, pork and other necessities . . . could be obtained." The store became a central gathering point for "Indians, Frenchmen, half-breeds, and restless wanderers from the East." In this same warehouse the first court session of the third judicial district of Minnesota Territory was held in 1849, and it was also the site in 1851 of the initial negotiations leading to the Treaty of Mendota.

Other buildings dotted the waterfront area — among them a ferryhouse and a frame warehouse where Mendota's first precinct elections were held in 1853. The Mendota ferry began operations at least as early as 1839 and provided transportation between the village and Fort Snelling until 1926. It was a vital service for both the military and the fur traders, predating Minnesota's first regularly scheduled steamboat line from Mendota to Galena, Illinois, in 1847, the area's first roads constructed in 1852, and the railroad that reached the settlement in 1865. During the Civil War years, especially, troops training at Fort Snelling were among the ferryman's most numerous passengers as they sought the diversions of Mendota's night life.

The village of Mendota was the county seat of Dakota County from 1854 to 1857. Despite the communication links with other communities provided by roads, river travel, and railroads, Mendota's golden years began to fade. Its decline paralleled the lessening importance of Fort Snelling, the disappearance of the frontier and the fur trade, and the increasing growth of neighboring urban areas. By 1887 it was described as a "quiet little village" well past its heyday. The area including the sites below has been designated the Old Mendota Historic District by the state legislature and is in the National Register of Historic Places.

OLD MENDOTA *appears as a fur trading center in a view from Fort Snelling about 1840 (above) and as the quiet location of the historic Sibley House and St. Peter's Catholic Church in 1971 (right). Oil above attributed to Seth Eastman; courtesy Thomas Gilcrease Institute of American History and Art, Tulsa.*

THE SIBLEY HOUSE has fittingly been called "the Mount Vernon of Minnesota." From 1836 to 1862 it was the residence of Henry H. Sibley — fur trader, member of the constitutional convention, delegate to Congress, civic leader, and first governor of the state. When it was constructed the house served as a center of hospitality in an unsettled wilderness; later, as the region developed, it was the governor's mansion.

The cultured and well-educated son of a pioneer Michigan judge, Sibley was a bachelor of twenty-three when he arrived at the mouth of the Minnesota River to take charge of the American Fur Company's operations in an area larger than the present state. The young man first saw the site of his future home on October 28, 1834. "When I reached the brink of the hill overlooking the surrounding country," he later wrote, "I was struck with the picturesque beauty of the scene." He went on to say that when he descended to "the hamlet" of Mendota, he "was disappointed to find only a group of log huts."

In 1835, after living for six months in the log cabin of Alexis Bailly, his predecessor as the American Fur Company's agent, Sibley gathered a crew of workers, which included both Dakota men and women, and began to build his new house. He also hired John Müller (or "Miller"), the stonemason who had built the large warehouse for the fur company.

Sibley's substantial house was built of limestone quarried on the riverbanks nearby. The outer walls and an inner one were two and a half feet thick. The beams, flooring, and window sills were fashioned of hand-hewn timber fitted together with wooden pegs. Some interior partitions were formed by placing smaller supports between the beams and then packing mud over a framework of willow branches. The ceilings were similarly made by bridging beams with lath of rushes and grass woven by the Indian women and then plastered with mud. It is thought that the house was completed in 1836.

Large for its time and place, the house had two stories, an attic, and a cellar. Originally it was probably divided into three rooms downstairs and three on the second floor. An outside stairway was constructed so that Indians could find shelter by day or night on the topmost floor of the house. At first all the cooking was done in the basement, where a stone fireplace and heavy iron hooks for hanging meat may still be seen.

A large front room on the first floor originally served as Sibley's office and trading quarters. There the Indians traded, "smoked their pipes, huddled around the stove, or lounged on piles of furs," one historian wrote. "There other traders came, some of whom had charge of posts in Sibley's vast district — Joseph R. Brown, Joseph Renville, Jean B. and Alexander Faribault, Henry M. Rice, Norman Kittson, and Joseph Rolette. There, too, the clerks sat at desks and did their bookkeeping for the fur company." A safe — "the first of its kind in the Northwest" — stood in one corner of the room.

From this substantial combination home and office, Sibley, often with "little time even to sleep or eat," as he put it, directed the fur trade of an area stretching from the Mississippi to the Missouri. Hundreds of voyageurs, Indians, and traders converged upon Mendota, bringing furs by canoe and oxcart, while workmen in the warehouse that once stood on the riverbank packed the peltries for shipment to Prairie du Chien or St. Louis. A year after Sibley's arrival the total value of the furs collected by his "Sioux Outfit," as it was called, exceeded $59,000.

The young bachelor spent his infrequent leisure time hunting with the Indians, visiting the fort across the river, or entertaining visitors. After Sibley married Sarah Jane Steele in 1843, the bachelor abode which John C. Frémont, one of the visitors, once said resembled "a hunting lodge" was transformed into a fashionable family dwelling. A small wing was added to the east side of the house for an office, and probably about this time a new section was constructed at the rear to provide a kitchen, dining room, and two additional bedrooms. From time to time Mrs. Sibley's sisters lived with the couple, and her mother

HENRY H. SIBLEY *arrived in the Mendota area as a young fur trader in 1834. He remained in Minnesota for the rest of his life, becoming one of the state's best-known citizens. This photograph was taken in 1859, when he was governor.*

THE SIBLEY HOUSE, *considered the oldest private residence in Minnesota, was built by Indian and white laborers in 1835–36. The building at right is the former washhouse, which was enlarged for a caretaker's home; beside it is the smokehouse.*

MUD FROM THE RIVER *and willow branches gathered and woven by Indian women were combined in an ingenious method of wall construction in both the Sibley and Faribault houses at Mendota.*

frequently occupied one of the bedrooms in the rear wing. The house became the center of family life, and there nine children were born to Mr. and Mrs. Sibley.

The many visitors who continued to arrive were entertained in the trader's former office, which had become the parlor. The rough walls were covered with flowered paper, and a Brussels rug and a piano, shipped from New York in 1845, testified to the home's new role as headquarters for Minnesota's polite society. When Alexander Ramsey arrived in May, 1849, to take up his duties as the first governor of Minnesota Territory, he, his wife, and infant son were the Sibleys' guests for about a month. During that time the Sibley house was the temporary capitol of Minnesota Territory, and from it on June 1 Ramsey issued the proclamation declaring the territory officially organized.

The "Squire of Mendota," as Sibley was known, was soon called upon to serve the people of the fast-developing region. He became the territory's first representative in Congress in 1849, an influential member of the convention that framed the state constitution in 1857, and the first governor of the state in 1858. In 1862, when he was named commander of the volunteer forces to put down the Sioux Uprising, he moved his family to St. Paul, where he made his home until his death in 1891.

After leaving Mendota he sold the stone house to the Catholic church, and from 1867 to 1878 the Sisters of St. Joseph conducted a parochial school there. In the 1890s it was the headquarters for a summer art school. After that it served as a merchant's warehouse and finally as an abode for tramps. The proud old house deteriorated until it seemed about to become a ruin.

It was rescued by the St. Paul chapter of the DAR, a group long interested in restoring it as a historic site. At the urging of Archbishop John Ireland, the church deeded the house to the St. Paul chapter, which then turned it over to the Sibley House Association, an organization of the state DAR. That group restored the house and opened it to the public in June, 1910.

The front room, which has been refurnished as a parlor, contains the Sibleys' music box, a melodeon that belonged to Mrs. Sibley's sister, Abbie Potts, and the chair in which Sibley was sitting when he died at his St. Paul home. In the central room on the first floor, a section of the wall has been exposed to show its construction of willow branches and mud. A walnut desk which Sibley used for twenty-two years as president of the St. Paul Gas Light Company is in this room, along with other family mementos. On the first floor, too,

THE PARLOR, *which Sibley used as his office until his marriage to Sarah Steele in 1843, has been restored to resemble the hospitable room where the Sibleys entertained.*

THE "CAPITOL ROOM," *which was added to the house in the 1840s, served as Territorial Governor Alexander Ramsey's headquarters in 1849. Sibley later used it as his office until 1862.*

are a dining room where the Sibleys' oval table and china may be seen, and a kitchen with utensils and a dry sink that belonged to the family, as well as a bird cage woven by an Indian woman as a gift for Mrs. Sibley. The office, called the "Capitol Room" presumably because Governor Ramsey made it his headquarters for a time, contains a large painting of General Sibley reviewing his troops, the family Bible, and Sibley's portable writing desk.

Three rooms on the second floor are furnished as bedrooms, and Sibley's guns, a portrait of his favorite dog, "Lion," and other items are displayed in the attic. Restored, too, on the spacious grounds are the stone icehouse, which now shelters a Concord stagecoach, and the smokehouse. The original washhouse was rebuilt and enlarged as a home for the caretaker.

THE FARIBAULT HOUSE — When Sibley arrived at Mendota in 1834, he found Jean Baptiste Faribault and his family living in a log house there. "Old Faribault," as he was affectionately known, was then a man of sixty who was well established as a fur trader. The Dakota, among whom he had traded for over thirty years, called him "Beaver Tail" because of his intelligence and fairness. Jean and several of his sons, who were also traders, were respected by the Indians, over whom they exerted great influence.

"Small of stature and gentlemanly in his bearing," Jean had been born near Quebec and had entered the Indian trade as a very young man. By the early 1800s he was trading in what is now Minnesota, where Zebulon M. Pike enjoyed his hospitality in 1805. It is said that he was loyal to the United States during the War of 1812 and that he was arrested and imprisoned by the British. After his release he is known to have lived for a time in the 1820s on Pike Island near Mendota. Apparently he moved to higher ground on the present site of Mendota about 1826, dividing his time for many years between his home there and his fur station at Little Rapids in Carver County.

On June 24, 1839, Jean Faribault contracted with John Müller "to proceed without delay to finish and perfect the stone dwelling," which was already under construction, "in the same manner" as the house he had built for Sibley. Work was to be completed "on or before the first day of June, 1840," with

THE HOUSE *Jean B. Faribault built in 1839–40 for a family dwelling and inn had been converted into a railroad warehouse by about 1907.*

at least two rooms ready for occupancy "before the winter of 1839–1840." Müller was to furnish all necessary materials and "to have the whole of said dwelling house completed at his own proper cost." If he fulfilled the terms of the contract, the mason was to be paid the sum of five thousand dollars. It is not known whether he met the construction deadline, but it is obvious that he followed building techniques similar to those he employed in erecting Sibley's home next door.

At various times the Faribault house was used as an inn, and it has been called "Minnesota's first hotel." The dual purposes of family home and inn dictated the interior arrangement of its rooms. On the first floor were a wide central hall, a billiard room, and a bar, as well as the family living room. On the second were three bedrooms and a sitting room, while the third housed a ballroom and a community meeting room. The cellar contained an auxiliary kitchen with a large fireplace, a dining room, a vault for ice storage, and storerooms for meat and vegetables. At one time the house had a wooden section at the back. In it were a dining room, kitchen, and bedrooms. Fireplaces heated the larger rooms of the home where Faribault lived with his mixed-blood wife and eight children. His eldest son, Alexander — for whom the Minnesota town of Faribault was later named — was a young man of twenty-eight when Sibley reached Mendota, and the two became lifelong friends.

Jean Baptiste was a devout Catholic, and his home was open to pioneer priests of the area. Both Father Lucien Galtier and his successor, Father Augustin Ravoux, lived for a time under his roof. For a brief period in 1842 the Faribault house served as a Catholic chapel.

Jean's wife died in 1847, and it appears that before long he moved to Faribault to make his home with Alexander. After Jean left Mendota, his grandson, George H., and others conducted a hotel in the old house for a time. Later it was sold to James McGronan, who is said to have rented out parts of it

THE FARIBAULT HOUSE, *shown at right as it looks today, was restored and opened to the public in 1937. It serves as a meeting place for the DAR and as a museum.*

until 1898. Like the Sibley house, it then degenerated to the lowly status of a storehouse.

Federal public works agencies, the Sibley House Association, and the Minnesota Highway Department rescued the home from neglect in 1934 and began to restore it as a museum. The state deeded its portion of the property to the Sibley House Association, which completed the restoration work and opened it to the public in 1937.

The house now serves as a meeting place for the DAR and as a museum of Indian artifacts. Also preserved in the home are a small commode, an octagonal table, and some dishes and flatware which belonged to the Faribault family. On the first floor are a large assembly hall, a committee room, and a library. Displayed on the second floor are the Indian artifact collections of Henry B. Whipple, a pioneer Episcopal bishop who made his home in Faribault, and of Mrs. W. O. Winston of Minneapolis.

St. Peter's Catholic Church at Mendota is the oldest church in continuous use in Minnesota. Apart from the remodeled steeple, its exterior looks much as it did when it was built in 1853.

St. Peter's Catholic Church is located on a hill immediately south of the Sibley house. The structure is the oldest church in continuous use in the state. Before it was built in 1853, Mendota Catholics worshipped in a log cabin presented to them by Jean Faribault, then in the Faribault house for a brief time in 1842, and from 1842 to 1853 in a wooden chapel constructed under the direction of Father Galtier. The new church, erected at the request of Galtier's successor, Father Ravoux, was built of limestone quarried nearby. Measuring 35 by 75 feet, it had a roof of hand-split shingles and a steeple topped by a cross. The original spire has been twice replaced, and the cross is now mounted over the door. The first pine pews have been removed, and other alterations have been made in the interior.

Pilot Knob, now the site of Acacia Memorial Park Cemetery, is located just off state highway no. 55 on state aid road no. 31 south of Mendota. The highest hill in the vicinity, it rises over two hundred and fifty feet above the Mississippi. Here Sibley probably stood when he first saw the Mendota settlement, and here Senator Stephen A. Douglas of Illinois was so impressed by the sweeping view of the countryside in 1848 that he suggested Mendota be made the territorial capital. Three years later Pilot Knob gained enduring fame as the site of the TREATY OF MENDOTA, by which the Wahpekute and Mdewakanton bands of Dakota ceded to the United States government their lands in Minnesota, Iowa, and South Dakota.

By the beginning of the 1850s, statehood for Minnesota was already on the horizon. The pressing need to open new Indian land to eager settlers and the desperate poverty of the Dakota Indians indicated to the government that the time was ripe to negotiate another treaty. The hard-fought bargaining sessions between the Mdewakanton and Wahpekute Dakota and the government commissioners began at Mendota on July 29, 1851, a few days after the Sisseton and Wahpeton bands had signed the Treaty of Traverse des Sioux (see p. 117). The council opened on the second floor of the American Fur Company's warehouse, but, oppressed by the heat and fearing the floor would collapse, the Dakota chiefs asked that the sessions be moved to Pilot Knob — their favored council ground. Consequently they adjourned to a leafy arbor built atop the hill to shield participants from the sun.

For four days great chiefs like Little Crow and Wabasha debated hotly with Luke Lea, United States commissioner of Indian affairs, and Governor Alexander Ramsey. Much of the Mdewakanton's reluctance to sign hinged on their bitterness over the government's failures to give them money stipulated in a treaty signed in 1837. Some spokesmen also feared (with good reason, as it turned out) that the new treaty would be changed once it reached Washington; others were dissatisfied with the reservation lands designated. After a three-day rest, the commissioners and chiefs reassembled on August 5. Again the Indians voiced their complaints and hesitations. Tired of the delay, the government representatives became threatening. "No man puts any food in his mouth by long talk," warned Lea, "but may often get hungry at it." The hint that provisions would be withheld was effective. Though still dissatisfied, Little Crow agreed to be the first to sign the treaty; he was followed by sixty-four other chiefs and braves.

Provisions of the treaty included a purchase price of $1,410,000; future payment in cash of annuities provided by the 1837 treaty, of which the Wahpekute would also get a share; and a reservation twenty miles wide and sixty miles long embracing the Minnesota River from Little Rock River to the Yellow Medicine. From the money, certain sums were to be expended for schools and farming supplies, for paying the Indians' alleged debts, and for provisions to see the bands through until they were settled on the reservation. The remaining amount would be invested for fifty years with the annual interest providing the cash, goods, food, and special funds that made up the yearly payment to the Dakota. At the end of the investment period, the principal sum would not revert to the Indians.

Before ratifying the two new treaties with the Dakota in June, 1852, the United States Senate removed the provisions describing the reservation lands and authorized the president to select a new home for the Indians outside the ceded territory. Later that summer Ramsey induced the chiefs to accept the amendments, despite the fact that they literally left the Dakota without a home. The next step toward implementing the treaties was to pay off the Indians' debts to traders (see p. 119). The Wahpekute had signed a traders' paper at Mendota and had paid without trouble. The Mdewakanton, however, had to be put into a cooperative frame of mind by delaying for "two or three weeks" the desperately needed annuities due them from the 1837 treaty.

Early in 1853, the president proclaimed the Treaties of Mendota and Traverse des Sioux and allowed the Dakota to move to the reservations designated in the original agreements — at least temporarily. For the first time in their long history, the Dakota Indians were to be confined within a reservation of limited size. It was surrounded by an estimated twenty-four million acres of land that now belonged to the white man.

A marker "to commemorate the Treaty at Mendota negotiated on Pilot Knob" was erected in 1922 by the Mendota chapter of the DAR.

Indian Mounds Park

Located at Mounds Boulevard and Earl Street in St. Paul.

AMONG THE FEW VESTIGES of Minnesota's prehistory located on public land are six mounds preserved in St. Paul's Indian Mounds Park atop a bluff overlooking the Mississippi River Valley. At the turn of the century, Minnesota had an estimated ten thousand artificially built mounds, most of which have long since disappeared — the victims of farming, road building, and public carelessness. The St. Paul mounds were excavated in the mid-nineteenth century and found to be burial places. Since then, widely divergent explanations of their origins have been offered.

The presence of these large mounds was first recorded by Jonathan Carver in 1766. One of the earliest white men to visit the area, Carver described them as "the burying-place of several bands of the Naudowessie [*Dakota*] Indians: though these people have no fixed residence, living in tents, and abiding but a few months on one spot, yet they always bring the bones of their dead to this place." He explained that the mounds area, which then extended all along the bluff, was the site of an annual council of chiefs, who met to "settle all public affairs for the ensuing summer." At the time of the meeting, said Carver, the Dakota brought their dead "for interment, bound up in buffaloes skins."

The mounds were first excavated in 1856 by Edward D. Neill, a St. Paul minister, historian, and founder of Macalester College. At that time there were eighteen of them; seventeen were round and one was elliptical. Neill dug into only the largest mound and found fragments of a human skeleton and some pieces of broken pottery. Ten years later four mounds were opened, and human bones, a broken earthen pipe, decayed mussel shells, charcoal and ashes, and some pottery fragments were found.

The most extensive investigation of the site was made by Theodore H. Lewis and William H. Gross from 1879 through 1883. At that time only sixteen mounds existed. One of the largest measured seventy feet in diameter and twelve feet in height. Three of the twelve mounds opened yielded extraordinary artifacts. In mound number seven the diggers unearthed a "well preserved bone implement, which had been rudely sharpened at one end as if intended to be used as an awl or perforator." A few feet deeper the men found what is believed to have been a log tomb, and below that were indications of a hearth. The second important discovery was made in mound number three. This "rare find," as Lewis termed it, was a skull which had been covered with red clay "thus producing an image of the original face." After removing the fragile clay impression, Lewis determined the skull to be that of a child about five years old.

THESE LARGE *prehistoric burial mounds in St. Paul have yielded artifacts some two thousand years old. Only six of the eighteen mounds that existed in 1856 survive today in Indian Mounds Park.*

What has been called the "most notable discovery" made by Lewis consisted of eight cists, or compartments, about seven inches deep and formed by flat pieces of limestone placed on edge. In each compartment were parts of a human skeleton; several also contained grave offerings — quantities of mussel shells, a perforated bear tooth, a crescent-shaped ornament of hammered sheet copper, about a dozen arrowheads, a lump of lead ore, and a piece of red ocher.

Later archaeologists, attempting to interpret the mounds on the basis of the scattered and fragmentary evidence available, feel that this group does not belong to any single prehistoric period. This belief contradicts an earlier theory, now considered to be folklore, that they are the work of the so-called "Mound Builders," a race which preceded Indians in the area. It is currently thought that the St. Paul mounds were built by various peoples over a long period of time, commencing perhaps with what has been termed a Hopewell culture dating from about the beginning of the Christian era. Such items as the log tomb, hammered copper, clay funeral mask, and lumps of lead ore and red ocher are related to this culture of two thousand years ago. Carver's report also leads some archaeologists to believe that the Dakota of the late prehistoric period placed their bundle burials (burials of the bones only) in mounds that had been constructed by an earlier people, and that they perhaps built some additional ones.

By 1881 more than half the mounds in this group had disappeared or had been leveled to make way for the construction of houses and streets. A move to preserve the few that remained began about 1887 under the direction of Joseph A. Wheelock, president of the St. Paul park board and editor of the *Pioneer Press*. Largely through his efforts, the park was acquired by the city

CARVER'S CAVE *was visited in 1867 as part of the observance marking the centennial of its discovery. This sketch was made at that time by Robert O. Sweeny.*

in small pieces from 1893 to 1914. It now comprises slightly more than twenty-five acres. Public picnic facilities are available.

CARVER'S CAVE — In the late autumn of 1766, Jonathan Carver, who headed one of the few British expeditions to visit the Minnesota country, arrived at what is now St. Paul. He intended to explore the area and to search for a Northwest Passage. About November 10 he stopped briefly at the foot of the bluff below Indian Mounds Park where, he later reported, he found "a remarkable cave of an amazing depth" in which there were "many Indian hieroglyphicks, which appeared very ancient." The Dakota called the cave "Wakon-teebe," meaning "dwelling of the Great Spirit." The following spring Carver returned to the cave, which was later named for him, to attend a council of some three hundred Indians. Carver says he addressed them in their native language, urging their alliance with the British.

Carver's Cave became one of Minnesota's earliest landmarks, for Carver journeyed to England, where in 1778 he published the first edition of his *Travels through the Interior Parts of North-America.* The book became a bestseller; fifty-three known editions, complete and abridged, have been printed in nine countries. It has been called "one of the most amazing travel books in American history." Carver's work was the first to advertise widely the upper Mississippi to the English-speaking world, and it aroused Europeans' curiosity about America as no other book ever had.

The volume made Carver's Cave a landmark in an unknown land, and it was sought and described by many later explorers. With the settlement of St. Paul nearly a century later, the cave became a popular tourist attraction. In the 1860s it was regarded as the foremost relic of antiquity in the region. Today Carver's Cave is inaccessible; most of it was destroyed by railroad construction in 1869 and the 1880s. A marker that tells in brief the story of the cave is located on Mounds Boulevard between Cherry and Plum streets.

The Chapel of St. Paul

Site marked on Kellogg Boulevard at the foot of Minnesota Street overlooking the Mississippi River in St. Paul.

THE CHAPEL OF ST. PAUL erected by Father Lucien Galtier in 1841 formed the nucleus of the future capital city of Minnesota and gave it a name. Today a granite boulder bearing two bronze plaques commemorates the pioneer chapel, which was abandoned as a church in 1851 and torn down at an undetermined date later in the 1850s.

The story of the chapel of St. Paul began in 1840, when Bishop Mathias Loras of Dubuque, Iowa, sent Father Galtier to Minnesota to open a mission. The young priest, who had left France for Dubuque less than two years before, began his Minnesota work in a log house at Mendota. In 1840 the commandant of Fort Snelling increased the population on the Mississippi River's eastern shore by driving squatters from the military reservation. Many of them took up claims on the future site of St. Paul. After that Galtier often crossed the river to celebrate Mass in the claim shanties. Since none of the cabins was large enough to accommodate the dozen or so Catholic families in the new settlement, Galtier decided to build a chapel.

He chose to erect it about two hundred feet from the riverbank, between present-day Cedar and Minnesota streets, on a site donated by pioneer settlers Vital Guerin and Benjamin Gervais. With an eye to the future, he rejected two other sites that were offered him — one on low ground subject to flooding and another where the shore was not suitable for a steamboat landing. "I was truly looking a head and for the future," he wrote later, and "the idea of having the church swept down towards St. Louis one day did not please me."

Settlers occupying the nearby claim shanties gathered in October, 1841, to build a chapel on the site Galtier had selected. In a few days they erected walls of rough logs fastened together with wooden pins, a steeply slanted roof fashioned of bark-covered slabs donated by a Stillwater lumberman, and benches and a floor of the same rude material. On November 1 the priest "blessed the new basilica" and dedicated it to "Saint Paul, the apostle of nations."

Galtier expressed a wish that the infant settlement be called by the same name. Since it was then known as "Pig's Eye" — the nickname of Pierre Parrant, a whisky seller with a squinting eye — the residents were quite willing to make the change. In the early years they used the name "St. Paul's Landing," then "St. Paul's," and at last simply "St. Paul." In 1850, the year after the booming town became the capital of Minnesota Territory, the region's first

THE CHAPEL OF ST. PAUL, *from which the state capital took its name, was portrayed in an oil painting by Robert O. Sweeny in 1852, eleven years after the log church was built.*

newspaper — the *Minnesota Pioneer* — recorded the change in clever verse:

> Pig's Eye, converted, thou shalt be like Saul,
> Arise; and be, henceforth — Saint Paul!

In choosing a site that could be used as a steamboat landing, Galtier was truly foresighted. Steamboats that had formerly stopped only at Fort Snelling and Mendota gravitated to the St. Paul landing, where an impressive array of warehouses soon appeared. By the 1850s, St. Paul was the busiest river town in the territory, and it proudly proclaimed that it was the "true head of navigation" on the Mississippi River. For many years it was to be the state's leading commercial city.

The town soon outgrew its pioneer chapel. Although the building was enlarged in 1847 and the bell from the sunken steamer "Argo" was installed in a belfry beside the chapel, St. Paul Catholics deserted it in 1851 for a new brick cathedral at Wabasha and Sixth streets. Before its abandonment, however, the little chapel had its moment of glory, for there in 1851 Joseph Cretin was installed as St. Paul's first bishop. For a few months after Cretin's arrival and before the completion of the new building, the log chapel bore the exalted name of the Cathedral of St. Paul.

After the new church was completed, the Sisters of St. Joseph used the chapel to house the city's first permanent Catholic school. When they, in turn, moved to new quarters in 1852, the old log structure continued to serve as the sisters' private chapel, and in 1854 they converted it into a temporary hospital when a cholera epidemic swept the city. Sometime later in the 1850s the original section of the chapel was torn down. Determined to preserve the pioneer church, Bishop Thomas L. Grace had the logs taken to the grounds of St. Joseph's Academy with the intention of rebuilding it at a later date. In 1862 or 1863, however, men working on the academy, ignorant of the bishop's intent, burned the logs to warm their coffee.

In 1941 descendants of St. Paul's pioneer settlers dedicated a marker near the site of the old chapel to commemorate the centennial of its construction. The plaques bear sketches of the chapel and of Father Galtier and the following words of the pioneer priest: "In 1841 and in the month of October I caused some logs to be cut, prepared and put up and soon after a poor church of logs and fitted so as to remind one of the stable of Bethlehem was built. Now the nucleus of Saint Paul was formed. This church thus remained dedicated to Saint Paul and I expressed the wish to call the place by no other name."

A MARKER *on the site of the Chapel of St. Paul at Kellogg Boulevard and Minnesota Street carries this likeness of Father Lucien Galtier, the city's first resident priest and the builder of its first church in 1841.*

MINNESOTA'S FIRST CAPITOL *(above), built of stone in 1853, housed both territorial and state legislatures. Two additions were constructed in the 1870s after this photograph was taken. The building burned during the legislative session of 1881.*

THE SECOND CAPITOL *(below), designed in the form of a Greek cross, was built in 1883 on the site of the first statehouse. It served only until 1904, when state offices were moved to the present capitol, and was razed in 1938.*

Minnesota Capitols

Earlier capitols were located at Tenth and Wabasha streets, St. Paul. The present capitol stands nearby at Cedar Street and Aurora Avenue. Accessible from Interstate highway no. 94, Marion Street exit.

ALTHOUGH ST. PAUL has been the seat of Minnesota government ever since Minnesota Territory was organized in 1849, the city officially received that distinction only after a struggle and retained it with some difficulty. The Organic Act establishing Minnesota Territory, which Congress passed on March 3, 1849, specified that the first legislature should convene at St. Paul. Accordingly the territorial officials appointed by President Zachary Taylor made their way to the village at the head of navigation on the Mississippi River. Governor Alexander Ramsey arrived in May from Pennsylvania, and Charles K. Smith of Ohio, the newly named secretary of the territory, followed in July. Secretary Smith secured rooms in the Central House, a hotel on the riverbank at the foot of Minnesota Street, and there the first territorial legislature met on September 3, 1849. In succeeding years the lawmakers gathered in two other privately owned buildings and in three structures erected specifically as capitols.

Congress had appropriated twenty thousand dollars for the construction of a permanent capitol on a site to be chosen by the territorial legislature. The three largest towns in the territory — Stillwater, St. Paul, and St. Anthony (now Minneapolis) — competed for the honor of being named the permanent capital, and the selection was not made until 1851. Meeting in a three-story building on Third Street in St. Paul, the legislators at last solved the problem by parceling out the territory's three plums: Stillwater received the penitentiary, St. Anthony became the home of the university, and St. Paul was named the capital.

In June, 1851, the problem of securing land for the first statehouse was resolved when Charles Bazille offered the young territory a block of property at Tenth and Wabasha streets for a token payment of one dollar. Within a month work began on a stone structure designed by N. C. Prentiss, who was paid fifty dollars for his plan. Completed in 1853, the first territorial capitol was an extremely plain, two-story building; its only adornments were a cupola on top and several Greek pillars on a portico facing Exchange Street. Its cost exceeded the $20,000 available, and Congress provided $12,500 more.

St. Paul remained in undisputed possession of the capital for only four years. On February 6, 1857, near the middle of what was understood to be the last session of the territorial legislature, a bill was introduced to remove the seat of government to St. Peter. The developers of that Nicollet County town promised

23

to donate a site and contribute a hundred thousand dollars toward the erection of a new capitol. The measure passed both houses of the legislature with little opposition, and although the newspapers of the day violently denounced the scheme, it seemed likely that the governor would sign the bill. Friends of St. Paul, however, succeeded in bottling up the approved measure in the senate committee where it had to be enrolled before it could go to the governor for signature.

As the close of the session drew near, Joseph Rolette, the committee's chairman, apparently disappeared into thin air taking the bill with him. The senate remained in continuous session for 123 hours, while the sergeant at arms futilely scoured St. Paul in search of Rolette. It is said that he did not appear until the clock was striking midnight — the hour when the senate by law had to adjourn. Although the speaker of the house and Governor Willis A. Gorman signed what was thought to be a true copy of the bill, the president of the senate refused to add his signature, maintaining that the copy contained numerous errors. Hoping that the document would be upheld by the courts, the St. Peter proprietors erected a frame statehouse. It was, however, destined to serve as the Nicollet County Courthouse rather than the capitol, for the courts ruled that the removal bill was not valid.

The question of where Rolette had been hiding during those five days remained for many years a well-kept secret. Then it was revealed that he had spent the week in a rear room on the top floor of a St. Paul hotel, the Fuller House. Well cared for, he comfortably played poker while the sergeant at arms ranged the town looking for him "in a manner so ostentatious that no complaint could be made of any lack of zeal in duty." Although attempts were again made in 1869, 1871, and 1893 to move the capitol to a lake-shore site in Kandiyohi County, they did not succeed, and St. Paul has remained the state's center of government, thanks to Joe Rolette.

The first capitol burned on March 1, 1881. Next morning the house and senate reconvened in hastily prepared rooms in a newly erected markethouse at Seventh and Wabasha streets. This structure served as the state's headquarters until the second capitol was built in 1883 on the same site as its predecessor (the block now occupied by the St. Paul Arts and Science Center). Although the state government quickly outgrew its new quarters, the handsome red brick capitol continued to serve until the present statehouse was ready for use in 1904; it was razed in 1938.

Efforts to build a new and larger capitol began only ten years after the second one had been completed. The legislature in 1893 passed a hotly contested bill creating a commission with authority to initiate the construction of the present capitol. Under the chairmanship of Channing Seabury, the seven-man commission took on the sometimes thankless task of raising funds and supervising the completion of construction with all its complexities. At the commission's invitation, architects throughout the United States anonymously submitted forty-one plans from which the commissioners, assisted by two architectural consultants, selected the Italian Renaissance design of Cass Gilbert, a St. Paul architect. Gilbert later moved to New York and became famous as the designer of such noted buildings as the United States Supreme Court Building in Washington, D.C., and the Federal Courthouse and the Woolworth Building, an early skyscraper, both in New York City.

Land for Minnesota's new capitol was secured at Cedar Street between University and Aurora avenues in St. Paul for a price of $367,161.98. Ground was broken on May 6, 1896, and on July 27, 1898, Alexander Ramsey, first governor of the territory and second chief executive of the state, officiated at ceremonies laying the cornerstone. Major construction was completed in nine years, and although the interior was not entirely finished, most of the state offices were moved into the new quarters late in 1904. The thirty-fourth session of the legislature, the first to sit in the present capitol, opened on January 3, 1905.

CASS GILBERT, *a young St. Paul architect later acclaimed nationally, designed the present Italian Renaissance statehouse. He is shown here on the roof of the capitol while the dome was being built in 1901.*

While some Minnesotans viewed the capitol as an extravagance (its total cost was nearly $4,500,000), many people throughout the nation acclaimed it as a lesson in design and decoration for generations to come. The *Western Architect* in 1905 called it "the latest expression in modern design," and commented, "Its art stands [as] a monument to its architect, but the securing of the necessary funds, their prompt use and careful expenditure (which is phenomenal in the history of state-houses) in the hands of Channing Seabury and the secretary [*Frank E. Hanson*] should be remembered with gratitude and appreciation by every citizen of the state."

Over half a century later the capitol was still considered one of the country's outstanding examples of eclectic architecture. Dominated by a gleaming dome, believed to be the largest unsupported marble dome in the world, the monumental structure rises 223 feet high and extends 433 feet in length and 228 feet in width. It has a framework of steel imbedded in walls of stone and brick which, with the floors, partitions, and roof, are fireproof. The exterior superstructure and dome are built of gray-white Georgian marble; the foundation, terraces, and steps are constructed of gray granite from St. Cloud. The building comprises a basement, ground floor (legislative hearing rooms, offices, cafeteria), first floor (rotunda, offices of the governor, lieutenant governor, and attorney general), second floor (senate chamber, house of representatives, and the supreme court), and third floor (law library, visitors' galleries, and senate offices).

Focal point of the interior is the rotunda, which is sixty feet in diameter and from which the massive marble staircases extend to upper floors. At the base of the rotunda an eight-point star is imbedded in the marble floor to symbolize Minnesota, the "North Star State." From the vaulted ceiling 142 feet above hangs a huge chandelier made of thousands of pieces of crystal and containing nearly a hundred light bulbs. Off the north corridor a unique, self-supporting stairway rises to the second and third levels.

Gilbert was determined to supervise both the construction and the decoration to ensure harmony in every detail, and his imaginative integration of architecture,

MINNESOTA's *present state capitol has been a landmark in St. Paul since its completion in 1904. Considered a masterpiece of integrated art and architecture, it required nine years to build and cost nearly $4,500,000. The impressive gilded figures (below) entitled "The Progress of the State" adorn the south façade.*

THE SENATE CHAMBER, *pictured during the 1971 legislative session, is decorated with French marble. It is located on the second floor of the capitol's west wing.*

THE ROTUNDA *rises 142 feet from a symbolic North Star on the first floor to the dome above. In this unusual photograph the entire expanse of the rotunda has been captured by using a fisheye lens.*

sculpture, and painting is often cited as the greatest achievement in the capitol design. The use of Minnesota stone — granite from St. Cloud and Ortonville, limestone from Kasota and Mankato, red pipestone from the sacred Indian quarries — serves the dual purpose of publicizing the state's resources and effecting a decorative interplay of color and texture. For additional richness more than twenty kinds of marble were imported from foreign countries. Mahogany and Minnesota white oak are used for the woodwork. All of the decorative art — oil paintings, frescoes, sculptures, and scrollwork — relates symbolically or historically to the state. The artists commissioned to execute it were among the most noted in the nation. The capitol's largest and most popular work is the heroic gold quadriga done by the eminent American sculptors Daniel C. French and Edward Potter and entitled "The Progress of the State." Located atop the south façade, the gilded figures symbolizing the triumph of government and prosperity are visible for miles.

Since 1970 the educational services department of the Minnesota Historical Society has been responsible for guided tours of the capitol. Trained guides tell more than 120,000 visitors a year of the state's history, the art and architecture of the capitol, and the functions of state government. Group tours may be arranged by reservation; visitors may join tours which begin on the hour at the base of the rotunda. There is no charge for the tours, which are available every day of the year except major holidays.

Alexander Ramsey House

Located at 265 South Exchange Street in St. Paul.

THIS HANDSOME LIMESTONE RESIDENCE was completed in 1872 by Alexander Ramsey, a bluff, hearty man who can truly be called one of the founders of Minnesota. Appointed by President Zachary Taylor as the first governor of the territory, Ramsey went to Minnesota in 1849 and remained a resident of St. Paul for more than half a century. When he died in 1903, Minnesota had become a modern state, and Ramsey had contributed much to its development. The house was occupied by members of the family until 1964, when it became the property of the Minnesota Historical Society. Now open to the public, it is one of the state's finest examples of Victorian architecture.

Ramsey became Minnesota's first governor at the age of thirty-four. A native of Pennsylvania, he was born of Scotch and German parentage in 1815. In 1839 he was admitted to the Pennsylvania bar and rose rapidly in the ranks of the Whig party, serving in the United States Congress from 1843 to 1847 as a representative from Pennsylvania. It was his work in support of the election of President Taylor that brought him the appointment as governor of newly created Minnesota Territory. Immediately Ramsey identified himself with the interests of Minnesota and worked skillfully to lay the foundations of government and open the vast Indian-held lands to white settlement. As governor he was also *ex officio* superintendent of Indian affairs in Minnesota, and he has been called the "essential and controlling factor" in the transactions leading to two treaties by which the Dakota ceded to the government some twenty-four million acres of land in 1851. Again in 1863 Ramsey, then a United States senator, was called upon to negotiate with the Chippewa for the sale of their lands in northern Minnesota.

Although he received his first Minnesota office through appointment, Ramsey was elected as the state's second governor in 1859 and re-elected in 1861. During his last term, as one historian put it, his "official duties were greatly complicated by the responsibilities connected with the Sioux outbreak of 1862 . . . and with providing troops for the Civil War." Ramsey happened to be in the nation's capital when Fort Sumter was fired on in 1861, and he offered the first troops to the Union Army. After the Republican party was born, he became its leader in Minnesota, and from 1863 to 1875 he represented his adopted state in the United States Senate. He then became the first Minnesotan to be named to the cabinet, serving from 1879 to 1881 as secretary of war under President Rutherford B. Hayes. Following his return to St. Paul in 1881, Ramsey

27

accepted appointments to the memberships of two special federal commissions and served until 1886.

Along with his political career, Ramsey became involved in land development schemes, the state's early railroads and flour milling companies, and made "large and judicious investments in real estate." He was a founder of the Minnesota Historical Society in 1849 and twice served long terms as its president. Ramsey County was named for him.

When Ramsey, his wife, and young son first reached Minnesota, they accepted the invitation of Henry H. Sibley to live in his Mendota home until a house in St. Paul was readied. After a month the Ramseys moved into a cottage on what is now Kellogg Boulevard, where they lived for about a year. Ramsey later recalled that St. Paul then consisted of "a dozen frame houses, not all completed, and some eight or ten small log buildings, with bark roofs." In 1850 the governor built a large frame house on a hill "a little out of the city" near what came to be known as Irvine Park, a fashionable residential district. Eighteen years later he and his wife, who had received a substantial inheritance, decided to replace the frame structure with a more elegant dwelling, and the first house was moved across the street to make room for the present one.

The "Mansion House," as the Ramsey family called it, was designed by Monroe Sheire, a St. Paul architect, who provided plans for a fee of $250. Late in 1868 Ramsey contracted with Leonard and Sheire, a local building firm, to construct the basement, which was completed the following spring. There followed a hiatus in the building while the Ramseys, who were then living in Washington, D.C., deliberated on materials, costs, and contractors' estimates. Further delays may have resulted from their absence in 1869, when Mrs. Ramsey took teen-age daughter Marion to Europe for the season and Ramsey was in France negotiating to lower rates in international postage. Construction apparently resumed in the spring of 1871, and the house was ready for occupancy — though not completely finished — in September, 1872.

The three-story French Renaissance mansion was built of the "best blue limestone available"; the total cost of the sixteen-room home exceeded forty thousand dollars. A century later, the house remains practically unaltered. On the first floor are the kitchen, pantry, dining room, library, sitting room, and the large parlor measuring 20 by 40 feet. The second floor has five bedrooms, two baths, and Ramsey's office. The third floor consists of three servants' rooms and a playroom; there are storage areas on the third and fourth levels.

Especially noteworthy are the fourteen-foot ceilings on the main floor and the extremely tall windows and doors with arched woodwork or carved cornices. Each window is fitted with folding butternut shutters. All the original woodwork remains — black walnut with butternut panels in the major rooms downstairs, and, in the other chambers, select northern white pine that was carved and painstakingly hand-grained by local artisans to look like walnut. Pine was also used throughout the house for flooring. At first the home was heated by a hot-air furnace and registers, which Ramsey replaced with steam heat and radiators. A modern heating system has been more recently installed. The original gaslight fixtures, including the Bohemian cut glass chandeliers, remain in the rooms, and many of them have been wired for electric lighting. The mansion also featured an early central plumbing system that provided hot and cold running water to the basement laundry, the kitchen, and the bathrooms. The water was heated in coils beside the big iron cookstove and stored in a forty-gallon tank in the kitchen.

Among the house's architectural features are the mansard roof of slate, dormers, bay windows, and three porches. The long, narrow piazza at the front was Ramsey's favorite spot for reading in fair weather. The large yard has many trees, some of which undoubtedly remain from the forty hard and soft maples

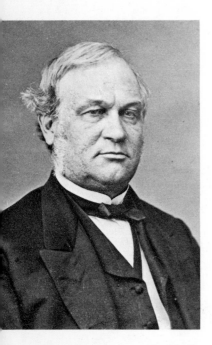

ALEXANDER RAMSEY *arrived in St. Paul in 1849 as governor of newly organized Minnesota Territory. During the next fifty years he served his adopted state in many capacities. This photograph was taken in 1865.*

and box elders that Ramsey bought for seventy-five cents each in 1872. An ornate cast-iron fence on a stone base encloses the property.

Mrs. Ramsey was one of Minnesota's leading hostesses, and she presided over numerous social gatherings from 1872 until her death in 1884. The first party held in the Mansion House was in November, 1872, when Ramsey bought ten gallons of beer for two dollars and entertained the men who built it — contractor John Summers, master carpenter Matthew Taylor, and some twenty-five laborers. A month later, on December 20, the public was invited to attend a musicale for the benefit of the House of Hope Presbyterian Church. Performing was Marion Ramsey, who played Chopin's "Valse Brilliante" on her new Steinway grand piano, which can still be seen in the large parlor. Three years later the same room, decorated with banks of Easter lilies, was the scene of a fashionable wedding when the governor's daughter married Charles E. Furness. In that Victorian era, when social calls were an obligation, it was not unusual for as many as a hundred visitors to drop in on the Ramseys as they did on New Year's Day, 1875.

President Hayes and his wife were entertained in the home in 1878, and in 1886 they returned for a week's visit. Each year on May 27, Sibley called to observe with his old friend and political opponent the anniversary of Ramsey's arrival in Minnesota, and other prominent Minnesotans were often guests. (In 1971 the large parlor was once again the setting for a gathering of Minnesota leaders when some seventy people attended a formal dinner for newly elected Governor Wendell R. Anderson.)

Mrs. Furness succeeded her mother as the mansion's hostess, and the activities of a new generation centered in the house — children's Christmas parties for her son and daughters, coming-out parties, musical matinees, and receptions

THE MANSION HOUSE *Ramsey built in 1872 served as the family's St. Paul residence until 1964, when it was willed to the Minnesota Historical Society. Now restored to its Victorian elegance, the house is a popular historic site visited by thousands of people annually.*

for as many as six hundred people. After she died in 1935 her daughters, Laura and Anna Furness, continued to live in the stately home until their deaths in 1959 and 1964, respectively. The last members of the family, the Furness sisters willed the house to the Minnesota Historical Society.

From 1965 to 1968 the society kept the house open to the public, but structural weaknesses demanded that it be closed for repairs. At that time a major program of restoration was initiated by the society's historic sites staff. The St. Paul Foundation and the Women's Organization of the Minnesota Historical Society contributed to the funding of the program, as did the Colonial Dames of the State of Minnesota. The latter organization, in which the Furnesses had been active, was given the responsibilities of restoring and maintaining the large parlor. Restoration of that room was completed by the historic sites staff in 1970. The result is a magnificent chamber decorated with reproductions of hand-blocked wallpaper, draperies of cloth woven to match a sample of the original fabric, and the same carpet and furniture, now carefully restored, that appear in a photograph of the room taken in 1884.

Meanwhile the restoration progressed with the plastering, painting, papering, and refinishing necessary to renovate other rooms in the house. Careful scraping through layers of wallpaper and paint revealed the original patterns and colors, which were closely matched with modern versions of Victorian decorating materials. Major restoration of the first and second floors was completed in 1971, and the third-floor rooms, where the servants lived and where Ramsey is said to have often watched boats on the Mississippi far below, are scheduled for future work. Much of the furniture the Ramseys purchased in New York and Europe remains in the rooms. One outstanding piece that is in excellent condition is the Steinway piano, which was purchased in 1872 for $1,400. Beautifully finished in rosewood, the piano is the largest model built in 1872 by the company and features a full cast-iron harp; it is the forerunner of today's concert grands. The carved legs and scrollwork music rack attest to the Victorian origin of the piece.

Throughout the house antiques, original carpets, portraits and family mementos, monogrammed Haviland china, family silver, and articles of personal clothing richly document the Ramseys' long residence. A tall grandfather clock thought

THE LARGE PARLOR has been restored to look as it did in 1884, the year Mrs. Ramsey died.

RAMSEY'S OFFICE, *a small room on the second floor, is simply furnished with his desk, chair, and bookcases.*

THE CARRIAGE HOUSE, *located behind the mansion, was reconstructed from the plans of the original building erected in 1883.*

to date from the 1700s and several mirrors are among the items Ramsey inherited from his family in the East. Two white marble fireplace mantels, designed and carved by J. F. Tostevin of St. Paul at a cost of $1,225, decorate the huge parlor just as they did a century ago. Other less elegant fireplaces, most of which never held a flame, also remain in their original condition. Bell cords used to summon servants from the kitchen have been replaced in several rooms, and the speaking tube of a simple intercommunications system is still evident in Ramsey's bedroom.

On the second floor, Ramsey's office or sitting room, as he preferred to call it, looks today much as it did when he welcomed friends and business acquaintances who entered the house by the side door and unobtrusively climbed the back stairs. A small chamber, it is furnished with Ramsey's own desk and chair, his books in glass-door bookcases, a Franklin stove, and a matched pair of spittoons. Down the hall from the office is the master bathroom, complete with a tin bathtub encased in a walnut cabinet, a porcelain lavatory, and Ramsey's tilting shaving mirror.

In 1970 the historical society reconstructed the carriage house which stood at the rear of the lot, using the plans drawn in 1883 by Denslow W. Millard. Razed in 1920, the original building had a hayloft, feed bins, and quarters for the grooms on the second floor; the ground level had stalls for horses and a cow and a storage area for carriages and buggies. The present building serves as a visitors' center. Exhibits relating Ramsey's long public career and a gift shop are on the first floor, and buggies, sleighs, and harnesses are displayed on the second.

The Ramsey House, which is in the National Register of Historic Places, is open to the public daily except Mondays and major holidays. Guided group tours are available by reservation made at the Minnesota Historical Society. There is an admission fee.

THE FALLS OF ST. ANTHONY, *sketched by Seth Eastman in the 1840s, looked much as they did in 1680 when Father Hennepin named them for his patron saint. This engraving is from a book written by Eastman's wife, Mary, entitled* Chicóra and Other Regions of the Conquerors and the Conquered, *which was published in 1854.*

The Falls of St. Anthony

Located in the Mississippi River at Minneapolis. Visible from the Third Avenue Bridge, the observation deck of the Upper Lock at the foot of Portland Avenue South, or the St. Anthony Falls Hydraulic Laboratory at the foot of Third Avenue Southeast.

A SCENIC WATERFALL sixteen feet high and several hundred yards wide was responsible for the birth and early growth of the state's largest city — Minneapolis. Beside the Falls of St. Anthony in 1821–22 soldiers from newly founded Fort Snelling built the first saw and grist mills in what is now Minnesota. Later the cataract's waters furnished power for the two industries most important in the early development of Minneapolis — sawmilling and flour milling. And in 1882 the falls powered the first hydroelectric central station in the United States. They are still used to generate electricity for the city they fostered. All remnants of the lumber era have disappeared, and many of the flour mills that once made Minneapolis the milling capital of the nation are also gone. The largest, however, still stands on its original site at Third Avenue Southeast and Main Street. It is the "Pillsbury A," a limestone structure designed by LeRoy S. Buffington and built in 1880–81 that was once touted as the biggest flour mill in the world. Although it can no longer claim this distinction, the mill is still in use.

The explorer who discovered and named the historic waterfall was Father Louis Hennepin, a Belgian friar who came upon it in 1680. In his wanderings through the North American wilderness Hennepin had already seen the splendor of mighty Niagara, but the falls in the Mississippi so impressed him that he described them as "terrible" and "astonishing." He named them for Anthony of Padua, the saint "we have taken for the Protector of our Discovery." (Lucy Wilder Morris Park at the foot of Sixth Avenue Southeast preserves the site from which Hennepin is thought to have viewed the falls. Although the cataract was near this spot in 1680, it has now retreated through erosion about four blocks upstream. The entrance to the small park is indistinctly marked by an iron gateway; the area was cleared in 1971 to provide a view of the river.)

Upon his return to Europe Hennepin wrote a book, first published in 1683, which spread the fame of the falls abroad. Seeking them out, explorers of the Northwest who came after Hennepin described their beauty in rich detail. As time went on, however, travelers less awed by the cataract's size scaled down the friar's generous estimate of height from sixty feet to a more accurate sixteen. (Today at the falls site there is a drop in the river of some seventy-five feet, but the decline is gradual over a distance of half a mile.)

By the early nineteenth century the falls attracted crowds of tourists whose

33

SAWMILLS AND FLOUR MILLS *at St. Anthony (right) and Minneapolis (left) flanked the falls about 1870. In the background is the first Suspension Bridge built between Minneapolis and Nicollet Island in 1854.*

enthusiastic reports made the site renowned among the scenic wonders of the Midwest. After the "Virginia" opened the upper Mississippi to steamboats in 1823, travelers from all over the nation flocked to St. Anthony on what was known as a "fashionable tour."

Although early-day tourists visited the falls only to observe their scenic beauty, other men living nearby viewed them as a potential source of water power. The first to use them for this purpose was Colonel Josiah Snelling, commandant of the frontier outpost that bears his name. In 1821 he ordered the construction of a stone gristmill and a frame sawmill on the west riverbank near the falls. These small mills furnished lumber and flour for the garrison at Fort Snelling.

When treaties with the Dakota and Chippewa opened the land on the east bank of the falls to settlement in 1838, men from the fort scrambled to secure sites that would give them control of the water power. Franklin Steele, a storekeeper at the post, was victorious in the land rush. He built his cabin on the eastern shore near the falls and held his claim against many predatory frontiersmen who tried to displace him. In 1847 his workmen began the construction of a dam and a sawmill above the falls, and in 1849, after buying some of the first Minnesota land sold by the government, Steele platted the town of St. Anthony.

Meanwhile the west bank of the falls was taken over by Robert Smith of Alton, Illinois, and his Minnesota partners. In 1849 they secured control of the old government mills which had fallen into disrepair. Settlers, who moved in behind them on the broad prairie that stretched far to the south and west, divided their claims into lots and blocks threaded by streets that are now main thoroughfares. They called their new town Minneapolis, combining the Dakota word for "waters" with the Greek one meaning "city." So rapidly did it grow that in 1872 Minneapolis absorbed St. Anthony, its older rival across the river. Since 1880, when it surpassed St. Paul, Minneapolis has been the largest city in Minnesota.

With the vast supply of timber available from the northern pineries, it was natural that the logs should be floated down the Mississippi to Minneapolis. There a large industry soon grew up at the falls. Two long rows of sawmills — at times numbering as many as sixteen — jutted into the river from both shores. In 1860 these mills sawed 28,900,000 board feet of lumber; ten years later production reached 118,233,113 board feet, and the output was still growing. Minneapolis surpassed Stillwater as the state's lumbering capital in the mid-1860s, and the mills remained at the falls until the 1880s when the industry gradually shifted upriver to north Minneapolis.

During the 1860s a flour-milling center had begun to evolve at the falls, and in the decade that followed it eclipsed lumbering as Minneapolis' largest industry. Miles of tunnels and canals riddled the lands along the river, draining water from the Mississippi above the falls to power the flour mills. Towering stone structures soon darkened the narrow streets in the falls district, crowding out the sawmills and other industries that tried to take root there. In 1880, when

Minneapolis' twenty-seven mills were producing over two million barrels of flour annually, the city surpassed St. Louis, Missouri, as the milling capital of the nation. It held this supremacy until 1930 when Buffalo, New York, claimed the honor.

One of the mills that helped make Minneapolis the flour-milling capital of the nation was the giant Pillsbury A, once the largest mill of its type in the world. When it was completed in 1881, the "A" had a daily capacity of five thousand barrels, which made it easily the biggest at the falls. Three years later its output was exceeded by only one other mill in the world, and by 1905, after it had been improved, its owners claimed that no two mills on earth could equal its production record. The building, which is owned by the Pillsbury Company, has been designated a National Historic Landmark. IT IS NOT OPEN TO THE PUBLIC.

The success of the falls as an industrial water-power site doomed them as a scenic attraction. In the 1870s engineers covered the face of the falls with a wooden apron to protect them and control the erosion that was slowly destroying them. A powerful flood in 1952 ripped the apron from its moorings, leaving a cataract of wild beauty. A few people suggested that it be left in its natural state, but practical men triumphed, and once more the falls were sheathed, this time with a concrete apron.

While the cataract was tamed as a power source and a gray phalanx of mills was etched into the skyline of nineteenth-century Minneapolis, a forgotten group of pioneers built the nation's first hydroelectric central station on Upton Island (now gone) near the west bank of the falls. (A marker commemorating the

NAVIGATION *to Minneapolis' industrial center is now facilitated by the Lower (foreground) and the Upper locks that allow Mississippi River traffic to bypass the falls. The Stone Arch Bridge, seen here with the truss span installed in 1962, is in front of the falls in this 1969 view. Courtesy U.S. Army Corps of Engineers.*

station was erected near the Upper Lock observation deck in 1969 by the Engineers Club of Minneapolis.) The small plant was constructed in 1882 to furnish lights for the nearby business district. The closing decades of that century saw the energy of the falls slowly diverted from the direct powering of flour mills into the generating of electricity — a change that took on speed after 1900. In 1923 the Northern States Power Company, which owns the properties today, purchased the companies that had first developed the falls, but it was not until 1960 that the last flour mill at the cataract converted to electricity.

Today the best panoramic view of the Falls of St. Anthony may be obtained from the observation deck of the Upper Lock. There the present-day tourist, should he see the falls at floodtime, will witness the mighty force of water that awed the Indians and moved early visitors to pen their impressions of beauty and grandeur. The Pillsbury A mill on the opposite bank and the few remaining mills that stand silently on the west bank evoke memories of the golden age of flour when Minneapolis was known far and wide as "the mill city." The hum of hydroelectric plants also recalls the past and testifies to the continuing utilization of water power. But now much of the excitement at the falls focuses on the Upper Lock — the culmination of a century-old dream of a river harbor in the industrial heart of Minneapolis. Completed in 1963, the Upper Lock is the last in a series of twenty-nine locks and dams that create a stepladder for river traffic from St. Louis to Minneapolis. By it the city is linked with the Gulf of Mexico, with the Missouri and Ohio river systems, and, via the Illinois Waterway, with the Great Lakes and the St. Lawrence Seaway. Now modern Mississippi River barges loaded with steel, grain, coal, sand, fertilizer, and many other commodities can easily slip past the cataract that seemed so awesome to Hennepin.

With the passing years, and especially with the execution of the Upper Harbor Project, the area embracing the falls has been dramatically altered. Because of its importance as the birthplace of Minneapolis, the area is included in the National Register of Historic Places as the St. Anthony Falls Historic District, and the Minnesota Historical Society is encouraging its preservation and interpretation. Visitors to the observation deck of the Upper Lock are introduced to a dozen nearby sites of historic significance by an informative plaque.

THE STONE ARCH BRIDGE below the Falls of St. Anthony is the oldest mainline railroad bridge in the Northwest. Built in 1882–83 by railroad magnate James J. Hill, it is believed to be the only stone arch bridge across the Mississippi and, next to the Eads Bridge at St. Louis, is the oldest railroad bridge anywhere on the river. Hill first envisioned such a bridge in the late 1870s as part of a plan to improve the Minneapolis facilities of the St. Paul, Minneapolis, and Manitoba Railway Company (later the Great Northern), of which he was president. His plan also called for the construction of a Union Depot (completed in 1885) on the west side of the river to be used by several rail lines that had stations scattered about Minneapolis. Coming at a time when Minneapolis was exerting itself to match the superior railroad facilities St. Paul had attracted in the 1870s, the bridge's construction was a celebrated event in the city.

When Hill announced plans for it in 1881, he said that he intended to build "the finest structure of the kind on the Continent." The Stone Arch Bridge is a magnificent fulfillment of his promise. Sweeping from bank to bank in a graceful curve below the Falls of St. Anthony, the bridge originally contained twenty-three limestone arches, measured 2,100 feet in length, and carried double tracks. It cost an estimated $750,000 and was so ambitious an undertaking for its time that incredulous Minneapolis residents called it "Jim Hill's Folly."

For nearly eighty years the landmark bridge stood unaltered except for general repairs and modernization of its tracks. Then in 1962 as part of the Upper Harbor Project two arches near its western end were replaced with a truss span to accommodate the passage of river traffic. Three years later swirling

THE PILLSBURY A MILL, *a giant of the milling industry for nearly five decades, still towers above the east bank of the Mississippi River.*

floodwaters undermined the base of the bridge's center piers, causing severe structural damage and a fourteen-inch sag over a distance of a hundred feet. For a period of six months the bridge was closed for extensive repairs; it opened again late in 1965 and continued to carry its normal traffic of thirty passenger trains daily. But travel by rail was already declining, and on May 1, 1971 — the day the National Rail Passenger Corporation took over operation of the nation's network of passenger service — the number of trains passing over the Stone Arch Bridge each day was limited to two.

Today the unusual bridge, which has often been compared to a Roman viaduct, is as popular a site as it was in the 1880s when Minneapolitans called it simply "The Great Bridge." It can be seen from the Tenth Avenue and Third Avenue bridges and from the Upper Lock observation deck.

Minnehaha Falls

Located in Minnehaha State Park in Minneapolis. Accessible from Minnehaha Parkway, West River Road, state highway no. 55, or from St. Paul, on Ford Parkway.

THREE DECADES before Henry Wadsworth Longfellow proclaimed to the world the beauties of Minnehaha Falls in his poem *The Song of Hiawatha,* the fifty-three-foot cataract had caught the fancy of nearly every explorer, trader, and settler on Minnesota's wild frontier. The waterfall in Minnehaha Creek was first called Brown's Falls, Little Falls, or Little River Falls to differentiate it from the more impressive Falls of St. Anthony not far away up the Mississippi River. Later it became more widely known as Minnehaha, the Dakota words meaning "laughing waters." By the 1840s "that little vision of exquisite beauty," as one visitor described it, attracted numerous viewers who traveled from the East and South to the healthy climate of Minnesota on what was known as the "fashionable tour." Today the falls, formed by the descent of Minnehaha Creek to the Mississippi River, are still internationally known and one of the most popular attractions in the Twin Cities.

As early as 1819 soldiers building newly established Fort Snelling hiked over the prairie to view Minnehaha Falls. In fact, the falls had been selected as the site of a government sawmill to provide building materials for the fort, but the water was so low that the mill was erected in 1821 at the Falls of St. Anthony instead. One of the soldiers, a youthful drummer boy named Joseph R. Brown (who was later to become one of Minnesota's best known pioneers), aided in tracing the source of the creek to Lake Minnetonka in 1822. Legend would have it that the waterfall thereby became known as Brown's Falls; it is more probable, however, that the name referred not to the young soldier but to Major General Jacob Brown, the commander of the United States Army at that time.

Within the next century word of the cataract's beauty was spread throughout the country by many distinguished visitors — among them Lewis Cass, whose expedition sought the source of the Mississippi in 1820; Stephen H. Long, who explored the Minnesota Valley and the Red River of the North in 1823; George Catlin, who painted the Indians of the region in 1835–36; Joseph Le Conte, a geologist who vacationed in the area in 1844; Frank B. Mayer, a Baltimore artist who worked in Minnesota in 1851; and Samuel L. Clemens (Mark Twain), who visited the falls with his family in 1886.

The cataract's greatest publicity, however, resulted from the publication in 1855 of Longfellow's *Song of Hiawatha.* According to the author, the poem was "founded on a tradition prevalent among the North American Indians,

THE LAUGHING WATERS *of Minnehaha Falls in Minneapolis (below) still draw crowds of visitors each year, just as they did in 1863 (left). Photograph below courtesy of Donald C. Holmquist.*

of a personage of miraculous birth, who was sent among them to clear their rivers, forests, and fishing grounds, and to teach them the arts of peace." Although the Indian was known among the various tribes by several names, Longfellow elected to use the Iroquois title, Hiawatha. Taking the story of Hiawatha as told by Henry R. Schoolcraft in his numerous publications on Indian lore, Longfellow wove into it "other curious Indian legends." There is no record, however, of a native tradition involving a maiden named Minnehaha, and it is thought that she is a romantic figure of Longfellow's imagination.

The poet never visited the falls, but he noted in the first edition of the poem that he had based his description of the area and the cataract on Mary H. Eastman's *Dahcotah, or, Life and Legends of the Sioux Around Fort Snelling.* Mrs. Eastman, the wife of Fort Snelling's commandant, published this work in 1849. In addition, it is known that Longfellow received a daguerreotype of the falls taken in 1852. The book and the photograph turned the poet's fancy to the "land of the Dahcotahs,"

> Where the Falls of Minnehaha
> Flash and gleam among the oak-trees,
> Laugh and leap into the valley.

Efforts to preserve Minnehaha Falls within a state park failed until 1889, when the legislature voted to sell some 120 acres in the falls area to the city of Minneapolis for $100,000. Although it is still designated as a state park, the land has since then been under the administration of the Minneapolis park board. Now enlarged to 170 acres, the recreation area includes the falls, thickly wooded groves, shaded lawns and picnic facilities, springs of pure water, and the creek that empties into the Mississippi River. It has been designated as Minnehaha Historic District and is in the National Register of Historic Places.

Statues and a historic house add to the park's interest. The bronze, life-sized figures of Hiawatha and Minnehaha, located on a small island just above the falls, are among the Twin Cities' best known statuary. They are the work of Jacob H. Fjelde, a noted sculptor who was inspired by the following lines from Longfellow's poem:

> Over wide and rushing rivers
> In his arms he bore the maiden;
> Light he thought her as a feather,
> As the plume upon his head-gear.

The statue was erected in 1911 with funds raised by Minnesota school children, who donated more than $1,000 in pennies.

A short distance south of the falls (near Minnehaha Avenue·and East Forty-ninth Street) are the house and statue of Colonel John H. Stevens, who in 1849 made the first claim in the original townsite of Minneapolis on the west bank of the Mississippi. The government allowed him to settle on what was then part of the Fort Snelling military reservation on the condition that he operate a ferry for the use of soldiers at the fort, and he stayed to become a civic leader, legislator, promoter of water-power development, and agriculturalist. In this small house, built in 1849–50 at the river's edge just below the present Burlington Northern station, occurred such significant events as the organization of Hennepin County, the naming of Minneapolis, early court sessions, and meetings of political, religious, and educational groups. The house was moved twice before 1896, when it was towed to its present location by nearly ten thousand school children working in relays. It is included in the National Historic Buildings Survey. The statue of Stevens standing nearby is a full-length figure in bronze taken from a clay bust created by Jacob Fjelde. It was a gift to the city in 1912 from Stevens' daughter, Mrs. Philip B. Winston.

MINNEHAHA DEPOT, located across Minnehaha Avenue from the Stevens house, is one of the oldest depots in the state and surely one of the quaintest in design. For nearly ninety years the small Victorian station served as the popular stopping place for suburbanites commuting to downtown jobs and for sight-seers and picnickers going to Minnehaha Park. It was closed in 1963 and presented by the Milwaukee Road to the Minnesota Historical Society; the Minnesota Transportation Museum restored the building and maintains it as a historic site.

The Minnehaha station (along with those at South Minneapolis Junction and Fort Snelling) was one of three stops on the first railroad line built out of Minneapolis. Completed to Mendota in 1865, the tracks were extended the following year to St. Paul. The line was built by the Minnesota Central Railway Company, previously known as the Minneapolis, Faribault and Cedar Valley Railroad. In 1862 the latter company had taken over the rights and property of the Minneapolis and Cedar Valley Railroad, which was the earliest forerunner of the Milwaukee Road. Thus the depot was on the heavily traveled line that first connected Minneapolis with Chicago and the East in 1866 and served as a mainline of the Milwaukee Road until a direct route between Minneapolis and St. Paul was constructed in 1880.

It is believed that the Minnehaha Depot was built at its country site in the mid-1870s to replace a temporary structure erected at the time the rails were laid. The cost of the building and its brick platforms was $2,410. It was designed by company engineers in a style called Carpenter-Gothic and featured elaborate

LONGFELLOW'S *Hiawatha and Minnehaha* are portrayed in this bronze sculpture by Jacob H. Fjelde which stands near the creek just above Minnehaha Falls.

gingerbread ornamentation made possible by the recently invented jig saw and precut or dimension lumber, which was another innovation. Called by railroad men "The Princess," the little frame structure, with its array of roof line cockscombs, ornamental eave triangles, fans, and spires, was as delicate and decorative as any of the ladies in bustled Victorian dresses who took shelter under the cedar-shingled roofs over its platforms.

Even after the city of Minneapolis encroached on its country setting, the Minnehaha Depot continued to be a busy stop on the line to Fort Snelling. Those who chose to travel by rail could select from three passenger trains that made eight round trips daily in 1910. Traveling time for the five-cent trip downtown was sixteen minutes. Other trains made five round trips a day carrying only freight. During the Spanish-American War and later critical war years (including the Korean conflict), the depot was a key agency handling shipments of supplies to Fort Snelling, and soldiers often worked side by side with railroad employees on an around-the-clock basis. Thousands of young men inducted into service during the Spanish-American War and both World wars either boarded trains at the old depot or rode past it on the way to the fort.

For several years after 1964 members of the transportation museum organization worked on the restoration of the depot, collecting items for its interior and repainting its exterior in the harvest-gold and maroon colors of the Milwaukee Road. Today the combined waiting room and office, measuring only 20 by 22 feet, looks much as it did about 1890. There are the hard wooden benches with their iron arm rests, the coal-burning, potbellied stove, the agent's roll-top desk, telegraph equipment, and levers that work the outdoor order board, which signaled trainmen to pick up changes in their operating orders. Near the depot stands a 1915 vintage heavyweight railway coach typical of passenger cars used in Minnesota from 1910 to about 1950. The Minnehaha Depot is open to visitors on Sunday afternoons during the summer. There is no admission fee. Information on group tours is available from the Minnesota Historical Society's historic sites department in St. Paul.

MINNEHAHA DEPOT *in Minneapolis, known as "The Princess" because of its small size and fancy Victorian design, was used for nearly a century before it was closed in 1963. The office and waiting room (above) have been fully restored and look as they did in the 1890s.*

Peter M. Gideon Homestead

Site marked in Gideon Memorial Park at Manitou near Gideon Bay in Lake Minnetonka. Accessible from state highway no. 7 to Hennepin County road no. 19 at Excelsior, then 1.4 miles north.

PETER M. GIDEON, a native of Ohio who took up a claim on Lake Minnetonka in 1853, devoted forty-one years of his life to developing fruit trees that would withstand northern winters. Although his accomplishments in fruit culture are numerous, the most famous and most important to Minnesota is the Wealthy apple, a variety he developed by 1868 from seeds obtained from Bangor, Maine, seven years earlier. The introduction of the Wealthy, which Gideon named for his wife, the former Wealthy Hull, marked an epoch in American apple growing, since it was the first full-sized variety to survive cold winters, bear regularly, and have good keeping qualities. To northwestern fruit growers the Wealthy was for decades unequaled as the most profitable apple for marketing.

Having inherited a love of horticulture from his parents, Gideon began growing seedlings when he was a very young child in Ohio. By the time he arrived in Minnesota he had a deep interest in the culture of many fruits, and in 1854 he planted on his Lake Minnetonka farm orchards of apples, peaches, pears, plums, and quinces. Within ten years, however, all his trees had died, leaving him little to show for his hard work.

There is an often-told story that at this time Gideon had only eight dollars in his pocket — money that might well have been spent for a badly needed suit of clothes. He determined, however, to spend it for seeds in order to continue his experiments. For the new suit he substituted a garment of his own making. He sewed together two castoff vests, cut the legs from an old pair of trousers and attached them to the vest for sleeves, and reinforced the patches on the rest of his worn clothing. Thus he made a suit that was described as "more odd than ornamental." With the money saved he obtained the means to continue the experiments that at last resulted in the Wealthy apple.

Never satisfied with his efforts, Gideon continued to test and improve the Wealthy and in so doing developed several additional strains, among them the hardy Peter and Gideon apples. In 1878 he became superintendent of the University of Minnesota's experimental fruit farm, which was established that year on a tract adjoining his property. Some of the trees he planted still flourish there. For years he was an indefatigable laborer who "loved to work, not for fame or for money," according to one acquaintance, "but for the benefit of his fellow men."

The Wealthy apple became a favored variety throughout America and was

42

even known in Europe; its fame brought Gideon wide acclaim as a horticulturist. Although his reputation as a fruit breeder was unchallenged, he was considered personally eccentric and a temperamental nonconformist. He was an outspoken advocate of temperance, abolition, woman's suffrage, and Universalism. On the other hand, he did not hesitate to decry horse racing, prayers at secular meetings, and men's beards. "No man had ever more the courage of his convictions," said his daughter at the time of his death in 1899. "He believed thoroughly in his work[,] and in his ideas as a man meant to accomplish the best results. . . . But his ideas were as often blighted and frost bitten as his beloved trees," she wrote. "His religion, his philosophy and his politics, which cost him so many sympathizers, were as truly his own production as the Wealthy apple."

Two markers commemorate Gideon's accomplishment in producing the Wealthy apple on his Lake Minnetonka farm. They stand at the junction of Hennepin County road no. 19 and Glen Road. The original Wealthy apple tree is believed to have stood about eighty rods north of the monument erected in 1912 by the Native Sons of Minnesota in Gideon Memorial Park. The second marker was erected in 1965 by the Minnesota Historical Society.

PETER M. GIDEON (right), a native of Ohio who arrived in Minnesota in 1853, devoted more than forty years of his life to the successful development of various fruit trees that would withstand the severe winters of the Northwest.

A MARKER at Gideon's homestead near Lake Minnetonka stands within view of the orchard where he developed the Wealthy apple.

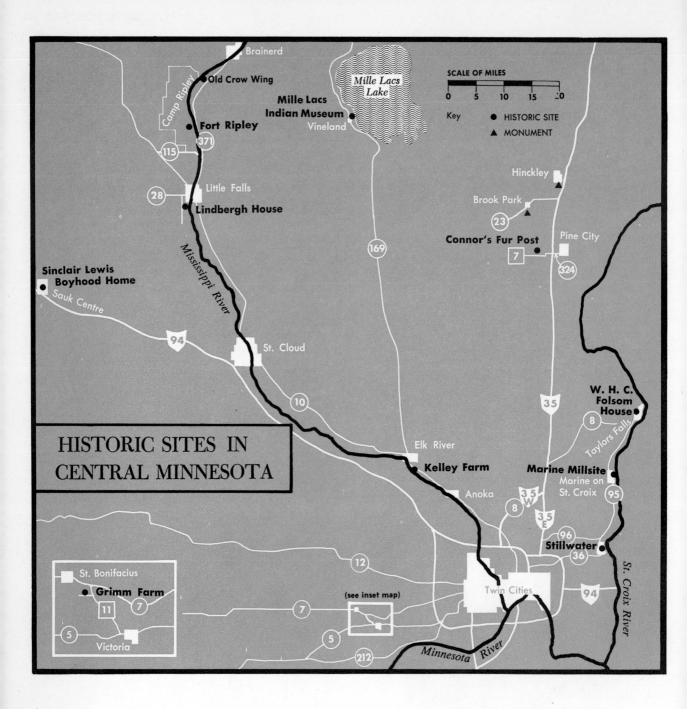

Brainerd

Old Crow Wing

Camp Ripley

Mille Lacs Lake

SCALE OF MILES

0   5   10   15   20

Key   ● HISTORIC SITE
      ▲ MONUMENT

Mille Lacs Indian Museum

Vineland

Fort Ripley

115

371

Hinckley ▲

Brook Park ▲

23

28   Little Falls

Lindbergh House

Mississippi River

Connor's Fur Post

7

Pine City

324

169

Sinclair Lewis Boyhood Home

Sauk Centre

94

HISTORIC SITES IN CENTRAL MINNESOTA

St. Cloud

10

35

W. H. C. **Folsom House**

8

Taylors Falls

Elk River

Kelley Farm

Anoka

35W   8

35E

Marine Millsite

Marine on St. Croix

95

St. Bonifacius

Grimm Farm

11   7

5

Victoria

12

(see inset map)

7

7

5

96

Stillwater

36

94

St. Croix River

Twin Cities

212

Minnesota River

Marine Millsite

Site located at Marine on St. Croix. Accessible from U.S. highway no. 95.

THE MAIN STREET in the village of Marine on St. Croix passes over a small, swiftly flowing millstream. A few hundred feet north of the bridge, a narrow roadway leads east to the St. Croix River and the site of the first commercial sawmill in Minnesota. The opening of this mill in 1839 marked the birth of Minnesota's important white pine lumber business and the beginning of over sixty years of logging activity in the St. Croix Valley. Only the ruins of an enginehouse, parts of two raceways, and a few partial foundations now remain to mark the site where commercial lumbering in Minnesota was born. A marker calling attention to the pioneer millsite stands in a small wayside park and picnic area along the highway in Marine.

To this spot late in 1838 came Lewis S. Judd and David Hone from the Illinois village of Marine Settlement. They claimed the land for a millsite and returned to Illinois, where with others they formed the Marine Lumber Company. The following spring the firm's eight active partners and a load of milling machinery set out for Minnesota on the side-wheel steamer "Fayette." Arriving at the Marine claim in May, 1839, they immediately began the construction of a sawmill. Under the direction of Orange Walker, a Vermont tanner who was to be the young settlement's chief man, it took just ninety days to complete the structure. On August 24, 1839, the slow and cumbersome muley saw, powered by water from the stream, cut the first commercial lumber in what is now the state of Minnesota.

When the Marine sawmill began operations, its pioneer owners could not legally purchase the millsite they claimed or the pinelands they cut. The land belonged to the United States government, which had bought it from the Dakota and Chippewa Indians by treaties negotiated in 1837, but it was not surveyed and offered for sale until eleven years later. In the meantime, the Marine loggers as well as many others who quickly followed them into the St. Croix Valley in the 1840s did not wait for such technicalities, and by the time the land was legally available many million board feet of lumber had been sent downriver to markets at St. Louis and elsewhere.

During the 1840s business at the settlement that was then called Marine Mills outgrew the capacities of the first crude mill, which cut less than five thousand feet a day, and in 1852 it was replaced by a larger one. Powered by a forty-foot overshot water wheel, the new mill had two upright saws, a rotary saw, and a lath machine which ran day and night. This structure burned

45

THE SITE *of Minnesota's first commercial sawmill at Marine had been enlarged and had been owned by several firms when this photograph was taken about 1880.*

to the ground in September, 1863, and three years later a still larger mill was constructed in its place at a cost of about fifteen thousand dollars. By 1873 this, too, was outmoded, and it was almost completely remodeled with new machinery. The enlarged mill could cut from twenty-five thousand to thirty thousand feet of lumber a day.

The decade of the 1870s was perhaps the most profitable for the Marine firm, which at that time was known as Walker, Judd and Veazie. In 1870 the company's general store, which had been in existence since the early 1840s, moved into a large new frame building on the main street near the millstream. The structure still stands, and it still houses a general store.

This prosperity, however, did not long continue. A widespread depression hit in the mid-1870s at about the same time that a succession of log jams occurred on the upper St. Croix, holding back timber and preventing the lumbering

A REMNANT *of the mill's old stone enginehouse now marks the birthplace of Minnesota's white pine lumbering industry. In the photograph above the enginehouse can be seen topped by a smokestack.*

firm from fulfilling its contracts. In addition, the supposedly limitless forests along the banks of the St. Croix were disappearing, and the loggers were beginning to seek new supplies of timber farther north. By 1885 the firm was bankrupt.

Several unsuccessful attempts were made to reopen the mill at Marine, but its end came in 1895, when the machinery was sold and the large frame buildings and numerous sheds were torn down. The mill produced about 197,000,000 board feet of lumber during the years it was in operation.

After nearly seventy years of neglect, the old millsite was recognized in 1964 by the Minnesota Outdoor Recreation Resources Commission as a historic site worthy of state acquisition. In 1970 a committee of Marine residents campaigned to preserve the site, and in 1971 the state legislature appropriated funds for its purchase. The Alice M. O'Brien Foundation contributed a half-acre tract to the state in 1972 which completed the acquisition. The site is administered by the Minnesota Historical Society; it is situated in the Marine on St. Croix Historic District and is in the National Register of Historic Places.

The most outstanding aspect of the millsite area is the stark ruins of the stone enginehouse built in 1873. Also visible, but more difficult to find, are the partial foundations of the sawmill, a sorting shed, and a smaller enginehouse, and segments of underground stone and wood-covered raceways. All of the millsite remnants except the 1873 enginehouse were uncovered in 1970 by the Marine committee members. They also located the sites of several other structures — primarily lumber storage sheds — atop the bluff overlooking the river. The society plans to erect identifying markers at the buildings' locations.

MARINE TOWNSHIP HALL — In the upper section of Marine village stands the township hall built in 1872 on land donated by Orange Walker. Morgan May, a township supervisor and farmer who had settled at Marine in 1858, provided two thousand dollars to finance the construction of the small three-room meeting house and jail. It was built of locally quarried stone by Gustaf Carlson, stonemason, and was maintained by the township board until 1895, when the residents of Marine voted to dissolve that governmental unit. For more than sixty years afterward, the building was put to varied uses as a schoolhouse, community meeting place, and a storage area. Widespread recognition of the hall came in 1934, when it was cited in the National Historic American Buildings Survey as an outstanding example of Swedish stonework typical of the masonry art of early Minnesota settlers. Since 1963 it has been operated as the Stone House Museum of local history by the Women's Civic Club of Marine. It is open to the public Saturday and Sunday afternoons in the summer or by special arrangement with the museum's volunteer staff. There is no admission charge. In 1968 the Minnesota Historical Society erected a marker at the hall.

Minnesota's Birthplace and First Lumbering Capital

Sites located at Stillwater. Accessible via U.S. highway no. 95 and state highway no. 96.

THE ST. CROIX RIVER TOWN of Stillwater has been called the birthplace of Minnesota and the cradle of the territory's white pine lumbering industry. Here in 1848 the initial steps were taken toward the creation of Minnesota Territory, and here for over forty years the extensive operations of sawmills and the St. Croix Boom Corporation made Stillwater one of the state's leading lumbering centers. Today a plaque affixed to a building at the northwest corner of Main and Myrtle streets calls attention to the spot where Minnesota was born. The "boom site," which was designated a National Historic Landmark in 1970, is marked in an attractive wayside park three miles north of downtown Stillwater on U.S. highway no. 95.

Minnesota Territory was born in a rather roundabout way. When Wisconsin joined the Union on May 29, 1848, the delta between the St. Croix and Mississippi rivers became a no man's land without government or law. That area, previously a part of Wisconsin Territory, was not included in the new state whose western boundary was declared to be the St. Croix River. Citizens of the omitted triangle decided to press for the formation of their own territory with laws and a government to protect them and to provide such needed services as mail and roads.

To this end they called on August 26, 1848, an extraordinary public meeting known as the "Stillwater Convention of 1848." It was attended by sixty-one delegates from the area. A key committee headed by pioneer settler Joseph R. Brown drafted memorials to Congress and the president asking for "the early organization of the Territory of Minnesota." The convention also chose fur trader Henry H. Sibley to go to Washington and lobby on behalf of the formation of Minnesota Territory.

Some of those who attended the meeting, however, realized that Sibley's informal appointment would not carry much weight in the halls of Congress, and they sought a way by which their delegate might be seated in the House of Representatives. John Catlin, former secretary of Wisconsin Territory, assumed the role of acting governor of the delta that had been omitted from Wisconsin. He established his residence at Stillwater, and from there, as though it were the capital, he issued a proclamation calling for the election of a delegate to Congress to represent the rump of Wisconsin Territory. Late in October, 1848, Sibley was again chosen delegate — this time by a vote of the people.

He went to Washington, where his campaign to establish Minnesota Territory was successful in 1849. Thus the future thirty-second state of the Union was born in the frontier lumbering settlement of Stillwater.

Lumbering — the new territory's leading industry — created Stillwater as well as many other Minnesota settlements. Stillwater's first sawmill was built in 1844. Ten years later the town had become the foremost lumbering center in the territory and the principal supply depot for the vast pineries to the north. White pine also made Stillwater one of Minnesota Territory's three largest towns (the other two were St. Paul and St. Anthony, now part of Minneapolis).

Stillwater seems to have retained its distinction as the lumbering capital of the state until the mid-1860s, when the industry began to seek supplies of timber farther north and the mills of Minneapolis exceeded those at Stillwater in total output. The town continued to be an important lumbering center until the 1890s, the decade which saw the final decline of logging in the valley. It can claim this distinction in part because of the activities of the St. Croix Boom Corporation.

This firm was organized in 1856 by a group of enterprising valley lumbermen sparked by Isaac Staples of Stillwater. Many St. Croix pioneers had migrated from the lumbering state of Maine and were therefore familiar with booms — collecting areas where logs were caught and measured. In 1856 Staples and his associates began the construction of a boom a short distance above Stillwater, where the river runs between steep bluffs and three long, narrow islands divide the stream into several channels.

To this spot went the huge spring log drives from the upper reaches of the St. Croix and its tributaries; here millions of logs were sorted according to ownership marks, scaled or measured, and rafted to downriver sawmills. Each log had been stamped in the pineries with its owner's characteristic mark or brand, and the extensive sorting operation at the boom has been compared to a cattle roundup. At the peak of one spring drive, the logs covered a stretch of river nine miles in length.

The St. Croix boom was indispensable to the lumber companies of the valley. During its existence, it handled over fifteen and a half billion feet of logs. The last log went through the boom on June 12, 1914, and one of the state's great economic institutions passed into history.

THE STILLWATER BOOM *on the St. Croix River teemed with the activity of a spring log drive when this photograph was taken in 1886.*

MINNESOTA'S FIRST PRISON, *built at Stillwater in 1851–53, is shown in a photograph taken in 1912. The warden's house (at left) is the only original building now standing. Sections of the wall are also still visible.*

THE FIRST COURTHOUSE *erected in Minnesota Territory continues to serve the residents of Washington County in 1972.*

MINNESOTA'S FIRST PRISON — In February, 1851, the Minnesota territorial legislature designated Stillwater as the site of the area's first prison. It was to be erected on the northern edge of Stillwater in Battle Hollow, so named from a bloody encounter between the Dakota and Chippewa that took place there in 1839. Plans for the new structure were provided by Jacob Fisher, a pioneer Stillwater resident. Construction began in 1851, and by early 1853 a three-story cell block, a workshop, and a home for the warden were completed of native St. Croix Valley sandstone.

During its more than sixty-one years of existence, the prison was usually crowded. Most famous of its inmates were the Younger brothers, who were captured after their raid on a Northfield bank in 1876. Although the prison's swampy location near the St. Croix was unsatisfactory from the beginning, it served until after the turn of the century when new buildings were erected at nearby Bayport. The old prison was not completely vacated until 1914.

Of the original buildings only the fourteen-room warden's house stands today. It is adjacent to and overlooks nine and a half acres of prison yard, where portions of the walls may still be seen. In 1941 the house became the museum of the Washington County Historical Society. Its collections contain articles used at the old prison as well as numerous artifacts relating to the history of Washington County. Notable are the many lumbering items which occupy several rooms in the frame addition at the rear. The museum is open Tuesday, Thursday, Saturday, and Sunday afternoons from May to November. There is an admission fee. Guided tours are offered.

WASHINGTON COUNTY COURTHOUSE — The first courthouse in Minnesota Territory, a three-room frame structure, was built in 1849 at the corner of Fourth and Chestnut streets in Stillwater. By 1867 it was inadequate for a burgeoning Washington County, and work began on an imposing a new two-story structure of native sandstone faced with red brick. Located high on Zion's Hill overlooking the countryside, this domed building stands on land donated by Socrates Nelson, a prominent Stillwater lumberman. It was designed by Augustus F. Knight, a pioneer St. Paul architect. Its façade has wide, balconied porticos with ten arches, and its floors are composed of imported English tiles. Completed at a cost of $46,500, it was first occupied during the winter and spring of 1869–70. Although some county offices have now been moved to a newer structure, the courts are still located in this building, making it the oldest Minnesota courthouse still in use. The Minnesota Historical Society erected a marker in 1969, and the courthouse was placed in the National Register of Historic Places in 1971. It is open to the public.

W. H. C. Folsom House

Located on Government Road in Taylors Falls. Accessible from U.S. highway no. 8 and state highway no. 95.

IN THE mid-nineteenth century the St. Croix Valley beckoned to westward-looking young men in the New England pineries, and they responded in large numbers. Among them was William Henry Carman Folsom, who arrived in the valley in 1845 and settled at Taylors Falls in 1850. The home he built in 1855 of lumber from the St. Croix forests stands today as an outstanding example of Greek Revival architecture interpreted by New Englanders in the St. Croix Valley. After being owned and occupied by members of the Folsom family for 113 years, the house was sold in 1968 to the state of Minnesota. It is maintained by the Minnesota Historical Society and is open to the public during the summer months.

The story of W. H. C. Folsom parallels in many ways those of other Yankees who settled in the St. Croix Valley in the 1840s. He was born in 1817 into a family that for generations had been engaged in milling, lumbering, and storekeeping. The Folsoms lived in various New England towns and finally settled at Bloomfield, Maine, about 1827. Already an experienced laborer on farms and in lumber camps by the age of fourteen, William decided he wanted to leave Maine for the western frontier. He persuaded his father to sell him his time — those years remaining until his financial obligation to his family was fulfilled. Within five years he had managed to save $250 to pay his father plus $200 to take him west.

Folsom's first stop on his western trek in 1837 was Prairie du Chien, Wisconsin Territory, where he remained for eight years. During that time he made two trips — one to Louisiana and the other back to Maine, where he married Mary Jane Wyman on New Year's Day, 1841. In the fall of 1845 Folsom left Prairie du Chien to investigate the supposedly more salubrious climate and the vast timber reserves of the St. Croix Valley. He settled first at Stillwater, and soon he was operating a pinery in the Clam River region of Wisconsin. He also pre-empted and then sold the embryo townsite of Arcola on the St. Croix in Minnesota and helped build a sawmill there.

In the summer of 1850 Folsom took a raft of logs to St. Louis where he purchased $5,000 worth of supplies and shipped them upriver. When the goods arrived in September, he opened a store in an old log cabin at Taylors Falls and a few months later bought a quarter interest in that townsite. In 1851 he doubled the amount of supplies and constructed a two-story building on what later became First Street. This new store, the first frame structure in

W. H. C. Folsom, one of many Yankee lumbermen to reach the St. Croix Valley in the 1840s, built this large frame home in 1854–55.

Taylors Falls, housed merchandise on the ground floor and provided living quarters for the Folsoms on the second level.

At that time there were perhaps only half a dozen log cabins scattered among the boulders and tree stumps of Taylors Falls, but the townsite was platted in April, 1851, and that brought in a light flow of new residents, most of them connected in some way with the lumber business. Folsom was encouraged by his store's success, and he optimistically determined to make Taylors Falls his permanent home. "If close application of mind and exertion to business will make my business profitable," he wrote in his journal, "I see not[,] by the aid of . . . Providence, why I should not get along comfortably."

For the site of his new residence, Folsom pre-empted a parcel of land high above the river on a natural bench midway up the hill. In 1853 he cleared the land and built a barn to prove up the claim. He, his wife, and two small sons, Wyman and Frank, lived in this shelter during the summer of 1854 before they left for an extended visit to Maine. Meanwhile construction of the big frame house got under way in May, 1854, with Elias H. Connor, a young carpenter from Maine, in charge. For his daily wages Connor received $3.50 while his laborers earned from $1.50 to $2.25 a day. The total cost of the house is not recorded; Folsom noted that he paid $4,828.22 for "All Carpenter Work," and it is probable that he used white pine from his own lumber camps, thereby keeping the price of materials to a minimum. The house was completed in a little more than a year, and the family moved in during the summer of 1855.

Like other homes built in Taylors Falls in the 1850s, the Folsom house reflects the strong ties of the owner with his native New England. In style it is Greek Revival blended with Federal — a combination popular in the East from 1820 to the Civil War era. Transplanted to the St. Croix Valley, the design retained its full triangular pediments with fan-shaped louvers at the gables, six-on-six windows, painted exterior shutters, and simple façades. Folsom broke with tradition by adding two delicately latticed verandas along the east side of the house as a reminder of the beautiful mansions he had once admired in Louisiana. He stayed with the New England custom of constructing the outbuildings close to the main house and built a two-story woodshed, outhouse, wagon shed and stable, icehouse, brick smokehouse, chicken coop, and well house. For years the well served not only the Folsoms but also many other nearby residents. All of the buildings and the spacious grounds were enclosed by a board fence.

The handsome two-story house sits on a foundation of local trap rock. Of interest to modern visitors are the huge, pegged and mortised timbers of the frame, the wide, pine floor boards, and the twelve-inch woodwork framing windows and doorways. Originally the ground floor was divided into two parlors connected by sliding doors, a library, a dining room, and a kitchen with two adjacent storage pantries — one housing the cistern pump and the other used as a summer kitchen and laundry. From the front entrance hall an extraordinarily wide staircase with a hand-carved rail leads to five upstairs bedrooms. Two rooms were finished on the attic floor.

Throughout the house wood-burning stoves were used instead of fireplaces as sources of heat. Light was provided by kerosene lamps, two of which hung in chandeliers in the dining room and parlor. One of the first pieces of furniture the Folsoms had shipped upriver was the large square piano that still stands in the northeast parlor. In the dining room is the family's oak ''draw table'' which is fitted with an unusual lock mechanism and hinged extension boards. Tables of this type are now rarely seen; this one is more than a hundred years old. Other furniture added during the years included the desk in the library.

All his life Folsom displayed a commitment to social progress, a keen eye for business, and, as a charter member of the town's Methodist Society, a pious belief in his religion. He was prominently involved in major projects

THE FOLSOMS *purchased a square piano in the East and had it shipped by riverboat to their new home on Angel's Hill. It stands in the northeast parlor of the restored house.*

that helped erase the rough frontier atmosphere of Taylors Falls — construction of the first bridge across the St. Croix River, and establishment of public schools, the Chisago Seminary, and the local public library. Among his business ventures were the St. Croix Boom Corporation, the St. Croix Bridge Company, and the Taylors Falls Copper Mining Company. Drawn into politics, he served at various times as sheriff, justice of the peace, deputy postmaster (he kept the post office in his store), and county treasurer. A Republican, he was a delegate to the state constitutional convention in 1857, and he spent seven sessions in the state legislature where he worked for the development of water power, the improvement of navigation on the St. Croix and Mississippi rivers, and the extension of railroads. He took great pride in the construction of the Methodist Episcopal Church on a lot which he donated along with $1,200 for materials. When the church was dedicated in January, 1862, it was entirely free of debt, due to Folsom's generosity and the fact that members were urged to purchase family pews. Folsom bought seven of them at $65 each.

Today the church stands just west of the Folsom house; both of them are listed in the National Register of Historic American Buildings as little changed, early examples of Greek Revival architecture in the St. Croix Valley. The two structures, with other homes built in much the same style during the 1850s and 1860s, are situated in an area of town called Angel's Hill. The houses and their surroundings have remained relatively unchanged, and the area has been designated the Angel's Hill Historic District to encourage its preservation and restoration.

In his business Folsom's "close application of mind and exertion" paid off handsomely. Writing of him in 1855 a correspondent to the *St. Croix Union* commented: "This gentleman, five or six years ago, was a '*logger.*' In other words, he was not worth the powder that would blow him up. Now, he has his 'pockets full of rocks,' and is considered independent." Folsom was beginning to ride the crest of the lumbering wave. By 1860 his real estate was valued at $50,000 and his personal property was worth $5,000. In ten years those figures multiplied to $150,000 and $27,000. In 1873, after more than two decades in the business, Folsom retired from the mercantile trade, but he continued for a time to operate his sawmill, a carriage factory, and the Chisago Boat Yard, all located at the foot of the Dalles in what was called "Milltown." In 1867 his boatworks produced a stern-wheeler, the "Wyman X," which was the first and largest steamboat built on the upper river.

About 1878 Folsom began closing out his businesses and turning to real estate, farming, and a long-standing interest in collecting and organizing historical data on the St. Croix Valley. He compiled a substantial book entitled *Fifty Years in the Northwest*, published in 1888 and advertised, sold, and delivered by the author. The volume remains a respected source of information on the region.

Folsom survived the financial crises of earlier decades, but the Panic of 1893 left him practically impoverished. The last quiet years of his life were spent gardening, visiting his farm lands, and jotting down philosophical thoughts on life, religion, and nature. His wife died in 1896, leaving him with lonely memories of the many days they had spent beautifying their lawn with trees, bushes, flowers, and vines. As a matter of habit he continued to note in his journal those things that were important to him — the state of his health, the amount of work he was able to do, the weather, and who preached at his church. Folsom died on December 15, 1900, and was buried in Kahbakong Cemetery, which he had helped establish in 1853.

After his father's death Wyman X. Folsom continued to live with several of his children in the old homestead. In 1914 Wyman's sons painted the house white (originally it was ocher) and built the portico at the front entrance. For several years after Wyman's death in 1929 the house was the residence of

FOLSOM'S DESK *still stands in the library where he probably wrote his history of the St. Croix Valley. Many of his records, diaries, and letters are preserved in the Minnesota Historical Society.*

AN OAK "DRAW TABLE" *is one of the rare antiques to be seen in the dining room of the restored Folsom House. The lock mechanism and hinged extension boards made it easy to expand the table's size to accommodate a large number of guests.*

his daughter, Mary. Then in 1940 his son, Stanley B. Folsom, undertook a major restoration of the estate. All of the outbuildings except the well house were razed, and a garage was constructed on the foundation of the wagon shed, utilizing timbers from the old buildings. Because the house had already been named an outstanding historic American building, Folsom carefully planned the renovation to preserve its original architecture. The project included adding electricity, plumbing, and a modern heating plant and remodeling the pantries into an enclosed porch and a bathroom. At this time, too, the wide pine boards in several rooms were covered with hardwood flooring, a few built-in cupboards were removed, and some of the interior woodwork was replaced. The Minnesota Historical Society is developing plans to restore the interior to its original appearance.

The Folsom House is open to visitors on a regular summer schedule. For more information and for reservations for group tours, contact the Minnesota Historical Society in St. Paul. There is an admission fee.

Wendelin Grimm Farm

Site located in Laketown Township, Carver County. Accessible from state highway no. 5 to the western outskirts of Victoria, then north on county road no. 11 for 2.2 miles, and west on a graveled road for .7 mile; or from state highway no. 7 to Carver County road no. 11, south for .5 mile, then west .7 mile to the site.

A BRONZE MARKER located near the driveway of the old Wendelin Grimm farm commemorates the significant contribution this persistent German immigrant made to American agriculture — Grimm alfalfa. When he emigrated from Külsheim, Germany, to Carver County in 1857, Grimm carried with him a bag of seed, weighing not more than twenty pounds. From this small amount of "Ewiger Klee," or "everlasting clover," as it was called, he developed the first winter-hardy strain of alfalfa in the United States. For some eighty years Grimm alfalfa reigned as the most important variety produced in this country.

Grimm purchased his farm of 137 acres shortly after he reached Chaska in 1857. The following year he planted his cherished seeds. Only a few of the clover plants survived the winter, but from these he carefully picked seeds for replanting. Year after year he followed this procedure, until he had developed a substantial field of alfalfa acclimatized to Minnesota's cold temperatures.

At first Grimm's remarkable alfalfa received little notice outside his own community, where his neighbors eagerly purchased seed from him for their own farms. About 1900 the head of the University of Minnesota agricultural experiment station at St. Paul learned of the thriving alfalfa grown in Carver County. He immediately began to test it at the university, and by 1904 other experiment stations became interested in obtaining the seed. By 1920 Grimm alfalfa had become a standard crop in Minnesota and was being grown in many other northwestern states and in Canada.

The German lived on this farm until about 1875, when he moved to another one nearby. His eldest son, Frank, then established himself on the Grimm homestead, and with his father's assistance replaced the original log house, barn, and granary. Wendelin Grimm died in 1890, leaving several heirs to carry on his agricultural work.

While other more desirable types of alfalfa have now been developed, Grimm's contribution is still recognized. One historian has written: "The production of a forage plant so hardy as Grimm alfalfa, with its permanence, enormous yields, high protein content, economy as a crop, and value as a soil builder and weed throttler, is almost without parallel in plant history. It is impossible to compute in dollars and cents what it has meant to the nation." In 1924

GRIMM ALFALFA, *the first winter-hardy strain in the United States, was widely adopted by dairy farmers throughout the Northwest and Canada. Courtesy Webb Publishing Company, St. Paul.*

THIS MARKER *stands near the drive-way to Wendelin Grimm's homestead in Carver County.*

the Grimm Alfalfa Growers' Association erected a commemorative plaque at Grimm's old homestead. The centennial of Grimm's arrival in Carver County was observed at the farm in September, 1957.

A living testimonial to the hardiness of Grimm Alfalfa was discovered in 1950. At that time Clarence Schwalbe, owner of the Grimm farm, dug into the ground for eight feet and found growing roots an inch in diameter. These are believed to be the original plants dating from Grimm's efforts in the 1850s.

THE OLIVER HUDSON KELLEY FARM *near Elk River is considered the birthplace of organized agriculture in the United States. Grangers from all parts of the nation contributed funds and furnishings to restore the house.*

Oliver H. Kelley Farm

Located on the Mississippi River about two miles southeast of Elk River. Accessible from U.S. highways nos. 169, 10, and 52. Turn west off the highway at the Kelley historic site marker and continue about .3 mile to the farmyard.

THE FARM Oliver Hudson Kelley homesteaded in 1850 is nationally known as the birthplace of organized agriculture in the United States. It was here in 1868 that Kelley, the principal founder of the Order of the Patrons of Husbandry, opened his office as executive secretary and began organizing local units called granges. For nearly three years vast amounts of printed material and letters promoting the infant organization were mailed from the Itasca post office (now gone) near the Kelley homestead. Sixty-five years after Kelley left the farm for Washington, D.C., the National Grange purchased the property as a shrine to the organization Kelley had originated. Since 1935 the house has been restored with furnishings representative of the 1880s and 1890s. In 1961 the farm of some 190 acres was presented by the National Grange to the Minnesota Historical Society. It has been named a National Historic Landmark.

Kelley was born in Massachusetts. In 1849 at the age of twenty-three, he gave up a brief career in telegraphy at Muscatine, Iowa, and moved with his bride to St. Paul. He carried a letter of introduction to Alexander Ramsey, first governor of Minnesota Territory. In it Kelley was described as a young man possessing "ample business capacity, with active mind" who was "anxious for steady employment." Perhaps at Ramsey's suggestion, Kelley became involved in local politics. He was elected messenger of the House in the first territorial legislature, and in 1851 he was commissioned an "aide-de-camp" to Ramsey. He also joined Minnesota's first Masonic lodge, an organization that was to influence his later work in establishing a farmers' fraternity.

During the 1849 legislative session, Kelley's attention was captured by the townsite of Itasca, located on the east bank of the Mississippi near the present city of Elk River. Although a bill to make Itasca the new capital of Minnesota Territory was defeated, Kelley joined the rush of settlers to the townsite. Early in 1850 he and his wife took up the present homestead and began to participate in the development of the frontier town. For the next few years Kelley postponed working his land to trade with the Winnebago Indians and promote the growth of Itasca. With his brother, Charles, Kelley also surveyed and platted the townsite of Northwood, located just above the mouth of the Crow River in Wright County. Like many of Minnesota's townsites, some of which existed only on paper, both Northwood and Itasca were doomed to disappear. By 1868 only the post office remained at Itasca.

In April, 1851, Kelley's young wife Lucy died in childbirth, and the infant daughter died the following October. Both are buried in unmarked graves on the Kelley farm. In 1852 Kelley married his second wife, Temperance Baldwin Lane, like him a Boston native, and they raised a family of four daughters.

When townsite speculation and trading proved unsuccessful, Kelley turned his energies to the business of farming. At this point his three major interests combined to serve each other: (1) his commitment to "book farming" based on scientific and experimental agriculture; (2) his firm belief in farmers' organizations to educate the men of the soil; (3) his faith in printers' ink as the most powerful tool he could use to promote any venture.

On his farm Kelley initially grew several crops — oats, corn, wheat, buckwheat, and the first timothy sowed for hay north of Minneapolis. He later concentrated primarily on horticulture, experimenting with melons, apples, asparagus, strawberries, and other garden vegetables. He is said to have owned the first mechanical reaper in the state; he built one of the first frame barns in Minnesota (it is still standing); and he installed a complicated irrigation system as early as 1863. To promote advanced agriculture among his neighbors, Kelley acted as agent for a nursery and seed store in St. Paul, for a farm implement company in St. Louis, for J. D. West's patented pumps, and for agriculturally oriented newspapers. He soon became widely known as the successful operator of a "model farm." He advertised his own success as a "book farmer" by sending complimentary samples of his produce to influential people, especially newspaper editors.

In 1852 Kelley helped found Minnesota's first county agricultural society, and he served that Benton County group as corresponding secretary for four years. He was instrumental in establishing the Minnesota Territorial Agricultural Society in 1854, and later he sat on the first executive committee of the Minnesota Fruit Growers Association. His support of county and state fairs became widespread. And at every opportunity Kelley set his prolific pen to paper to promote his adopted home. "I have since 1849," he noted in 1864, "written and had published, out of our State, over eight hundred letters regarding Minnesota." He also was at various times agricultural editor of the *Sauk Rapids Frontierman;* the regular correspondent for the *National Republican* in Washington, D.C., and for the *Anoka County Union;* the author of several series of articles that appeared in the *Boston Post*, the *St. Paul Press,* and the *Sauk Rapids Sentinel* (which he also served as associate editor).

It was his writing that introduced him to the agencies of the federal government in Washington. In 1863 his ten-page essay on Minnesota was printed in the report of the commissioner of agriculture. The same year a severe drought brought such financial hardship to Kelley that he sought and received an appointment as clerk under the commissioner. Kelley returned to his farm in 1865 with an assignment from Commissioner Isaac Newton to report on Minnesota and its agricultural prospects.

In 1866 the federal bureau of agriculture sent Kelley on a tour of the rural South which planted in his mind the seed that finally blossomed into the National Grange. His mission was to gather statistical data on the desperate post-Civil War condition of southern farmers and to assemble information to aid reconstruction and foster immigration. Immediately sympathetic to the farmers' plight, Kelley concluded that it was due largely to their outdated thinking, apathy, and lack of communication. While his reception in the South was generally friendly, he was especially aware of the warmth and helpfulness of fellow Masons, and he began to foresee a similar fraternity of farmers that would erase ill feeling between the North and South. "The idea of association was fast getting fixed in my mind," he recalled in 1875, "and I remember comparing the Mississippi and its tributaries to a national organization and its subordinates."

Before returning to his Minnesota farm, Kelley discussed his ideas with Caroline Hall, his wife's niece, who lived in Boston. She offered him encourage-

ment as well as the radical suggestion that membership be open to women. By the time Kelley returned to Washington in the autumn of 1866, he had mentally mapped out a secret organization for farmers constructed along the lines of the Masonic order. Its purposes would be to provide members with opportunities for ''social and intellectual advancement'' and to encourage education in all branches of agriculture.

At this time Kelley was employed as a clerk in the post office department, and he discussed his ideas with friends in Washington. Six men joined his cause; on December 4, 1867, four of them met with him to frame and adopt a constitution establishing the National Grange with Kelley as executive secretary. The selection of a name had been a problem, Kelley later wrote, but it was finally decided ''that the name of the Order be 'PATRONS OF HUSBANDRY,' and the branches of it be known as GRANGES, instead of Lodges.''

Kelley's imagination was fired by the prospects of an organization of farmers that would ''Encourage them to read and think; to plant fruits and flowers — beautify their homes; elevate them; make them progressive.'' He resigned his clerkship in February, 1868, and devoted the next two months to perfecting the rituals of the order. Then he returned to Minnesota, where he immediately established his office in the farmhouse and launched an advertising campaign to acquaint the state with his new organization. (The present Kelley house is not the original home in which the Grange office was established. Little is known about the construction of the second house, except that it was completed sometime after 1870.)

The first Minnesotan besides Kelley to be instructed in the complex rituals was his daughter, Julia. The second was Caroline Hall, who as Kelley's assistant became nationally known for her contributions to the organization's growth. Progress was often slowed by a lack of money to pay printing bills and other expenses, but Kelley persevered and with sheer hard work and a remarkable ability to convince others of the value of his organization he succeeded. ''Almost discouraged'' in July, 1868, he was exuberant in September with the formation of Minnesota's first grange chapter at St. Paul. Four months later he founded the State Grange of Minnesota, the earliest such state-wide organization in the nation.

While traveling in the East in 1870, Kelley became suddenly and severely

THE FIRST FARMHOUSE, *shown here in an undated photograph, served from 1868 through 1870 as the office of the secretary of the National Grange. The people in the photo are probably Kelley and one of his daughters.*

OLIVER H. KELLEY, *who home-steaded in Minnesota in 1850, conceived the plan that developed into the Order of the Patrons of Husbandry in 1868.*

ill. After a troublesome trip home, he determined "to either give up the work or move my family to Washington, and putting all other things aside, give exclusive attention to the Order." He left Minnesota in December, 1870, and, typically, had to borrow the money to move his wife and children to Washington early the next year. "You said the Order must sacrifice one martyr," Kelley wrote a friend, "and I am going in" for that position.

Kelley's martyrdom soon ended, however, for the following year saw rapid progress with chapters organizing in many states. The Grange was well on its way to becoming the leader in a national agrarian reform movement that reached its peak of influence during the mid-1870s. Kelley remained as executive secretary of the order until 1878. During the last decades of his life, he was involved in land-development ventures in Florida; he died at Washington in 1913.

Following the Kelleys' departure from Minnesota, the farm was owned by various members of the Kelley and Hall families until 1901. In 1932 the Minnesota Historical Society marked the then run-down homestead as a historic site. Two years later the National Grange voted to investigate the purchase of the property; in 1935 its executive secretary, Eugene A. Eckert, wrote a personal check for $7,500 to buy it. Grangers from all over the nation contributed funds to restore the farm as their shrine. The eleven-room house received a new roof, front porch, windows, and extensive interior remodeling. The ceilings, still noteworthy for their height, were lowered about a foot.

Between 1950 and 1954 the National Grange transformed the Kelley house into a farm home of the 1880s and 1890s. Grange members provided rag rugs for many rooms, straw ticks, feather beds, and handmade quilts for the four bedrooms, and toys for the nursery. In the parlor an antique lamp hangs above rocking chairs, an ornate sofa, a nickel-plated stove, a reed organ, and appropriate tables. The dining room has eight chairs upholstered in leather and a massive oak extension table. The kitchen and pantry are also furnished. Much of the restoration work was spearheaded by Mr. and Mrs. Frank A. Archer of Minneapolis, in whose memory a new gateway to the farm was dedicated in 1970.

The Minnesota Historical Society plans to develop the Kelley homestead into a working farm of the 1860–70 era. As a first step, the original barn will be reconstructed as a focal point for future activity at the site. The Kelley Farm is open to the public daily from May through September. During the month of October group tours with reservations are accommodated. There is an admission fee. Reservations should be made with the Minnesota Historical Society.

A BEDROOM *of the Kelley House, like the other rooms, has been restored with furnishings of the late Victorian era.*

Mille Lacs Indian Museum

Museum located on the southwestern shore of Mille Lacs Lake near the village of Vineland. Accessible from U.S. highway no. 169.

THE DAKOTA OR SIOUX INDIANS did not always ride horses and hunt buffalo on the Great Plains of the West.* For centuries before the white man entered the region, the Dakota controlled the vast forested area of northern Minnesota between the Red River and Lake Superior. Eventually the center of this empire was at Mille Lacs Lake. Perhaps by the mid-seventeenth century, several bands of Dakota apparently had moved south and west, leaving the Mille Lacs region to the Indians known as the Eastern Dakota — the Sisseton, Wahpeton, Wahpekute, and Mdewakanton bands. The migration continued, and by the 1740s the most populous band remaining in the vicinity was the Mdewakanton, who maintained villages near the headwaters of the Rum River at Mille Lacs Lake.

Indicative of their long residence in that area, the Mdewakanton band took its name from the Dakota words for Mille Lacs Lake — "Mde wakan" — which mean "wonderful lake" or "spirit lake." This band lived along the Rum River and the southwestern shore of Mille Lacs, where they had at least three major villages of considerable size. One of these was at the base of Cormorant Point; another was located several miles south at Aquipaguetin Island. (This island, named for a Dakota chief, is now marshland.) A third large village may have been situated on the south shore of Ogeche Lake, not far from the outlet of Mille Lacs Lake and near a spot identified by archaeologists as a prehistoric village site (see map).

The first European to leave a record of his visit to Mille Lacs was the French explorer Daniel Greysolon, Sieur du Luth. In 1679 he traded with the Dakota there and planted the Fleur-de-lis to claim the land for France. In his memoirs Du Luth recorded his visit to the "great village of the Nadouesioux, called Izatys, where never had a Frenchman been." Later the word "Izatys," which Du Luth applied to the entire Dakota community at Mille Lacs Lake, was erroneously transcribed from the explorer's manuscript as "Kathio." Use of the incorrect name was long perpetuated by white people, who for years considered it the oldest village name known in Minnesota.

*The Indians known by white people as Sioux call themselves "Dakota," meaning "friends" or "allies." The Ojibway or Chippewa Indians called them "Nadouessioux," meaning "snake" or "snakelike enemy," which French traders in the 1600s shortened to "Sioux."

The second white man to report a visit to Mille Lacs Lake was Father Louis Hennepin, one of three members of an exploring party sent up the Mississippi River by La Salle. In the spring of 1680, Michel Accault led the priest and Antoine Auguelle to the upper Mississippi, where they were captured by the Dakota and taken to Mille Lacs Lake. There Hennepin was befriended by Chief Aquipaguetin and allowed to live and roam about with the Indians throughout much of the summer. Du Luth, learning that the Dakota were holding three white captives, returned to the upper Mississippi and found Hennepin in the company of a hunting party. The two men accompanied the Indians to Mille Lacs Lake, where Du Luth secured the release of the three prisoners.

Du Luth and Hennepin found at Mille Lacs a thriving Indian community in a land of beautiful lakes and forests bountifully supplied with wild rice, fish, and game. The Indians gathered wild rice, which was their principal food, obtained meat and furs by means of bow and arrow, and cultivated small gardens. They cooked their foodstuff in handmade earthen pots, fashioned tools from stone or wood, and constructed dwellings of bark supported by a framework of poles. Well-worn trails branched out in every direction from Mille Lacs. Over them, hunting parties traveled as far as the shores of Lake Superior, where the Chippewa Indians were living. Ambassadors from the two groups visited back and forth regularly for a generation or so before relations between them became strained, partly as a result of the Chippewa's intrusions into Dakota hunting territory.

The growth of the fur trade upset long-established relationships among many North American Indians. As furs became scarcer, eastern tribes pushed westward in search of new hunting grounds. Such was the case with the Chippewa, who had obtained guns from the French and migrated from the east to the Lake Superior area of Minnesota by the late seventeenth century. It was only a matter of time before they found themselves in conflict with the Dakota. Intermittent warfare between the two tribes apparently came to a head about 1745 in a

MAJOR DAKOTA VILLAGES, *battle sites, and archaeologically important places are shown on this map of the Mille Lacs area, which is also known as Kathio.*

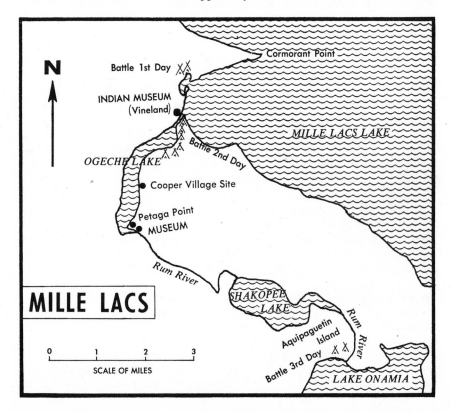

three-day battle at Mille Lacs that has been called one of the turning points in the history of Minnesota. What prompted the Chippewa to stage the attack is not definitely known. Their legend says that it was made to gain revenge for the murder of innocent Chippewa visitors to Mille Lacs. It is probable, however, that the true cause of the battle was the Chippewa's desire to gain control of the wild rice lakes and the fur resources of the country dominated by the Dakota. The real story will never be known; the version related here is from a history of the Chippewa by William W. Warren, whose Indian ancestors had passed it down orally through generations.

According to Warren, a large Chippewa war party armed with guns marched westward to Mille Lacs from Lake Superior. Early one morning they launched an attack on the unsuspecting Dakota at Cormorant Point. So numerous were the invaders and so effective were their firearms that before all the warriors got into the battle, large numbers of Dakota had been killed or had retreated by canoe south to "the greater village located at the entry."

By the following morning when the Chippewa descended upon the village to renew their attack, the Dakota had taken refuge inside semipermanent lodges. To force them out, the Chippewa threw bags of gunpowder into the holes on top of the dwellings through which smoke normally escaped. The powder exploded in the fire below, killing or wounding the occupants. The few Dakota who survived the second day of fighting escaped under the cover of darkness to the village on Aquipaguetin Island. There they made a last stand against the overwhelming firearms of the Chippewa. At the end of the third day of battle, the Dakota were routed. They fled by canoe during the night down the Rum River.

Never again did the Dakota regain possession of lovely Mille Lacs Lake. Eventually the Mdewakanton band settled around the junction of the Mississippi and Minnesota rivers. The other Eastern Dakota bands moved up the Minnesota Valley and beyond the state's present borders. As the Dakota advanced westward, they adapted their way of life to cope with the prairie environment. No longer could they secure fish and wild rice from the northern lakes. With fewer animals easily obtainable, they were forced to hunt over larger areas, to gather wild berries, fruits, nuts, and roots, and to plant gardens. Only a part of the year could be spent in semipermanent villages of bark houses. The only large game abounding on their new lands was the buffalo, and it became their chief source of food, clothing, and shelter. The pursuit of the buffalo, which was facilitated by the acquisition of horses, made the Dakota a nomadic plains people. Adjusting to a life of travel, they utilized the tepee, which was constructed of buffalo hides and could easily be taken down and moved while on the hunt. Still the Dakota longed for their old homeland and until 1862, when the eastern bands were expelled from Minnesota after the unsuccessful Sioux Uprising (see p. 129),

ITEMS *from the Ayer collection are used in the museum to compare the ways of life of the Chippewa and Dakota Indians.*

EXTERIOR *of the museum operated by the Minnesota Historical Society.*

they made sporadic attempts to recover parts of the territory lost to the Chippewa.

The story of the Dakota and the Chippewa at Mille Lacs as it is known at present is told in a museum operated by the Minnesota Historical Society near Vineland, nine miles north of Onamia. The Mille Lacs Indian Museum exhibits a valuable collection of Indian artifacts presented to the society by Mr. and Mrs. Harry D. Ayer, who lived in the area from 1914 to 1966. Along with the collection, the Ayers' gift in 1959 included a new building, about a hundred acres of land, and a trust fund to establish and maintain the museum. Guides are on hand to explain displays that compare the ways of life of the Dakota and Chippewa, showing the effects of the decisive battle and the influence of the fur trade on both tribes. An addition to the museum, completed in 1970, houses life-size dioramas that depict in realisitic detail the seasonal activities of the Chippewa in former days. The museum is open daily throughout the summer. There is an admission fee.

Since 1965 University of Minnesota archaeologists have been investigating ancient village sites within the nine thousand acres of Mille Lacs-Kathio State Park. At the picnic grounds on Petaga Point the first Old Copper habitation site to be excavated in Minnesota is identified by a marker. There archaeologists found scrapers and knives probably fabricated by prehistoric Indians from local raw copper deposits between 3000 B.C. and 1000 B.C. The same site yielded evidence of later occupation dating from 500 A.D. to 1700 A.D. Excavations also were conducted at the Leland R. Cooper Village Site near the park campground on the south shore of Ogeche Lake. Careful digging disclosed a large late prehistoric and early historic village site inhabited from about 1400 A.D. to 1750 A.D. This site is significant as a habitation of the Eastern Dakota and is probably one of the villages occupied by them at the time of Hennepin's captivity in 1680. According to state archaeologist Elden Johnson, it is the type site for a newly defined archaeological complex and an example of how characteristic patterns of the Mississippian culture, moving into central Minnesota from the south and east, influenced the life of and were adapted by Indians in a more northern environment. The Cooper Village Site is also marked, as are several burial mounds in the same part of the park.

EXHIBITS *in the Mille Lacs Indian Museum portray the former life of the Chippewa Indians during the four seasons of the year.*

AN INTERIOR VIEW *of a Chippewa bark house shows the tools and articles used in the summer.*

In 1972 an interpretive center focusing on the archaeology of the Mille Lacs Lake area was being constructed on Petaga Point by the parks and recreation division of the Minnesota Department of Natural Resources. Exhibits illustrating the various cultures represented by sites in this region will be opened to the public in 1973.

An area encompassing Mille Lacs-Kathio State Park plus additional lands southeast of the park's boundary has been established as the Kathio Historic District and is a National Historic Landmark.

Today Vineland is the largest Chippewa community within the Mille Lacs Reservation, which since its establishment in 1855 has dwindled to some 3,500 acres of undeveloped, Indian-owned land on the west shore of Mille Lacs Lake. The band's governing body is the Mille Lacs Reservation Business Committee, whose major emphasis is on improvements in the social and economic condition of the people. Located near the museum are the Mille Lacs Community Training Center, opened in 1968, and an electronic components factory, under Indian management, constructed in 1970. In an effort to retain their tribal heritage, the Mille Lacs Chippewa continue to make and market maple sugar products and handicraft items of birch bark and buckskin. They also perform ancient tribal dances on summer Sunday afternoons at the community center.

Fort Ripley

Site located on Infantry Road within the grounds of Camp Ripley. The camp is accessible from U.S. highway no. 371 and state highway no. 115 between Brainerd and Little Falls. Visitors MUST STOP at the administration building near the main gate.

FORT RIPLEY, Minnesota's second military post, was built in 1848–49 on the west side of the Mississippi River opposite its junction with the Nokasippi and a few miles below the mouth of the Crow Wing. It was erected just beyond the fringe of settlement to keep peace among the Winnebago Indians, newly removed from Iowa to Minnesota, and the warring Dakota and Chippewa. The post served its intended purpose until 1855, when the Winnebago were transferred to a new reservation in southern Minnesota. After that Fort Ripley stabilized relations between the Chippewa and the white settlers who moved into the area in the 1850s and 1860s. By 1877 the post was no longer needed, and it was abandoned. None of the original buildings remain; only the ruins of a powder magazine may still be seen at the location of the old fort. Its name, however, is fittingly perpetuated in present-day Camp Ripley, established in 1930 as a training center for the Minnesota National Guard. The site of the state's second military post is now within the grounds of Camp Ripley. Visitors must check in at the main gate and get directions to avoid firing ranges and maneuver areas.

In 1848 the spot for the army's new fort in Minnesota was personally selected by Brigadier General George M. Brooke, commander of the Department of the West. He chose a sandy, open plateau on the west bank of the Mississippi River. The government set aside a thousand acres for the fort, and reserved another 57,618 acres across the river. Civilian workmen arrived by steamboat in the fall of 1848, built log huts for their own use, and immediately put a sawmill into operation.

Then they proceeded to erect a fort of wood, totally unlike Fort Snelling, the state's first military post, which was made of stone. Fort Ripley's buildings were frame, covered with clapboard. At first a wooden stockade ten feet high partially surrounded them, but this had disappeared by 1868. The buildings faced on three sides of a 450-foot-square parade ground. The fourth side opened onto the Mississippi.

In 1868 the post surgeon noted that Fort Ripley's barracks occupied "the whole of the northwest side of the parade, while on the remaining two sides are located the hospital, chapel, offices, quartermaster and commissary storehouses and officers' quarters; four sets of the latter on each side nearest the river." He reported that the officers' quarters, barracks, and hospital were one-story structures with attics and that a portico about eight feet wide ran along the entire width of the buildings. The barracks, intended to house two companies of soldiers, were 263 feet long by 22 feet wide. They were divided into two sections, each of which contained quarters for married soldiers as well as dormitories and kitchens for the single men. Although Fort Ripley lacked the grandeur of Fort Snelling, an observer commented that the "handsomely painted" buildings gave it "a very pleasant and comfortable appearance."

First to garrison the fort were the soldiers of the Sixth United States Infantry, who arrived in April, 1849, under the command of Captain John B. S. Todd, for whom Todd County is named. These men continued the work of constructing the new post, which was then called Fort Gaines. Soon after Todd's arrival, however, the war department changed the name to Fort Ripley, possibly in honor of Eleazar W. Ripley, an officer who served in the War of 1812 and later become a congressman from Louisiana.

At the time of its erection Fort Ripley's location was very isolated; no roads ran to it and at first all supplies had to be brought up by river boat. By 1853, however, a passable military road on the east side of the Mississippi connected the post with St. Paul. A ferry plied between the fort and the road on the opposite riverbank.

For almost a decade after it was built, Fort Ripley dominated the peaceful countryside of central Minnesota. Convinced that the Chippewa were a friendly tribe and pressed by the need for economy in the depression of the late 1850s, the war department decided to evacuate Fort Ripley in July, 1857. A third Minnesota post — Fort Ridgely — had been established four years before on the Dakota reservation in the Minnesota Valley, and it was thought that Ripley would no longer be needed to watch over the seemingly tractable Chippewa. This supposition quickly turned out to be wrong.

"The report of the abandonment of Fort Ripley," wrote the commandant who later reoccupied the post, "spread like wildfire among the Indians, producing a marked change in their conduct." Almost at once the Chippewa "became insolent and reckless in their bearing towards the whites." Killing cattle, robbing settlers, and threatening the missions at nearby Gull and Leech lakes, the Indians demonstrated how effective Fort Ripley had been in preserving peaceful conditions. Indian-white relations reached a crisis when three Chippewa murdered a settler near the Gull Lake mission. The three murderers were captured and turned over to the sheriff at Little Falls, but before they could be tried a party of white men seized and lynched them. The Chippewa threatened reprisals, and the war department in September retaliated by reoccupying Fort Ripley with a company of the Second United States Infantry.

Regular army troops remained at the post until the outbreak of the Civil War. From 1861 until 1865 the fort was garrisoned by Minnesota volunteers — among them the famed First Minnesota Regiment which did frontier duty there in June, 1861. It fell, however, to soldiers of the Fifth Minnesota to preserve order at Fort Ripley when the Sioux Uprising broke over the southern half of the state in 1862. While the Dakota were ravaging the Minnesota Valley, the Chippewa, who had been peaceful since the 1857 disturbance, again threatened to cause trouble. Fear ran high that the Chippewa would join the Dakota in their war against the white man.

Preparing for a siege, volunteer troops at Fort Ripley "set at work by candlelight making cartridges" and threw up an additional stockade around the post. Settlers from the surrounding area hurried to Ripley, until the handful of soldiers there faced the unhappy prospect of defending over a hundred and fifty refugees, most of them women and children. "Had the Indians made an attack," wrote a man who was on the scene, "they might have killed the greater part of us, for we could not dare to shoot on account of the danger of killing our own people." Fortunately, the attack never came. Additional troops of the

THIS BLOCKHOUSE *of wood once protected a corner of Fort Ripley's parade ground. Like the fort's other buildings, it has disappeared.*

Seventh Minnesota reinforced the garrison, and the government successfully dissuaded the Chippewa from joining the Sioux Uprising.

From the close of the Civil War until 1877, a small force of regular army men again occupied Fort Ripley. By that time the country around the post was well settled, and the government decided to abandon the fort. A few months before the troops were withdrawn, fire destroyed some of the buildings. After the soldiers left, the remaining structures slowly decayed. Some were hauled away by settlers who squatted on nearby lands even before part of the military reserve reverted to the public domain in 1880.

Today the only visible remains of the frontier post are the ruins of the powder magazine. A marker located on U.S. highway no. 371 across the river from the old post calls attention to its role in defending the Minnesota frontier. The site of Fort Ripley is now about seven and a half miles north of the entrance to Camp Ripley. In 1971 it was named to the National Register of Historic Places.

In front of the Camp Ripley administration building near the gate stand three steel-rifled cannon — interesting mementos of the state's military history. They were presented to the First Minnesota in 1862 by the Honorable Henry S. Sanford, then United States minister to Belgium. Of foreign manufacture, they were sent to the United States as a testimonial of Sanford's pride in the valor

THE CRUMBLING RUINS *of a brick powder magazine are all that remain of old Fort Ripley, the second military post erected in Minnesota.*

displayed by the First Minnesota in the Civil War battles at Bull Run and Ball's Bluff. Today the Forty-seventh Infantry Division, a descendant of the First Minnesota, is one of several military elements that train at Camp Ripley, where the First did a short tour of duty before departing for the battlefields of the Civil War.

OLD CROW WING — When Fort Ripley was established, Old Crow Wing, on the opposite bank of the Mississippi River a few miles to the north, was the only settlement nearby. (The site of Old Crow Wing is now within the confines of Crow Wing State Park, accessible from U.S. highway no. 371 seven miles south of Brainerd. Turn off the highway at the Old Crow Wing sign and drive one mile west to the park.)

Many strands in the fabric of Minnesota history are woven into the story of this scenic spot at the junction of the Crow Wing and Mississippi rivers. It is one of the state's oldest and best-known ghost towns; the site of a significant battle in which the Chippewa defeated the Dakota in 1768; the location of fur trading posts dating back to 1771; the place where the Red River oxcart trail between St. Paul and Pembina (North Dakota) crossed the Mississippi River; the scene of well-established Catholic and Episcopal missions founded in the 1850s by Father Francis X. Pierz and the Reverend E. Steele Peake; the home of the Reverend Ottmar Cloeter, a Lutheran missionary in the 1860s; and a Chippewa center that was the dwelling and burial place of Chief Hole-in-the-Day the Younger.

Allan Morrison and William A. Aitken, for whom Minnesota counties are named, and others conducted profitable fur trading stations at the junction of the two rivers. Gradually a flourishing town grew up about the traders' stores and warehouses, and hotels, boardinghouses, saloons, churches, and a blacksmith shop catered to the needs of Indians, oxcart drivers, soldiers from Fort Ripley, and travelers on the stagecoach line connecting the settlement with St. Paul. At the height of its prosperity in the 1860s, the village had over thirty buildings and a population of about six hundred. The largest and most imposing house apparently belonged to Chief Hole-in-the-Day. Hopes that the village would continue to prosper were dashed when the Northern Pacific Railroad was built across the Mississippi at Brainerd rather than at Crow Wing. By the late 1870s the town was virtually abandoned, and as its people disappeared, so did the buildings they had occupied.

Realizing the historic importance of the old ghost town, Bishop Peter W. Bartholome of the Catholic Diocese of St. Cloud purchased about 92 acres of the site in 1946–47. Seven years later the Knights of Columbus marked the location of Father Pierz's mission. Meanwhile citizens in Crow Wing and Morrison counties organized the Crow Wing Park Association, which raised funds to match an appropriation by the state legislature in 1959 for purchasing the former townsite. Crow Wing State Park was opened to the public in 1961 and, with subsequent additions of land, now comprises 1,308 acres. Admittance to the historic area is by state park vehicle permit available at the entrance. Campgrounds, hiking trails, and a public boat access to the river are maintained in the park.

Excavations conducted by the Minnesota Historical Society in 1957 and 1964–65 located the sites of several fur warehouses, the Morrison trading post, the ferry, the Catholic mission, and other structures. The depressions of many basements are still visible, and several are identified by markers. What are believed to be rifle pits thrown up during the Indian battle may also be seen. The present memorial chapel honoring Father Pierz was built in 1968 by the Knights of Columbus on land owned by the Diocese of Duluth, which also holds title to the Catholic cemetery nearby. Old Crow Wing is listed in the National Register of Historic Places.

THREE GENERATIONS *of Lindberghs are represented by August (above), a pioneer who emigrated from Sweden to Minnesota in 1860; C. A. (below, left), a political maverick who represented Minnesota in Congress from 1907 to 1917; and Charles, shown here at about age ten, who later became a pilot and made the first solo flight across the Atlantic Ocean.*

Charles A. Lindbergh House

Located in Charles A. Lindbergh State Park. Accessible from Little Falls on Lindbergh Drive (Morrison County road no. 52) south from the city. A directional marker stands at the junction of U.S. highway no. 10 and state highway no. 28.

THE 110–ACRE FARM AND HOUSE of Charles A. Lindbergh, Sr., now constitute a beautifully wooded memorial park which was given to the state of Minnesota in 1931 by the Lindbergh family. The area is dedicated to the memory of the senior Lindbergh, a distinguished lawyer, an outspoken congressman, a controversial political writer, and the father of Charles A. Lindbergh, the "Flying Colonel," who made the first solo trans-Atlantic flight in 1927. On this farm the younger Lindbergh spent his boyhood summers from 1907 to 1920. The restored house and an interpretive center near it are open to the public. This site is in the National Register of Historic Places.

Charles A. Lindbergh, Sr., was born in Sweden in 1859 and was less than a year old when his parents emigrated to Minnesota and settled on a farm in Stearns County. There he attended rural schools and later went to the University of Michigan law school from which he was graduated in 1883. After a short period of employment in St. Cloud, Lindbergh moved to Little Falls and began his own practice. He was firmly established as an active trial lawyer, community figure, and family man by 1898, the year he purchased the land on the west bank of the Mississippi River that is now a park. In that year, too, his wife, the former Mary LaFond, died, leaving him with two young daughters.

The land with its stands of beautiful pines and hardwoods lay idle and untenanted for two years. Then in 1901 Lindbergh married Evangeline Land, a young schoolteacher from Detroit, Michigan, who taught in Little Falls. Following a trip to the West, the couple lived in a cabin on the bank of the Mississippi River while their three-story frame house was under construction. (About the same time a house for the tenant farmer, a barn, and other outbuildings were constructed across the road. None of these remain.) The impressive country home was a graciously furnished dwelling of seven bedrooms, billiard room, living room, dining room, study, reception hall, and kitchen. To this house the Lindberghs brought their son, Charles, a few weeks after his birth in Detroit on February 4, 1902.

Three years later, on a hot August Sunday, the youngster watched as billowing smoke and flames engulfed the mansion. Neighbors who rushed to help were able to rescue some furniture, books, and china before the burning structure became too dangerous to re-enter. When the fire was out at last, the splitstone foundation and two chimneys were all that was left.

The present house was constructed in 1906 on the same foundation, which still carries the black scars of the blaze. Because no fire protection was available, Lindbergh rebuilt on a much smaller scale, employing Carl Bolander, a partner in his real estate business at Little Falls, to design the house and take charge of its construction.

The new two-story home was never the full-time residence of the entire Lindbergh family, for the conflicting personalities and philosophies of the married couple resulted in their estrangement and the decision to maintain separate residences. In 1907 "C.A.," as he was called, moved to Washington, D.C., as the newly elected Republican representative of Minnesota's Sixth Congressional District. He retained his seat in the House for five terms, and when he returned to Minnesota, he opened an office in Minneapolis and divided his time between it, his office in Little Falls, and travel to Florida, where he had business interests. Although he did not reside with his family, Lindbergh maintained a close relationship with his son, who frequently visited his father, or welcomed him back to the farm. Together they spent many hours swimming in Pike Creek and the Mississippi River, hunting, or tramping over the fields. When they were separated, they often communicated by letter.

Throughout his career Lindbergh's support of causes that were often unpopular and sometimes in conflict with his own party stamped him as a controversial figure in political circles. In the House he refused to yield to party discipline, preferring to stand with whatever group supported the social and financial reforms he championed. He vociferously denounced the "money trust" and fought against the Payne-Aldrich protective tariff bill as strenuously as he supported the Underwood tariff with its income tax provisions. He was the moving force behind the resolution that ultimately resulted in the famous Pujo Committee's investigation in 1912 of a few financiers' control over the national economy. As the author of three privately published books criticizing the American economic system, he was labeled a "Gopher Bolshevik." The books — *Banking and Currency and the Money Trust, Why Is Your Country at War,* and *The Economic Pinch* — were published in 1913, 1917, and 1923, respectively.

At the close of Lindbergh's fifth term as congressman, he entered Minnesota's primary race for the United States Senate and lost. The next year, 1917, he allied himself with Arthur C. Townley's Nonpartisan League, an agrarian reform movement flourishing in the Dakotas and Minnesota. With league backing, he became a gubernatorial candidate in the Republican primary election of 1918. Throughout this stormy campaign, he courageously spoke in every county that would have him, often enduring harassment, physical assault, and even arrest. The opposition press branded him a "traitor" because of his economic views, his pacifistic stand before the United States entered World War I, and his association with the radical league. Not unexpectedly, he lost the primary election.

Five years later, Lindbergh again ran for the Senate in a special election following the death of Senator Knute Nelson. As one of three candidates seeking the nomination of the Farmer-Labor party in the primary, he campaigned vigorously, calling for nationalization of railroads, state ownership of public utilities, grain elevators, and mills, and the abolition of the Federal Reserve system. When his campaign hit a slump, he called on his son to provide transportation with his recently purchased airplane, which it was hoped would help draw crowds. Just ten days before the election, however, the plane cracked up on take-off and had to be grounded. By the time Charles could get it repaired, primary election day had passed and Lindbergh had been defeated. The following year he again tried for the Minnesota governorship. This was his last campaign; he died on May 24, 1924, before the election took place.

While Lindbergh served in Congress, Mrs. Lindbergh and Charles spent winters in Washington and summers at "the farm," as the family always referred to the place. For three years, from 1917 until the fall of 1920, young Lindbergh worked the farm, taking full responsibility but having the assistance of a tenant

farmer or a hired hand. Intrigued with the idea of mechanized farming, Charles persuaded his father to buy a three-wheeled La Crosse tractor and a two-bottom plow with which the boy broke a field north of the barn and planted it to crops. A short time later, Charles installed a milking machine and became an agent for its manufacturer, traveling by horseback, auto, and motorcycle throughout his sales territory. To make the farm productive, the elder Lindbergh bought small herds of western cattle and sheep — although his son was determined to establish purebred herds of Guernsey cattle, Shropshire sheep, and Duroc-Jersey hogs, along with flocks of Leghorn chickens and Toulouse geese.

When he was not attending Little Falls High School, from which he was graduated in the spring of 1918, Charles was kept busy with farm chores. One of his experiments in concrete construction is the duck pond he built south of the house. Still visible on its sloping sides are the inscriptions ''Moo Pond'' (according to Charles, ''moo'' was the Chippewa word for ''dirty'' — which he assumed the pond would be if ducks used it); ''1919,'' the year of construction; ''Lindholm,'' the formal but seldom used name of the farm; his initials; and ''Wahgoosh,'' the name of his fox terrier. (The suspension bridge now spanning Pike Creek is a reconstructed version of one Charles built using barbed wire, cedar posts, and ironwood crossbars. No date of original construction can be determined, but it was probably built sometime between 1917 and 1919. The site of the chicken coop was located by archaeologists in 1971, and the old icehouse still stands north of the present house.)

Although Charles loved his work on the Little Falls farm, he also developed during the war years a desire to become an aviator. In addition, his parents had suggested that he enroll in college. By 1920 he had made a decision: he would quit the farm. World War I had ended, forcing him to postpone his dream of becoming a fighter pilot, so he entered the University of Wisconsin. There he studied mechanical engineering for three semesters before embarking on a career in aviation, first as a student and mechanic, barnstormer, and Air Corps cadet, and in 1926–27 as an air mail pilot.

After Charles and his mother left the farm in 1920, the house remained empty and largely ignored until the spring of 1927. On May 22 radios around the world flashed the news that young Lindbergh had successfully flown nonstop and alone from New York to Paris. Immediately the youthful aviator was an

THE LINDBERGH HOUSE *now looks much as it did from 1906 to 1920 when young Charles and his mother lived there.*

THE RESTORED KITCHEN *has the wood box that Charles kept filled and a stove like that on which his mother prepared meals.*

IN 1919, *when Charles was operating the farm, he built this "moo pond" of concrete for his ducks. The inscriptions are still legible.*

international hero. Hordes of newsmen and curiosity-seekers traveled to Little Falls to see the place where he had grown up. And when they left the farm, they took with them anything that could be carried away as a souvenir of their pilgrimage. When Charles returned briefly to his Minnesota home, he found it unkept and vandalized.

Through the efforts of a group of Little Falls citizens, a move was launched to preserve the Lindbergh estate. The family agreed to give the property to any organization that would take care of it, and in 1931 the state legislature voted to accept it and develop it as a state park. At that time Lindbergh asked that the park be named for his father.

With his co-operation and that of his half-sister, the former Eva Lindbergh now Mrs. G. Howard Spaeth, the division of state parks, the Works Progress Administration, and the Minnesota Historical Society began to restore the house. It was repaired, painted, and enclosed by a steel and wire fence. The Lindbergh family generously donated many of the original furnishings of both the first and second houses and aided materially in replacing those pieces that had been damaged or lost through the years. Mrs. Lindbergh also shipped furnishings back to Minnesota from her home in Detroit, and after her death in 1954 additional items were returned by her son.

In 1969 the house and the property between the river and the roadway through the park came under the administration of the Minnesota Historical Society. At that time another phase in the restoration project was initiated, and plans were developed to build an interpretive center to house exhibits relating to the Lindbergh family. Completed in 1972, the center is designed to illustrate the lives of three generations of Lindbergh, — Ola Månsson, who served in the Swedish Riksdag before emigrating to Melrose, Minnesota, in 1860, when he changed his name to August Lindbergh; and the two Charles Lindberghs. The distinguished accomplishments of the younger Lindbergh in later life that are often overshadowed by his famous trans-Atlantic flight have a prominent place in the exhibits. After 1930 much of his time and energy was devoted to aviation and rocketry, and he was also active in the field of medical technology. Up to the time of his death in 1974, he was deeply involved in wildlife conservation. In 1954 Lindbergh was awarded the Pulitzer Prize for his autobiographical work, *The Spirit of St. Louis*.

Guided by the detailed recollections of Charles A. Lindbergh, the society's staff renovated the interior of the house and restored the rooms to their 1907–20 appearance. The steel and wire fence was replaced with one of woven wire and cedar posts, similar to the original erected at the turn of the century.

All three levels of the house — garage and basement, first floor, and second floor — are open to visitors. In the garage is the 1916 Saxon automobile in which Charles chauffeured his campaigning father and which was badly defaced by souvenir-hunters in 1927. It was restored by the men of the 747th Maintenance Battalion, a Minnesota National Guard unit training at Camp Ripley. Two damaged propellers from Charles' first airplane are evidence of crack-ups that occurred during the 1923 campaign. Also displayed are the outboard motor used by father and son on a trip down the Mississippi River from Itasca State Park in 1915 and toys, tools, and rocks belonging to Charles.

Because the house was used primarily as a summer home until 1917, it was never completely finished inside. The walls, for example, were never painted and curtains were not hung at most windows. Charles usually slept on the screened porch — summer and winter — even though the upstairs was finally divided into bedrooms just before he and his mother spent their first winter there in 1917–18. (In earlier years young Charles used the second floor for a playroom on rainy days.) The original hot-air furnace installed in 1917 may still be seen in the house.

Mementos of the Lindberghs are on view throughout the house, and on the grounds are other remembrances. A bronze plaque on a boulder near the front gate tells of the family's gift to the state. Trees and shrubs have been planted to restore the area to the condition of rare beauty that first attracted the elder Lindbergh. Footpaths take the visitor into the woods where Charles played and worked.

The Lindbergh House and interpretive center are open to the public daily from May through October. There is no admission fee.

THE INTERPRETIVE CENTER, *built on the Mississippi riverbank in 1971, houses exhibits describing the lives and careers of three generations of the Lindbergh family.*

CONNOR'S FUR POST, *located on the Snake River near Pine City, is a reconstruction of the wintering post Thomas Connor built and occupied from November, 1804, to April, 1805, while he traded with the Chippewa Indians.*

Connor's Fur Post

Located on the southeast bank of the Snake River in Pine County. Accessible from Interstate highway no. 35; exit at Pine City and proceed west on county road no. 7 for about 1.5 miles. The entrance to the site is marked.

SIX WEEKS after landing on the banks of the Snake River in late autumn, 1804, fur trader Thomas Connor and his voyageurs completed the building of a six-room trading post surrounded by a stockade. There Connor and his men stayed until spring, trading with the Chippewa Indians for furs. Connor's establishment was probably the southernmost of about a dozen wintering posts operated by the British North West Company's Fond du Lac department in the area south and west of Lake Superior. As such it was a small but important link in the vast trade network extending over much of Canada and the northern United States, where the North West Company in this period competed with the Hudson's Bay Company and the XY Company for dominance in the fur trade. Now reconstructed in its entirety, Connor's fur post is open to the public.

When Connor received his assignment to establish a wintering post in the Snake River region, he was a six-year veteran of the fur trade. Born in Great Britain about 1779, he emigrated to what is now Canada in his nineteenth year and took a position as a clerk with the London-based Hudson's Bay Company. He soon left that organization to work for the rival North West Company in the Lake Superior area. By 1804 he had apparently displayed the intelligence, loyalty, and stamina to merit a more responsible assignment, taking charge of the new post and keeping the records.

Connor kept a diary, which fortunately has been preserved. It begins on September 15, 1804, as he was en route from Lake Superior to the Snake River (via the Brule and St. Croix rivers) with five canoeloads of supplies and trading goods. By October 1 he reached Cross Lake on the Snake River, his progress having been hampered by delays to gum leaks in the canoes with spruce pitch, by rainy weather, and by meetings with Chippewa eager to trade their furs, wild rice, and meat. At Cross Lake Connor met with his "principal Men" to "fix on a place for my Winters abode." There, too, he gave out goods on credit to Indians who soon left for their hunting grounds.

The site for the wintering post was carefully chosen by Connor to meet the necessary requirements. It was on a high, sandy ridge about a hundred yards from the river and accessible to that stream for transportation and fishing. Equally important, it was in the midst of a heavy stand of timber for use as fuel and building material, there was abundant game in the area for food, and the site was within easy reach of the Indian villages.

On October 9 Connor's men began clearing the grounds and felling trees. The trader gave them each a dram of liquor ''morning and Evening & promised to do the same till our Buildings are Compleated provided the[y] exert themselves.'' Spurred on by this promise and faced with oncoming winter, the men began erecting the walls of the fort's single, long building, which could be finished one room at a time. Within a week they had completed the storage area, where with some relief Connor ''put all the provisions & Goods under Lock & Key.'' When the walls were up, the men finished the roof, the clay and rock lining of the fireplaces and chimneys, the floors of clay and sand, and the chinking of the walls. After the storage room, top priority went to Connor's quarters and his store, and on the same day that he moved into his two rooms he put the ''provision Store in Order.'' The men then finished their own sleeping room and a workroom before beginning the fifteen-day job of raising a stockade to protect the post. On November 20, the ''Doors of the Fort where [sic] fixd & Shut,'' and the following day Connor hoisted the British Union Jack over his wilderness post.

The construction method used for the building was a ''timbers on timbers'' technique that required few precious nails and no foundation. Ends of the logs were tenoned and slipped horizontally into large, vertically grooved upright posts firmly imbedded in the ground at the corners and at each end of the interior partitions. The structure thus formed was adequate for a short-lived wintering post. Measuring 18 by 77 feet, the elongated building was divided into six consecutive rooms whose entrances all opened onto the southeast side facing away from the river. Many of the rooms had glass windows (a fact archaeologists determined by the discovery of broken glass at specific locations along the wall line), and several of the outside doors were protected by small storm porches; four rooms had a fireplace. The building was secured against unwanted visitors and cutting winter winds by the stockade, which measured about 60 by 108 feet. Access to the fort enclosure was by a large gate in the southeast stockade wall and a smaller gate near the north corner. At the south and east corners of the stockade, there were two bastions from which the exterior walls could be defended.

How many men were involved in the speedy construction of Connor's fort is a matter of conjecture, since the trader failed to note this fact in his diary. Perhaps all the voyageurs who manned his supply canoes stayed to help, or perhaps Connor hired Indians, as did other clerks in the company. The trader also failed to record how many men lived in the fort that winter, though he mentions the typically French-Canadian names of six apparent employees. These men were not necessarily living at the fort, however, for winterers often elected to stay in the villages of their Indian wives.

The daily routine at the fort centered on Connor's major purpose — to collect furs — and branched out into other areas of necessity. Throughout the long winter, Indians regularly appeared at the store with furs and foodstuffs to exchange for blankets, cloth, trinkets, kettles, powder and shot, beads, body paint, tobacco, rum, high wine, and other goods in Connor's stock. When not occupied with trading, Connor had to make sure the fort's demands for food and fuel were met. Early in the season he employed a hunter who was ''accounted the best of all Indians of this Department'' to supply game; he regularly sent his own men out to hunt and seine fish as well. A major staple in their diet was wild rice, for which the locale had long been famous. Over the winter some fifty bags of ''oats,'' as wild rice was called, were brought in by Indians and stored in pits under the fireplaces to keep them safe from thieves and free from mold. Administering to the sick and keeping the peace in his small domain also took up Connor's time, while his men were assigned to collect furs from Indian lodges, make sledges and snowshoes, repair canoes, and cut firewood. The routine was broken by All Saints' Day, Christmas, and New Year's, each marked by a day of rest and gifts of rum and tobacco from the trader.

A FUR PRESS *like this one helped voy-ageurs pack animal pelts into ninety-pound bales. A birch-bark canoe hangs overhead in the workroom.*

Two threats to the success of Connor's winter season lay in the contest between the Chippewa and the ousted Dakota over the Snake River territory and in the competition from an XY Company trader located a short distance to the north on the Kettle River. Over the former Connor had no control, except to offer the Chippewa such safety as he could in case the constantly feared attacks by the Dakota became a reality. It was the threat posed by the rival trader that plagued him most, and he strongly suspected that the "XY Banditti," as he called his competitors, would "poison the Minds of the [Indian] Women by offering to sell Cheaper" and thereby gain the loyalty of his Chippewa hunters.

Competition from the smaller XY Company had increased markedly since 1802. Consequently the North West Company made a special effort to outnumber the XY traders in the interior by establishing as many wintering posts as it had clerks to operate them. (Connor's assignment in 1804 may have been part of this plan.) As the rivalry sharpened, both companies had authorized the use of liquor as a major item of barter instead of giving it to the Indians only on special occasions as had been the earlier practice. It was not long before high wine and rum, watered down to extend their trade value, were recognized as "the root of all evil" in the fur trade country. Connor and other agents apparently felt pressured by their employers to use any trading methods that brought results, for, besides having to best the opposition, each trader owed a personal debt to the company which he attempted to pay off at the end of the wintering season. Connor, for example, owed the North West Company £ 1,026.3 in 1805.

On December 31, 1804, Connor received word from company headquarters in Montreal that the North West Company had merged with the XY organization to put an end to the bitter competition. Effective with the outfit of 1805, the agreement was to give 25 per cent of the trade's profits to the smaller company.

CRUDE BUNKS, *hanging lanterns, and handmade snowshoe frames can be seen in the employees' sleeping quarters reconstructed at Connor's Fur Post.*

PEWTER, *glassware, and ivory-handled utensils, like these in Connor's reconstructed quarters, were supplied by the North West Company to its chief traders living in isolated wintering posts.*

Connor, who saw the merger as the destruction of his competitors, arranged to meet with the neighboring XY agent in order to make "a settlement with him respecting his future Conduct with the Indians." The following day the XY man left Connor's post "much discouraged," and Connor continued as before to forbid his Indians to trade with his rival, at least for the remainder of the winter.

With the coming of spring the fort became alive with preparations to end the trading season. Food supplies were desperately depleted, and when the weather warmed, Connor sent Indian women into the bush to boil down "maple juises," while his men seined for fish and retrieved caches of flour and wild rice downriver. On April 23 the last of the Indian hunters came to the fort to settle their accounts. The trappers had made "a pitifull Hunt," in Connor's opinion, and he seemed disappointed in the total of more than five hundred beaver skins he collected for the season. These, with muskrat, deer, and bear skins, were packed in ninety-pound bales and sent by canoe to the collecting post on Lake Superior for shipment eastward. That year the Fond du Lac department produced 10,350 pounds of furs, of which 4,426 pounds were beaver skins — then the most preferred pelt among the fashionable elite of Europe whose social status was indicated by the height of their beaver hats.

Connor left his post on April 27, 1805. Whether he ever returned to it is not known. He probably remained with the North West Company until 1816, when it was forced to stop trading within the United States. Thereafter he joined the American Fur Company and set up a post on the south shore of nearby Pokegama Lake, where he, his Chippewa wife, and eight children were living in 1840. Not long after, he removed his Catholic family from the influence of the Protestant mission at Pokegama and began trading in the St. Croix Valley. With the encroachment of loggers and the depletion of fur resources, Connor deserted the valley for the less settled shores of Lake Superior. There in St. Louis County, according to the census records for 1860, he lived into his eighth decade, having labored for half a century in the fur trade.

Connor's diary ends with his departure from the wintering post in 1805. All further information about the fort had to be pieced together by archaeologists nearly 160 years later. In the long interim the fur trade died out and gave way to lumbering, which cleared the land for the farmers who followed. Long after the voyageurs were gone, a dam was built on the Snake River, taming its challenging upper rapids into a quiet stream.

In 1963 Joseph Neubauer, who resided near Pine City, brought to the attention of a professional archaeologist some bits of charred wood, fired clay, and trade artifacts he had picked up each year in a field adjacent to his home on the Snake River. Preliminary investigation of the field convinced the archaeologist that a building once stood there, and after consultation with the Minnesota Historical Society, the site was tentatively identified as Connor's fur post. Its identity was confirmed by excavations begun that year and continuing for another four summers under the direction of Leland R. Cooper, emeritus professor at Hamline University.

As the digging progressed, the shape and location of the six rooms, fireplaces, cache pits, and surrounding stockade gradually emerged. Placement of doors and windows also was determined, and about the only dimensions of the post that remained in question were the exact heights of the building's walls and of the stockade. The hundreds of artifacts uncovered included an engraved lock plate and other gun components and part of a bale seal. Also salvaged were sections of baling wire, bits of ornamental beads and metals, and fragments of utensils, china, bottles, and clay trade pipes. Some artifacts were badly damaged in a fire that destroyed the fort at an unknown date, while other metal pieces were preserved in excellent condition.

During the peak years of the fur trade, hundreds of temporary wintering posts were in operation, but most of their locations remain unknown. Because

Connor's post could be unquestionably identified by the trader's diary, the Minnesota Historical Society urged that it be reconstructed. The state purchased the site in 1965, and with later additions now owns approximately forty-three acres, including a thirty-acre plot on the opposite riverbank. The state legislature appropriated funds for the reconstruction project in 1967 and rebuilding began in 1968 under the administration of the historical society.

Guided by unearthed artifacts, Connor's diary, and the writings of other fur traders, Professor Cooper and his associates were able to reconstruct the fort without major changes in the original design but with methods that resulted in a more permanent structure. From Chengwatana State Forest over 1,500 tamarack logs were hauled to the site to be stripped of bark and treated with a preservative. Workmen raised them in the "timbers on timbers" construction technique for the building and imbedded them three feet into the ground for the stockade. Cedar shakes were used on the roof — both for permanence and because the original material is not definitely known. Tinted cement replaced clay for the floors and chinking mortar. The reconstructed fireplaces are similar to the originals in that they are built of mortared rocks in the lower section, but the vertical poles forming the chimneys are lined with cement blocks instead of clay. Hinges, hardware, and rosehead nails simulating those found at the site were fashioned by the blacksmith at restored Fort Snelling especially for use at Connor's post.

The rooms contain authentically duplicated crude furniture and equipment like that the trader may have used. Connor's quarters have a bed, benches, a floor cache for personal belongings, and a table set with the pewter, glassware, and ivory-handled silverware that a chief trader rated. The employees' quarters are crowded with bunks, a table set with tinware, snowshoes, and other accessories. In the workroom a huge birch-bark canoe, a replica of those used in the trade, hangs above a fur press used in forming bales.

Since its reconstruction was completed in 1970, Connor's fur post has been open to the public daily from May through September, and by reservation only in October. There is an admission fee. Guides garbed in the colorful costumes of the fur trade era conduct visitors through the fort, explaining structural features in the reconstruction and pointing out replicas of trade goods. Modern exhibits describe the development of Minnesota's first industry — the fur trade.

THE "TIMBERS ON TIMBERS" *method of construction, shown here in detail, was used by both Connor and the men who reconstructed the post more than 165 years later.*

Sinclair Lewis Boyhood Home

Located at 812 Sinclair Lewis Avenue in Sauk Centre. Accessible from Interstate highway no. 94 and U.S. highway no. 71.

SINCLAIR LEWIS, the first American author to receive the Nobel Prize for literature, was one of the nation's most popular writers from 1920 to 1940. He lived in this modest frame house from the age of four until he left to attend college at the age of eighteen. With the publication in 1920 of Lewis' first major novel, *Main Street*, the author's home town of Sauk Centre was thrust into notoriety as the prototype for "Gopher Prairie," the small midwestern town so roundly criticized in the novel for its provincialism. The townspeople were, at first, angry at the treatment they received, but their anger soon waned, and Sauk Centre claimed as its own the boy who brought it international fame. Not only has the city forgiven Sinclair Lewis, it has refused to let the world forget him. In 1960 a group of Sauk Centre citizens established the Sinclair Lewis Foundation, a nonprofit corporation "dedicated to the furtherance of knowledge about Sinclair Lewis, and to the fostering in his name of creative activity in the literary world." Its first project was to purchase and restore Sinclair Lewis' boyhood home, which was opened to the public in 1970. The home is a National Historic Landmark.

Harry Sinclair Lewis, whose middle name honored a close friend of his father, was born at Sauk Centre on February 7, 1885. (His first home was at 811 Third Avenue, across the street from the present Lewis house. The family moved into the house at 812 Third Avenue in 1889.) He was the third son of a successful country doctor, Edwin J. Lewis, and a chronically ill mother who died when Harry was six. A year after their mother's death, Harry and his older brothers Fred and Claude were placed in the care of the second Mrs. Lewis. She was the former Isabel Warner of Chicago, whom Harry later described as a "pleasantly ambitious" woman of some cultural taste who read to her youngest stepson "more than usual" by Sauk Centre standards.

The new stepmother apparently adjusted well to the household, which ran on a rigid schedule dictated by the stern doctor. Year after year it remained the same; in fact, it was said that the people of Sauk Centre could set their clocks by the almost compulsive, methodical routine followed daily by Dr. Lewis. A man of little imagination or open affection, the doctor nevertheless was held in high regard by his family and his associates. He showed great respect for proper behavior, for education, and for professional responsibility and hard work.

84

There was no doubt that he expected his sons to conform to his standards and thereby to succeed. For two of the boys this presented no problem. Fred, the oldest, was allowed to quit dental school after an unsuccessful try, and he spent the remainder of his quiet life working in the milling trade in Sauk Centre. Claude, popular, ambitious, good-looking, and athletic, attended Rush Medical College, his father's alma mater, and became a respected doctor in St. Cloud. His father's favorite, Claude was the model for Harry to emulate, and the author once admitted that for sixty years he had tried to impress his older brother.

Life for young Harry, however, was not so easy. Given to tantrums and extraordinary behavior to attract attention, the lanky, red-haired Lewis boy soon found more friends in books than on the streets of Sauk Centre or even, perhaps, in his own home. He had trouble pleasing his father, whose reprimanding "Harry, why can't you do like any other boy ought to do" could never be forgotten. He sought the companionship of his brother Claude and his gang, but repeatedly discovered it was a pseudo friendship based on his own gullibility and availability as the butt of crude pranks. And so he turned increasingly to books. He read everything in his father's limited library at home, then absorbed all that caught his fancy in the Bryant Public Library. He read during the day, at night, while mowing the lawn, while chopping wood. He read while other boys his age were hunting, fishing, trapping, swimming — not because he did not enjoy those pastimes, but because he was seldom invited and he was not good at any of them. (Brother Claude once saved him from drowning.)

Neither did he excel in school, except in such extracurricular activities as debate and drama. Despite his dedication to books, an extremely wide vocabulary, and an ambition to grasp knowledge, his grades suffered from a lack of ability to apply himself and from his disruptive behavior in the classroom. As a youngster, he moved in a world of fantasy — tiring the patience of his few playmates with long and complex games, or, by himself, manipulating the lives of make-believe people symbolized by a variety of old keys. Much later in life Lewis recalled his boyhood "eagerness for anything out of Sauk Centre usual, or special in town." His objection to the town was, he said, that he could "find no ruined castles"; it was dull, unromantic. It was also rather unfriendly toward this uncommon child, though he never said so.

When Harry Sinclair Lewis was born in 1885, the village of Sauk Centre was less than ten years old. The combined population of the township and the village was 2,807. Streets were unpaved, often rutted, muddy tracks in rain and slush; plank sidewalks ran along five or six blocks of false-fronted business places. The town had an academy and a business college in addition to the public schools, a small but thriving library, an opera house, a hotel, a flour mill, the depot, and two newspapers. It received a city charter in 1889.

Despite its small size, Sauk Centre offered its citizens some cultural entertainment. There were concerts by visiting musical groups and soloists, a lyceum course, the University of Minnesota extension lectures, traveling elocutionists who illustrated their talks with stereopticon views, and theatricals performed by touring professionals and home-talent groups. The Lewis family attended many of these events. In addition the doctor was involved in civic affairs, and Mrs. Lewis was active in the Gradatim Club, whose members were devoted to self-improvement and community betterment.

Looking back, Sinclair Lewis tended to fantasize his childhood just as he had, as a boy, fantasized adult life. He somehow recalled a "totally normal boyhood — dull school routine, skating, sliding, skiing, swimming, duck-hunting." But his biographers and childhood acquaintances disagree with those recollections. Harry Lewis was considered by many to be odd — odd in his looks and odd in the way he acted. Tall for his age, he had a short body and long, thin legs that emphasized his height, carrot-red hair, ice-blue eyes,

SINCLAIR LEWIS *lived with his family in this house at Sauk Centre from the age of four until he went east to college at the age of eighteen.*

and a rather flushed, puffy face. He seemed to show off most of the time, talked unceasingly, and was generally unpopular. He had only one close friend, Irving Fisher, during his adolescence.

As early as age eleven, Harry decided to be a writer. At thirteen, he succumbed to a sudden humanistic urge to save the Cubans and ran off to join the Spanish-American War. With dreams of becoming a drummer boy, he walked some nine miles to Melrose, where his plans to board a train for the city were cut short by the appearance of his angry father who took him home forthwith. At seventeen, after graduating from high school and working for the local newspapers, Harry talked his father into helping him enter Yale University instead of the University of Minnesota, which the doctor had favored. Thus, in the fall of 1902, Harry left Sauk Centre to spend six months in preparatory study at Oberlin Academy in Ohio before beginning his collegiate career at Yale in 1903. It was at Yale that his literary efforts began in earnest.

From that time, Harry, who was by then commonly known as "Hal" or "Red," was to be only a visitor in his Sauk Centre home. He returned for the summer of 1905, during which, he recalled, he conceived a story about "The Village Virus" which would emerge as *Main Street*. The same year he published an essay under the name Sinclair Lewis. Eleven years later, after three of his novels had been published and he had become a full-time writer, he brought his first wife, Gracie, home to meet his family. The local newspaper marked his arrival late in April with these headlines: "Noted Young Writer of American Fiction Spending Summer as Guest of Parents and Friends in Sauk Centre." The couple took up residence in the back bedroom of his parents' house and stayed for about three months. During that time, the author worked at writing in a rented room above a hardware store, lectured at various club meetings, and renewed his acquaintance with childhood haunts. He and his wife took leisurely walks through the town and the countryside, often returning late and upsetting the schedule that still governed the Lewis home.

In October, 1920, *Main Street: The Story of Carol Kennicott* was published and met with immediate and phenomenal success. Sauk Centre's initial reaction to the novel was one of indignant rage at the lashing it received from the home-town boy. The resentment subsided by 1922, the year businessmen capitalized on the wide publicity and opened the Gopher Prairie Inn and the Main Street movie theater. It was not long until Sinclair Lewis was publicly acclaimed as the town's "chief ornament," a title in keeping with the nationwide praise he received as "the spokesman of a literary generation."

For two decades Lewis remained very much a popular figure watched and reported by the press as he published, traveled, married and divorced twice, and occasionally visited Minnesota. In 1926 his refusal to accept the Pulitzer Prize for his novel, *Arrowsmith*, caused a storm of comment. Then in 1930 the former Sauk Centre misfit won international acclaim when he accepted the Nobel Prize for literature — the first American to receive the honor. At that time he was the author of thirteen novels (including those mentioned above as well as *Babbitt, Elmer Gantry*, and *Dodsworth*) and numerous short stories, plays, essays, reviews, and poems. Lewis was to write ten more novels before his career ended in 1951.

Since 1920 Lewis' place in American literature has been debated by authors, critics, teachers, and the general public. His admirers would agree with Carl C. Van Doren's appraisal in 1933 that he was "the quintessence of the United States." As late as 1959 he was termed by John R. Dos Passos "a sort of folk-hero of his time." Others consider him a man with an insignificant mind who turned out highly overrated fiction. The debate will undoubtedly continue.

Sinclair Lewis last visited his home town in 1947. By then both his health and his literary prowess were on the decline. At the age of sixty-six Lewis died of heart disease and alcoholism in a hospital outside Rome. In the end he returned to Minnesota — where he had so often gone back, he said, to re-establish his roots. His ashes were brought to Sauk Centre, where on January 28, 1951, funeral services were held in the high school auditorium. On that frigid, windy afternoon, about a hundred people watched as Claude Lewis placed the ashes of his brother in a small grave beside that of their father. A simple stone marks the site in Greenwood Cemetery located a mile east of the city. It reads: "Sinclair Lewis 1885–1951 Author of 'Main Street.' "

Minnesota celebrated Sinclair Lewis Year in 1960 by proclamation of Governor Orville L. Freeman. A summer festival marked the seventy-fifth anniversary of the author's birth, the fortieth anniversary of the publication of *Main Street*,

ON A VISIT *to his former home, probably in 1916, Lewis (seated at right) gathered with friends for an outdoor breakfast served by his wife Gracie, dressed as a maid. Courtesy James Taylor Dunn.*

and the thirtieth anniversary of Lewis' Nobel Prize. Sauk Centre noted the occasion by renaming its major thoroughfare "The Original Main Street"; it also decided to designate Third Avenue as Sinclair Lewis Avenue and gave the author's name to a city park.

In 1966 the Sinclair Lewis Foundation purchased the house at 812 Sinclair Lewis Avenue and began a restoration project in co-operation with the Minnesota Historical Society. Following the death of Mrs. Lewis in 1921, the elderly doctor had been cared for in the house by Mr. and Mrs. Charles W. Rotert. When he died in 1926, the home was inherited by the three sons, who then sold it to the Roterts; it changed owners three more times before it was purchased by the Lewis Foundation. No construction date has been determined for the house, but it probably was built in the mid-1880s. Throughout its history, the home had undergone several remodelings — stucco had been added to the exterior probably in the 1920s; the roof line had been altered and the front porch enclosed; a bathroom had been installed in 1905; interior walls had been added or removed at various times; and the second floor had been turned into a three-room apartment. More than three years of carefully researched restoration work were required to bring the home to its present appearance. Much of the information that guided the work was obtained from photographs, interviews, and the writings of Lewis and his wives, Grace Hegger Lewis and Dorothy Thompson. Funds

A RADIO SET *Sinclair gave to his father is in the restored office used by the doctor. The photograph above it shows Sinclair at four years of age.*

THE SMALL BACK PARLOR *of the restored Lewis home is furnished with the family's platform rocking chair and mirrored bookcase.*

THE ORIGINAL *Main Street in Sauk Centre flaunted signs in 1957 to remind the world of the Sinclair Lewis book that first brought it fame.*

for the project came from a sale of stock in the foundation, from donations, and from a $12,500 grant appropriated by the Minnesota legislature in 1969.

A few original Lewis furnishings remain in the home — a platform rocking chair and a mirrored bookcase in the small back parlor; a radio receiver set, given by Sinclair Lewis to his father, in the restored doctor's office (the desk and physician's bag in this room belonged to Dr. Claude Lewis); a clock and a buffet in the dining room. The remainder of the furnishings are illustrative of small-town homes in the early 1900s.

In the back yard stands the original stable and carriage barn, which housed neither horses nor automobiles, since Dr. Lewis always rented the necessary means of transportation for his trips into the country. Plans are under study to restore the structure to its early 1900s appearance when, so the story goes, young Harry Lewis used its second floor as a quiet hideaway for writing.

Opened to the public in 1970, the Sinclair Lewis Boyhood Home is considered an outstanding example of historic restoration. The foundation in 1970 received an award of merit from the American Association for State and Local History "for restoring the author's boyhood home as nearly as possible to the appearance it had when Lewis lived there." The home is open to the public daily during the summer and on an irregular schedule the remainder of the year. There is an admission charge. Scheduled to open in the summer of 1975 is the new Sinclair Lewis Museum built by the foundation at a wayside on U.S. Highway 71 at its junction with Interstate Highway 94. In it will be exhibited collections of photographs, letters, diplomas, and other Lewis memorabilia, along with copies of many of the author's manuscripts. The original manuscript of Mark Schorer's extensive biography entitled *Sinclair Lewis, An American Life* will also be displayed. There will be no admission fee.

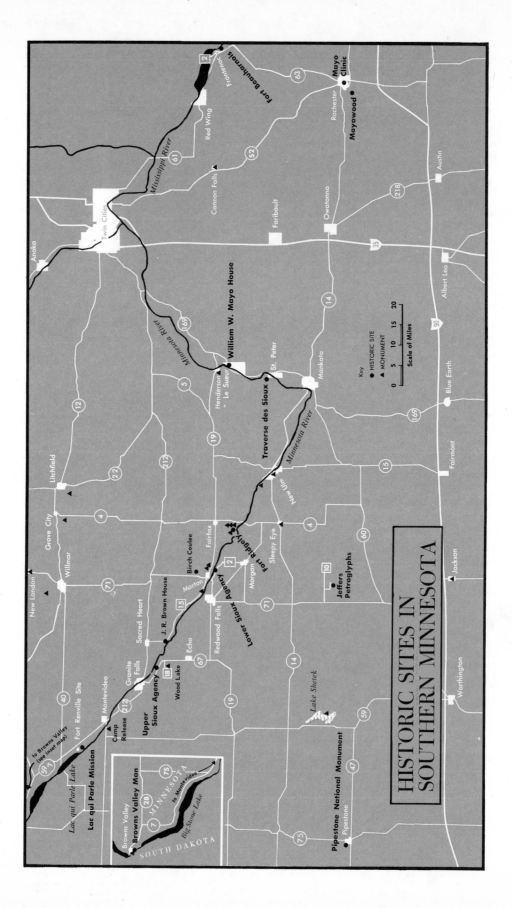

HISTORIC SITES IN SOUTHERN MINNESOTA

Fort Beauharnois

Mayo Clinic

Mayowood

Red Wing

Rochester

Austin

Cannon Falls

Faribault

Owatonna

Albert Lea

Twin Cities

Anoka

William W. Mayo House

Le Sueur

St. Peter

Traverse des Sioux

Mankato

Blue Earth

Key
● HISTORIC SITE
▲ MONUMENT

Scale of Miles
0 5 10 15 20

Henderson

Litchfield

Grove City

Willmar

New London

Fairmont

New Ulm

Birch Coulee

Fairfax

Fort Ridgely

Sleepy Eye

Jackson

Morton

Jeffers Petroglyphs

Minnesota River

J. R. Brown House

Sacred Heart

Redwood Falls

Lower Sioux Agency

Morgan

Echo

Wood Lake

Lake Shetek

Granite Falls

Upper Sioux Agency

Montevideo

Fort Renville Site

Camp Release

Worthington

Lac qui Parle Lake

Lac qui Parle Mission

to Browns Valley
(see inset map)

Pipestone National Monument

Pipestone

MINNESOTA

SOUTH DAKOTA

Browns Valley

Browns Valley Man

to Montevideo

Big Stone Lake

Mississippi River

Fort Beauharnois

Site located on Pointe au Sable immediately east of Villa Maria Retreat Center in Frontenac State Park. Accessible from Goodhue County road no. 2, about a mile north from U.S. highway no. 61.

IN THE CENTURY BEFORE 1763 when France gave up its claim to what is now Minnesota, adventurous men like Jolliet and Marquette, Du Luth, and La Vérendrye carried the French flag into the center of the continent. Other Frenchmen followed them to build fortified posts from which to explore the headwaters of the great Mississippi River. The Minnesota country was on the outer fringe of French activity, but some temporary posts were erected there after 1695. One Minnesota site of French occupation, however, was intended to be permanent. It was Fort Beauharnois on Lake Pepin, a widening in the Mississippi River between Red Wing and Wabasha. The fort was one of the earliest and also one of the last French outposts in the state. Within its stockade stood what seems to have been the first Christian church on Minnesota soil — the Mission of St. Michael the Archangel. Although these structures have long since disappeared, their history is recalled in appropriate markers.

Fort Beauharnois was to be the first step in a grand plan adopted by the French government in 1723. From this outpost on the Mississippi, the French hoped to reach the lucrative fur trading area of the Dakota Indians, secure an alliance with that powerful tribe, and establish a jumping-off place for further explorations in search of the Western Sea. Since the Dakota had earlier indicated that they would welcome missionaries to their villages, the French sent messengers of the gospel as well as soldiers and skilled workmen to the new post.

The notion that the fort could be used to further explorations toward the Western Sea was undoubtedly a powerful motivating force in its establishment. The pursuit of a route across North America to the Pacific Ocean was one of the dominant objectives of the period. Many men searched for it, all of them unaware of the vast width of the continent that balked their success.

The plan adopted by the French in 1723 was not executed until four years later because hostilities between the Fox Indians of Wisconsin and the Dakota made passage through the area dangerous. But in 1727 temporary peace prevailed between the tribes. With a party of thirty to forty men, René Boucher, a distinguished officer in France's colonial troops who bore the title Sieur de la Perrière, set off from Montreal for the upper Mississippi in June, 1727. With him went two missionaries, Michel Guignas and Nicolas de Gonnor. After passing safely through the land of the hostile Fox, the little party reached Lake Pepin the following September. There, in the largely unexplored Minnesota wilderness, Boucher probably landed on a low point of land now known as Pointe au Sable, Sand Point, or Long Point below Villa Maria Retreat Center.

The men began at once to erect a substantial stockade "with two good bastions." It was a hundred feet square, constructed of tree trunks set on end and extending twelve feet above the ground. Within the enclosure were three log buildings — a chapel, 25 by 16 feet in size, and houses for the commandant and the missionaries. Outside the stockade the men built cabins for themselves, a blacksmith's shop, and a warehouse. When the little village was completed in late October, the missionaries said Mass in the new chapel, dedicating it to Saint Michael the Archangel. The fort itself was named for Charles de la Boische, Marquis de Beauharnois, who was then governor of New France.

Its inhabitants spent the long winter without serious mishap, but with the coming of spring the fort was flooded. Boucher, who was then nearly sixty years old, found his health seriously affected by the rigors of the wilderness. When the flood subsided, he turned over his command to his nephew, Pierre Boucherville, and with Father de Gonnor made the long voyage back to Montreal.

Meanwhile the Fox had again taken the warpath, and the new commandant soon decided to quit the post. He set off with Father Guignas and eight men by canoe down the Mississippi. The party was captured by the Kickapoo and Mascouten Indians, who were allies of the Fox, but ultimately the men escaped or were released. The Frenchmen who had chosen to remain at Beauharnois successfully held the fort for another year. But prospects for a profitable trade with the Sioux seemed slight, and sometime in 1729 the fort was abandoned. The plan to launch an expedition from Fort Beauharnois in search of a Northwest Passage was never carried out.

Two years later French traders, again accompanied by Father Guignas, returned to the upper Mississippi and spent some five years on the Wisconsin shore in what is now Perrot State Park near Trempealeau before moving upriver to Lake Pepin in 1736. Reaching the site of Fort Beauharnois, they probably

THE CHAPEL OF ST. MICHAEL, *built at Fort Beauharnois in 1727, was probably the first Christian church erected on Minnesota soil. Courtesy St. Paul Seminary.*

FORT BEAUHARNOIS, *constructed on Lake Pepin by French fur traders in 1727, probably looked much like this charcoal drawing by Fletcher Sultzer. Courtesy Goodhue County Historical Society.*

selected a higher location for the new fort, perhaps where Villa Maria now stands. But the continuing Fox wars doomed this post to a short life, and it was abandoned and burned in the spring of 1737.

Not until 1750 did conditions become peaceful enough for the French to try again. In that year Paul Marin or his son Joseph built still another fur post on Lake Pepin, probably on or near the site of the first Fort Beauharnois. From it the Marins carried on a flourishing trade with the Dakota until 1756, when all outlying French garrisons were recalled to defend New France against Great Britain in the French and Indian War. The French did not return to the Minnesota country, which passed into the possession of Britain and then the United States.

Today nothing remains of the old French forts. But in 1887 two cannon balls of ancient make were found near Frontenac, and ten years later about a hundred lead bullets were recovered from the waters of Lake Pepin near Pointe au Sable. A marker calling attention to the old French mission stands on the grounds of Villa Maria. It was placed there in 1927 by the Goodhue County Historical Society. Another marker on U.S. highway no. 61 reminds the modern visitor of Fort Beauharnois. The French heritage of the area is further recalled in the name of the town, which was called Frontenac in honor of Louis de Buade, Comte de Frontenac, the successful governor of New France from 1671 to 1698.

Mayos of Minnesota

Three sites of historic interest associated with the Mayo Family are the Mayo House, located at 118 North Main Street (U.S. highway no. 169), Le Sueur; Mayo Clinic historical area in Rochester; Mayowood near Rochester.

THE MINNESOTA NAME probably best known throughout the world is Mayo. The accomplishments of this family in the field of medicine have brought fame both to its members and to the state. The name has come to mean the Mayo Clinic at Rochester, but two other sites — one in Le Sueur and one near Rochester — are also intimately associated with the lives of the Mayos. A small frame house in Le Sueur was the family's early Minnesota home, while Mayowood, built by Dr. Charles H. Mayo in 1910–11, was occupied by members of his family until 1968.

W. W. MAYO HOUSE — The first member of the family to become a resident of Minnesota was William W. Mayo, who emigrated from England in 1845 and earned a degree in medicine in 1850. Four years later at the age of thirty-one, he left his wife and small child in Indiana and traveled to St. Paul in search of relief from the effects of malaria. Finding the rude capital of Minnesota Territory to his liking, he soon established his family there. Mrs. Mayo operated a successful millinery shop, and her husband became actively involved in Minnesota politics — an interest he retained throughout his long life.

In 1856 the Mayos moved to an abandoned farm at Cronan's Precinct, a settlement on the Minnesota River across from the village of Le Sueur. Dr. Mayo resumed his medical practice, competing with other doctors, midwives, grandma's remedies, and the patent medicines with which the settlers dosed themselves. In the spring of 1859, when the Minnesota River overflowed its banks and marooned the settlers of Cronan's Precinct, Dr. Mayo decided to move to Le Sueur, where he had purchased property.

There, with the help of his brother James, the doctor built a house and a barn during the summer of 1859. The home was a modest, two-story frame cottage with a gabled roof and three small rooms on each floor. One of the rooms upstairs — a low-ceilinged nook under the gable — served as an office for the physician who, because of his short stature, was called the "little doctor." In it he arranged his medical books, a large roll-top desk, and medicine-mixing equipment. The Mayo's first son, William James, was born in this house in 1861.

When the Sioux Uprising exploded the following year, Dr. Mayo joined his neighbors in the defense of New Ulm. For two strenuous weeks the physician cared for the sick and wounded who survived the Indians' attacks on the town and surrounding area. Meanwhile, his wife and three children remained at home, fearing every moment that the Dakota would fire upon Le Sueur, but the settlement was never attacked. Instead, it became a refuge for settlers fleeing from the embattled region upriver. Mrs. Mayo and her children shared their little home with eleven families who occupied every inch of space in the house and barn. She received occasional news of her husband from the refugees, who told her the little doctor had dressed their wounds.

After the successful evacuation of New Ulm, Dr. Mayo returned to Le Sueur, and within a month the Sioux Uprising was quelled. The Civil War continued, however, and in May, 1863, Dr. Mayo went to Rochester as examining surgeon of the enrollment board for the first Minnesota district. The thriving town impressed him, and early in 1864 he moved his wife and children to Rochester, where he intended to set up his private practice.

The little house the Mayos left behind in Le Sueur has an obscure history after 1864. It had at least half a dozen owners before 1932, the year the *Le Sueur News-Herald* began to advocate its preservation. That year, too, a historic marker was erected at the house by the Minnesota Historical Society and the state highway department. Two years later Dr. Mayo's sons, William J. and Charles H., purchased the property and presented it to the city of Le Sueur. The house was opened in 1935 as the Le Sueur Public Library, and the little doctor's office upstairs was restored with the furniture and equipment he had used there.

In 1970 the city of Le Sueur transferred ownership of the Mayo house to the Minnesota Historical Society and removed the library from the building. Loren C. Johnson, the society's restoration expert, completed a detailed analysis of the structure and found it to be in serious need of repairs. He also determined

DR. WILLIAM W. MAYO, *who arrived in Minnesota in 1854, founded a family medical practice in Rochester that his sons developed into the famed Mayo Clinic. Courtesy Mayo Clinic Archives.*

THE MAYO HOUSE *was built in Le Sueur by Dr. William W. Mayo in 1859. Often altered and added to over the years, the house has now been restored to its original eight-room size.*

that the original house had been enlarged several times and that the Mayo family had built only a small six-room house in 1859 and possibly added two rooms at the rear the following year. Successive additions to the home were constructed by 1912, and some interior improvements were made about 1914, when the house was owned by Carson N. Cosgrove, a founder of the Minnesota Valley Canning Company. Since 1972 the house, which is in the National Register of Historic Places, has undergone extensive restoration. Additions built after 1860 were removed, as was exterior ornamental woodwork. Each room, including the doctor's office upstairs, is furnished appropriately for the 1860s. Public dedication of the Mayo House occurred in June, 1974. It is open on summer weekends or by reservation. There is an admission fee.

MAYO CLINIC — The Mayos' first home in Rochester was a frame structure on Franklin Street. There in 1865, their second son, Charles Horace, was born. The little doctor's reputation became widespread, due perhaps as much to his energetic activities in local and state affairs as to his healing prowess. Within ten years the doctor's practice proved lucrative enough to afford the purchase of a small farm on the outskirts of Rochester. On it he built a large, two-story house that featured a tower with an observatory for Mrs. Mayo's study of astronomy. On this farm the Mayo boys grew up, and as soon as they were old enough, they traveled with their father to treat patients living in the surrounding countryside. As youths, the Mayo brothers helped out in the doctor's office at Rochester, doing the work of today's interns and nurses. It never occurred to them that they would be anything but doctors when they matured, and it seemed to be understood that they would practice with their father when they had received their medical degrees. Young Will returned to Rochester with his in 1883 and Charles in 1888. The family practice prospered and grew. Like their father, the Mayo brothers insisted on being in the vanguard of progress in the medical fields, especially surgery, and all three doctors traveled widely to consult with innovative physicians and surgeons.

In 1883 a tornado ripped through the Rochester area, leaving in its wake thirty dead and scores of injured. Dr. W. W. Mayo asked the Sisters of St. Francis to oversee the emergency medical care of the victims, and as a result the Sisters later decided to build and operate a much-needed hospital in Rochester. When St. Mary's Hospital opened in 1889, Dr. Mayo headed its medical staff, which also included his two sons. The volume of operations performed by the Mayos at St. Mary's mounted each year, totaling nearly four thousand in 1905. By that time the little doctor had retired from the staff to pursue two other interests — travel and politics.

Since 1855, Dr. Mayo had led a somewhat erratic and often controversial political life. Outspoken and uncompromising, he seldom missed an opportunity to publicize his views as a freethinker, devotee of Darwinism, founder of the Minnesota and Olmsted County medical societies, antiprohibitionist, antimonopolist, opponent of woman's suffrage, and local leader in the agrarian crusade. He was elected justice of the peace in Le Sueur and mayor, alderman, and member of the school board in Rochester. He joined the Farmers' Alliance, and with the support of that organization and the Democrats, he was elected to the state senate in 1890. From time to time Mayo had switched party loyalty, but for the last forty years of his life he was a staunch Democrat. He died in 1911 shortly before his ninety-second birthday.

The Mayo brothers recruited several other doctors to join their practice, and eventually they left to their new associates all diagnostic procedures while they concentrated on surgery. As early as 1903 medical men referred to this group as "the Mayo Clinic of St. Mary's Hospital." In 1914 they opened new offices in a large building constructed on the site of the Mayos' first home in Rochester. The opening of this clinic marked the emergence of a distinctive private medical institution based on the central idea of specialists working in a group practice.

THE TWO YOUNG MAYO DOCTORS, *Charles H. (left) and William J., are shown in 1904 in the operating room of St. Mary's Hospital. Courtesy Mayo Clinic Archives.*

Under the administration of the Mayos, the clinic continued to expand its programs of medical care, teaching, and research. In 1928 a second building was constructed adjacent to and interconnected with the first. Together these two integrated structures are called the Plummer Building, which was designated a National Historic Landmark in 1970. Located in the Plummer Building is the clinic's historical area, which includes the archives, the old board of governors meeting room, and the last offices of Dr. Will and Dr. Charlie. Exhibits contain personal items and hundreds of photographs belonging to the two doctors and displays of their numerous honorary degrees and citations. Dr. Will's office has been completely restored with the simple furnishings he preferred plus favorite photographs of his wife and of Dr. Joseph Lister. Dr. Charlie's original office, located at the rear of the board of governors room, was taken over by his son, Dr. Charles W. Mayo, who used it until his death in 1968. An office across the hall from Dr. Will's has been furnished with Dr. Charlie's desk, books, and accessories and is open to the public. His original office, undisturbed since his son's death, is not currently open to visitors. Free public tours of the clinic, including the historical area, are offered weekdays at 10 A.M. and 2 P.M. and begin in Judd Hall in the subway of the Mayo Building.

Today the Mayo Clinic complex consists of five major buildings housing treatment and diagnostic facilities, laboratories, medical records, and libraries. In the Damon Parkade is located the Mayo Medical Museum which is open to the public without charge. The clinic, which is still affiliated with St. Mary's Hospital and with the newer Rochester Methodist Hospital, serves each year more than 200,000 patients from all over the world. The medical staff comprises over five hundred physicians and medical scientists, as well as some seven hundred doctors receiving advanced training. The nonmedical staff numbers nearly three thousand people. In 1971 the clinic announced plans to open an undergraduate school of medicine.

HONORARY DEGREES, *awards, and citations received by Charles H. and William J. Mayo line the walls of the old board of governors room in the present Plummer Building. Courtesy Mayo Clinic Archives.*

MAYOWOOD, *the country home Dr. Charles H. Mayo built in 1910–11, clings to a hillside overlooking the South Fork Zumbro River Valley. The thirty-eight-room house, shown here in the late 1930s, is owned by the Olmsted County Historical Society. Courtesy Mayo Clinic Archives.*

MAYOWOOD — The private lives of Dr. Charlie and Dr. Will Mayo were never far removed from their professional careers or from each other. While their personalities differed greatly, there was a bond between them that was never broken. Both men married Rochester girls. Will wed Hattie Damon in 1884; Dr. Charlie married one of the city's first trained nurses, Edith Graham, in 1893 and took her on a honeymoon to visit eastern hospitals. For years the two families lived with or near each other. In the evenings the brothers met for a chat and they left together for work every morning. Dr. Will, the decision maker and disciplinarian, essentially ran the clinic, while Dr. Charlie, the warmhearted wit, put doctors and patients alike at their ease. Together they were an unbeatable team, a living example of their father's favored saying that "no man is big enough to be independent of others."

Typically they built new houses — then the largest in Rochester — at about the same time. Dr. Will's residence is now part of the Mayo Foundation and IS NOT OPEN TO THE PUBLIC. The home Dr. Charlie called Mayowood is owned and operated by the Olmsted County Historical Society.

In 1907 Dr. Charlie and his wife purchased a 340-acre farm about four miles from Rochester. Originally it was to provide a place where their sons could work during the summer. But as the doctor's interest in conservation and agriculture grew, so did the size of the farm, eventually totaling more than three thousand acres. The permanent residence at Mayowood, built in 1910–11, was designed largely by Dr. Charlie in a style based on English country houses. Set on a knoll in the midst of rolling hills, meadows, and woodlands, it has been described by his son as "a slightly daft, rambling, haphazard arrangement of . . . big-windowed charming rooms that spill around trees and down a hillside." It was constructed of poured reinforced concrete, an innovation at the time, under the direction of contractor Garfield Schwartz.

The four-story house, which cost an estimated $60,000, comprises thirty-eight rooms. The garage, workshop, and furnace room occupy the ground floor, where the Mayo children once kept goats for two weeks before their parents discovered them. On the second level are the main dining room, living room, gallery, kitchen, library, music room, and foyer. Bedrooms and a nursery make up the third floor, and from the fourth-floor ballroom a stairway leads to a patio on the roof. The narrow driveway to the house is edged by a long, low, stone wall resembling one Dr. Mayo had admired in England. A double staircase rises to the home's front terrace, which is connected by a walkway with the summer teahouse. To enhance the view from his home Dr. Mayo built a dam in the South Fork Zumbro River to create an island-dotted lake spanned by swinging bridges. While these landscape features have disappeared, still standing (in altered form) is the greenhouse that became famous for thousands of glass X-ray plates that lined its interior, causing a variety of reactions in guests who suddenly recognized the clearly revealed body parts.

Within the estate Dr. Mayo developed a wild animal park, an experimental farm, excellent herds of Guernsey and Holstein cattle, and beautiful gardens of chrysanthemums. Many of his money-making schemes, however, failed at a sometimes staggering cost, a fact he dismissed philosophically. He was, he readily explained, an agriculturist and not a farmer. The difference was that a farmer made his money on the farm and spent it in the city, while an agriculturist made his money in the city and spent it on the farm. Some of his experiments, such as an animal laboratory and improved methods of dairy farming, were directly related to progressive medicine and public health.

Mayowood became a cultural and social center of the Rochester area. Along with local residents and clinic staff members, guests of Dr. Charlie and his wife numbered hundreds of distinguished surgeons and prominent Americans, including President Franklin D. Roosevelt. When his son, Dr. Charles W. Mayo, and his wife moved into the big house in 1939, they continued to welcome such notable visitors as Adlai E. Stevenson, King Faisal of Saudi Arabia, and Mahendra Bir Bikram, the king of Nepal, and his queen. But the expense of maintaining Mayowood in the manner established by his father became a financial burden for Dr. Chuck, as he was called, and he sold a large portion of the estate. In 1965 the family gave Mayowood and ten surrounding acres to the Olmsted County Historical Society with the provision that Dr. and Mrs. Mayo would continue to live there. (Dr. Mayo was killed in an automobile accident in 1968. His wife had died eight months earlier.) The home has been

THE FRONT COURTYARD *at Mayowood connects with a summer teahouse visible in the background.*

THE SUNLIT LIBRARY *is paneled with wood doors taken from Rochester's Central School, which opened about 1868 when Dr. William W. Mayo served on the school board.*

open to the public since 1966. It was added to the National Register of Historic Places in 1970.

The mansion retains much of the flavor of the home enjoyed by three generations of Mayos. It still contains the French, Spanish, English, and early American antiques selected by both Mayo families. Some of the outstanding features of the house are the paneling in the library, which was fashioned from the doors of old Central School built in Rochester about 1868; several large, gold-framed Mexican mirrors; portraits and sculpture of family members; the large canopied bed in the master bedroom; ornately carved baroque panels, framing a doorway to the living room, which were salvaged from a bombed castle in Germany; a Tiffany grandfather clock in the foyer; and an Aeolian player pipe organ in the music room. The large dining room, with its Georgian furniture and Limoges china, can accommodate fifty-two guests; an alcove in the gallery overlooking the courtyard was the dining area for Dr. and Mrs. Charles W. Mayo and their children.

Dr. Will and Dr. Charlie died within a few months of each other in 1939. Their legacy lives on in the clinic, in Mayowood, and in the civic improvements they gave to the city of Rochester.

Information regarding bus tours to Mayowood may be obtained at the Olmsted County Historical Society in Rochester. (Private autos are not allowed on the estate grounds because of inadequate parking space.) Mayowood is closed from December through March. There is an admission fee for public tours, which are conducted on a varied seasonal schedule. Group reservations are available by special arrangement made well in advance of the desired tour date.

THE DINING ALCOVE, *looking out over the lantern-lit courtyard at the back of the house, is reflected in one of Mayowood's many large mirrors.*

Browns Valley Man

Site is located .5 mile east of Browns Valley on U.S. highway no. 28.

BROWNS VALLEY MAN, a fragmentary skeleton discovered in Traverse County in 1933, dates from the Paleo-Indian culture of the first people known to have inhabited Minnesota at least eight thousand years ago — the prehistoric big game hunters who roamed the United States before 6000 B.C. and produced distinctive and finely made projectile points. Two such points found with the skeleton enabled scientists to arrive at an approximate age for Browns Valley Man and to define a new type of projectile point associated with the Big Game tradition named the Browns Valley point.

The discovery of this important skeleton was a fortunate accident. On October 9, 1933, amateur archaeologist William H. Jensen recognized several pieces of human bones and a beautifully made projectile point in fresh gravel dumped near the grain elevator he managed at Browns Valley. He immediately went to the gravel pit on the edge of town where he and others picked up more bone fragments, a stone knife, and another point. Jensen then spotted a U-shaped streak of reddish-colored gravel about four and a half feet from the top of the excavation wall. It proved to be a prehistoric human burial pit lined with red ocher and containing additional artifacts. Realizing the importance of his discovery, Jensen had the site photographed before digging it; he also notified Albert E. Jenks, an anthropologist at the University of Minnesota. The following summer Jenks directed the re-examination of the site by student archaeologists. They unearthed seventeen more bone fragments, some of which fitted together with those already retrieved, and another projectile point similar to one of the five Jensen had found.

The bones and flint artifacts were taken to the university for study, and the skeleton was reconstructed. It was determined to be that of a male between the ages of twenty and forty years. The carefully restored skull exhibited some distinctive characteristics: long head; broad, short face; narrow nose; strong brow ridges; and an extremely wide lower jaw.

Among the artifacts were six projectile points, two stone knives, two sandstone fragments that appeared to be abraders, and a large, unworked flat stone which may have been a grinding implement. Two of the points, skillfully chipped from brown chalcedony, are similar to others found in the Plains region and grouped into a broad category called parallel flaked points. According to Elden Johnson, state archaeologist, these two are the most recent in a sequence of projectile points associated with big game hunting and are the type specimens

The U-shaped burial pit that held the remains of Browns Valley Man was photographed with its discoverer, William H. Jensen, in 1933. Reproduced by permission of the American Anthropological Association from its Memoirs, *Number 49, 1937.*

A knife (below) and a projectile point (left) found in association with Browns Valley Man are similar to points that are almost eight thousand years old. Courtesy University of Minnesota Archaeology Laboratory.

for what is now called the Browns Valley point. Earliest points of the Big Game tradition, called Clovis and Folsom fluted points, have also been found in Minnesota, where it is assumed they were used to hunt elephantlike mammoths and giant bison before 8000 B.C. The Browns Valley points are thought to date from a later time when the mammoths had become extinct. They are similar to points found at a Wyoming site which were dated to almost eight thousand years ago. Using the points from Wyoming as evidence, it seems likely that Browns Valley Man dates from about 6000 B.C.

Much of the mystery that veils the origin of Browns Valley Man stems from its discovery in a gravel ridge. For many years it was believed that the ridge had been laid down during the Tintah beach stage of Glacial Lake Agassiz eight to ten thousand years ago. The grave chamber itself was devoid of humus, although the ridge had eight to ten inches of topsoil in 1933. This indicated that the burial was intruded into the gravel sometime after Glacial River Warren, the southern outlet draining the lake, had become inactive, but before abundant vegetation had developed there. More recent data, however, negates the Tintah beach association of the gravel ridge and places its origin much earlier. It has been determined that the ridge is a remnant of the Big Stone moraine, which was formed during the retreating phase of the Des Moines ice lobe about thirteen thousand years ago. This new evidence offers the possibility that the maximum age of Browns Valley Man could be greater than was previously considered probable.

After studies of them were completed, Browns Valley Man and its associated artifacts were returned to Jensen. For years they were kept in his home, where they were prized possessions in a large archaeological collection. Fearing for its safety, Jensen put the skeleton in a secret hiding place. He died in 1960 before revealing its location, and its whereabouts remains unknown to this day.

In 1968 the Minnesota Historical Society, in co-operation with the Traverse County Historical Society, the village of Browns Valley, and the state highway department, erected a marker in a landscaped wayside park east of the village. While the gravel pit has undergone much change since 1933, the plateau on which it is located is still visible about half a mile south of the marker.

Jeffers Petroglyphs

Located in northeastern Cottonwood County. Accessible from U.S. highway no. 71, three miles east on county road no. 10, a mile south on county road no. 2, then .3 mile east. The route is marked.

THE LARGEST known concentration of aboriginal rock art in Minnesota occurs at the Jeffers Petroglyphs located near the town of Jeffers in the southwestern part of the state. Set in the midst of rare virgin prairie close to the banks of the Cottonwood River, the petroglyph site consists of more than two thousand figures and designs pecked into an outcrop of red quartzite measuring about 700 feet long and some 150 feet at its widest point. The outcrop is part of a twenty-three-mile ridge that traverses Cottonwood, Brown, and Watonwan counties. Although isolated groups of rock carvings are scattered along this ridge and exist in at least ten other Minnesota areas as well, nowhere have they been found in such abundance and variety as at this site.

Rock art — paintings, carvings, boulder effigies — is found on every continent in the world, with major sites in Europe, Africa, Australia, and North America. Within the state of Minnesota, rock art exists in various forms, but at the Cottonwood County site it appears only as figures pecked into rock surfaces. These are called petroglyphs, a term derived from the Greek words "petra," meaning rock, and "glyphe," meaning carving. (There is inconsistency among anthropologists in their use of the terms "petroglyphs" and "pictographs." Some refer to both rock-incised figures and rock paintings as "petroglyphs"; others use "pictographs" to describe only rock paintings; still others maintain that "pictograph" refers specifically to a form of picture writing or the probable antecedents of written language. In the present discussion, the term "petroglyphs" refers only to figures carved or pecked into rock surfaces.) Rock carvings occur more often than rock paintings, at least in part because carvings are less subject to erosion by wind and general weathering.

The origins of Minnesota's petroglyphs are lost in the darkness of prehistory. Local Indians who were aware of existing petroglyphs when the first Europeans arrived related their legends and myths about the glyphs' makers. At Nett Lake in northern Minnesota, for example, where some five hundred petroglyphs occur on the smooth rock surfaces of what is now Picture Island, the Chippewa attributed them to creatures that were half sea lion and half fish. Other legends speak of great floods and fiery monsters that were responsible for the glyphs. Some Chippewa perhaps correctly considered them the work of the area's former occupants, the Dakota.

When, why, and by whom the Jeffers Petroglyphs were made cannot be stated with certainty. Current studies indicate a possibility that they were made by several groups of peoples inhabiting the region over a very long period of time. A large portion of the carvings may have been made by hunters as early as 3000 B.C. This date is based in part on the presence of figures representing different types of atlatls, or hunters' throwing sticks, known to have been used in various forms from about 5000 B.C. to about 900 A.D. Other glyphs at this site appear to be the work of Siouan peoples — Siouan here referring to the major language family which includes the Dakota Indians — and could span the centuries between 900 A.D. and the mid-1700s. These carvings include certain characteristic symbols and motifs that appear in the design elements used on Siouan beadwork, tepees, pipe bags, and clothing and in the "winter counts" of the Teton Dakota. (Winter counts are a type of calendar, a chronology of events recorded in symbols or ideographs.)

Among the typical Siouan symbols found at the Jeffers Petroglyphs are turtles, which denote fertility and maturity; bison, which are intimately associated with the Dakota people and as inscribed here closely resemble the Yankton representations; horned humanoids representing shamans (spiritual leaders); thunderbirds portrayed with the distinctive Siouan heart; and three-pronged objects, sometimes

THE JEFFERS PETROGLYPHS *occur on an outcrop of red quartzite set in the midst of virgin prairie. The interpretive center is the tepeelike structure to be seen in the background.*

IN ONE *of many groupings that appear on the outcrop, the petroglyphs range from identifiable figures to abstract designs. The inch-rule in these photographs indicates the size of the glyphs.*

called bird tracks. A possible horse figure suggests that the tradition of pecking inscriptions into rock continued into the mid-1700s, when that animal was introduced into the high plains area.

Archaeologists also point out that the Jeffers Petroglyphs strongly resemble and may be closely associated with those at Pipestone National Monument. It is thought that the Pipestone carvings may be the work of the Iowa or Oto Indians, who controlled that region perhaps in the 1600s and into the 1700s, when the Yankton Dakota gained dominance. If the Cottonwood County petroglyphs are associated with those at Pipestone, they may be of similar recent origin. In any case, it is believed that the petroglyphs in Minnesota, along with some found in neighboring Wisconsin, Iowa, North and South Dakota, and Nebraska, were probably done by groups of people with similar cultural affiliations. The rock paintings farther north on the Minnesota-Ontario border, however, are believed to be the work of other peoples.

As for the "why" behind the petroglyphs, four possible reasons have been suggested. (1) The carving of symbols interpreted as "name pictures," which could represent individual chiefs, shamans, or hunting leaders. (2) Carvings and peckings possibly done as a form of amusement or to pass the time. (3) Carvings as a form of hunting magic associated with ceremonies performed to increase the supply of game and hunting success, as in the famous Ice Age cave art in France and Spain. At least two authorities — Campbell Grant and Emory Strong — believe petroglyphs found in the western United States are definitely associated with hunting because of their proximity to known or probable game trails. It should be noted that the rock ridge on which the Cottonwood County petroglyphs are located would have provided hunters a natural trail with a panoramic view on all sides. (4) Carvings that may have played a part in special rituals. Rock carving is known to have been associated with puberty rites among the Quinault Indians of Washington, the Nez Percé of Idaho, and the Luiseño and Cupeño of southern California.

There is still a great deal of controversy and uncertainty over the origins and meanings of petroglyphs. In the past, many exotic and bizarre explanations of their origins have been suggested. But most anthropologists believe that distinctive cultural groups all over the world developed rock carvings and rock paintings spontaneously, naturally, and independently of other cultures. When the groups shared a common linguistic origin, as did the Siouan people, they also shared common symbols, and it is probable that there was some cross-cultural

THESE FIGURES *are atlatls, which were weighted sticks used to throw spear points with great force.*

A BISON *and a turtle are two typical Siouan symbols.*

exchange of traits over vast areas as populations moved about. Most anthropologists warn, however, that because the same symbol was used by different groups does not indicate a common meaning for that symbol or even that it had a meaning at all. Handprints, for example, are found in petroglyphs all over the world, but their widespread appearance may only indicate that there is a natural tendency for people to trace the outline of their hands. The cross is another symbol which undoubtedly had different meanings for various cultural groups. Investigators also warn against trying to interpret the petroglyphs as a form of language, picture writing, or hieroglyphics, or indeed, against attempting to read any meaning into them.

The petroglyphs in Cottonwood County were first brought to public attention in 1885, when the *New Ulm Review* reported that a party of six unidentified men had visited the outcrop and noted nine inscriptions. Four years later Theodore H. Lewis, a surveyor turned archaeologist, studied the petroglyphs, took field notes, and painstakingly made rubbings of thirty designs. His notes were later edited by Newton H. Winchell and published in 1911 by the Minnesota Historical Society in *The Aborigines of Minnesota*. Lewis estimated there were at least two hundred and perhaps as many as five hundred pecked figures. More thorough investigation of the site, headed by Minnesota Historical Society archaeologist Gordon Lothson in 1971, revealed at least two thousand.

Over the years erosion and vandalism began to take their toll of the petroglyphs. In 1960 Leota M. Kellett, director of the Brown County Historical Society, again called them to the Minnesota Historical Society's attention and suggested that the carvings be preserved. The state society purchased the petroglyph site in 1966. A small interpretive center, built in 1970, houses exhibits on North American rock art and on the geology and plant life of the Cottonwood County region. This site is now in the National Register of Historic Places.

Geologic features of interest at the site include glacial striations gouged into the extremely hard quartzite clearly showing the southeasterly direction of the most recent ice mass as it advanced about fifteen thousand years ago. These striations, made by harder rocks and sand grains carried along by the glacier, surfaced a few thousand years later when the ice retreated. Large glacial boulders known as "erratics" are strewn about the area. These are composed of rock

A ROW *of spear points (at right) appears with an atlatl, animals, and unidentified glyphs.*

FOUR PETROGLYPHS *at the Jeffers site have been identified as (from top left, clockwise) a shaman or spiritual leader, a Siouan thunderbird, a possible horse, and a handprint.*

that is foreign to the immediate region — in this case, granite — and were probably carried from some distance farther north.

Also visible on the outcrop are ripple marks, the result of wave action in the vast shallow sea that inundated the region 1.4 billion years ago. These ripple marks were covered with a red clay similar to catlinite or pipestone, and the pressure of the mud and succeeding layers of sediment preserved the impressions seen today.

Surrounding the Jeffers Petroglyphs is one of the few areas of natural prairie remaining in the farmland of southwestern Minnesota. At the time white men arrived on this continent, about a third of the land area was virgin prairie. In Minnesota a large part of forty of the eighty-seven counties at one time consisted of prairieland. Over the years much of Minnesota's virgin prairie has been drastically altered by farming, overgrazing, the introduction of alien weeds, or industrial and residential development. The gently rolling prairie near the petroglyphs is a living museum of plant species, a sanctuary for wild flowers and grasses which have flourished on the prairies for centuries. Incredibly rich in variety, these plants present a panorama of color that continuously changes from early spring to late autumn. In just one season of study, Florence E. Roefer, manager of the site, collected samples of eight different grasses and nearly sixty flowers and plants — many of them unique to virgin prairies. Some of these have special historic significance, for example the pomme blanche or prairie turnip and the prickly-pear cactus, which were used for food by early inhabitants and later pioneer settlers of the region.

The Jeffers Petroglyphs site is open to the public daily during the summer. Self-guided tours are offered; group tours may be arranged in advance at the Minnesota Historical Society in St. Paul. There is no admission charge.

Pipestone Quarry

Located in Pipestone National Monument. Accessible from U.S. highway no. 75, about a mile north of the city of Pipestone.

> On the Mountains of the Prairie,
>   On the great Red Pipe-stone Quarry,
> Gitche Manito, the mighty,
>   He the Master of Life, descending,
> On the red crags of the quarry
>   Stood erect, and called the nations,
> Called the tribes of men together.

HENRY WADSWORTH LONGFELLOW thus immortalized in *The Song of Hiawatha* one of America's best-known Indian sites — the Pipestone Quarry in southwestern Minnesota. Here Indians gathered for centuries to obtain the unusual red stone from which they carved their large highly prized calumets, or ceremonial pipes. Both the quarry and the artistic pipes fashioned from its stone have associations with Indian religion and mythology. Today the quarry is preserved in Pipestone National Monument, a picturesque prairie area of 283 acres.

The "site of the quarries," said John Wesley Powell, director of the Smithsonian Institution's Bureau of Ethnology in 1898, "was a sacred place, known to the tribesmen of a large part of the continent. . . . It is not too much to say that the great Pipestone Quarry was the most important single locality in aboriginal geography and lore." Although Powell's statement is sometimes used in exhibits at the monument, anthropologists now believe it to be extreme. They point out that most of the legends attached to the quarry are white men's romanticized versions of minor themes in native mythology. Longfellow, for example, gleaned many of his poetic ideas from Iroquois and Algonquian myths; neither of these groups was ever anywhere near the Pipestone Quarry.

In the romanticized legends that have come down to us, the quarry was believed to be the center of creation, the birthplace of all the Indian peoples of the earth. Although the legends vary in details, many focus upon the divine origin of the stone. A version known to the Indians of the upper Missouri relates that a great flood threatened to destroy all the nations of the world. To escape the rising torrents, the tribes assembled on the Coteau des Prairies (Highland of the Prairies), a striking geographical feature dividing the watershed of the Mississippi from that of the Missouri. But the water continued to rise, covering them and converting their flesh into the red stone. Only one young

108

woman was rescued from the flood by a war eagle, and her children, fathered by the eagle, again peopled the earth.

There is no doubt that the smoking of the ceremonial red pipe was a sacred ritual performed by Indians of the Great Lakes region to make offerings to various deities, to seal solemn promises, and to propitiate the weather gods. Many legends concerning the rite, which have doubtless been distorted by the white men, dwell on the importance of the pipe. One, which influenced Longfellow, says that soon after the creation of man, the Great Spirit called all the Indian nations together at the quarry. Standing on a precipice, he broke a piece from it and made a huge pipe by turning the stone in his hands. He then smoked the pipe over the people, pointing it to the north, south, east, and west, telling them that the red stone was their flesh, and that they must use it for their pipes of peace.

Legend would also have us believe that the quarry was sacred or neutral ground to which many tribes came in peace, but there is little historical support for this view. On the contrary, there is evidence that the quarry was jealously guarded by the tribes living nearest it. In historic times, the Dakota controlled the Coteau des Prairies. The quarry, located on its western slope, remained Dakota land, specifically the property of the Yankton Dakota, until 1929, when title to it passed to the United States government.

Just when the Indians began to quarry the red stone is not known. A tradition, which seems to have some historical foundation, has it that the quarry was discovered by the Indians when a buffalo trail was worn into the earth, exposing the pipestone to view. Archaeological excavations at the monument by the National Park Service in 1949 indicate the presence of late prehistoric Oneota and Woodland cultures (1500 A.D. to 1700 A.D.). Various investigators report evidence of ancient pits and stone mauls, indicating that the quarry was in use at least as early as 1200 A.D. Although similar stone has been discovered in South Dakota, Wisconsin, and Ohio, it appears that after the mid-1600s a large portion of the ceremonial pipes used by the Plains Indians and other tribes was produced from the Minnesota rock. Traders and explorers visiting the area comment on the widespread use of the red pipes by Indians of the Great Lakes and the Mississippi and Missouri valleys.

The first white man to record his trip to the quarry itself was Philander Prescott, a fur trader who lived among the Minnesota Dakota for more than forty years. In 1831 he accompanied a band of Indians to the site and worked with them a full day, quarrying enough stone for twenty pipes. He remarked that the Indians "labored here verry hard with hoes and axes" and "large stones which they use forr breaking" the relatively soft pipestone. After clearing off the dirt, he said, the men got "stones as large as two Indians can lift and throw it down so hard as th[e]y can and in this way break or crack the rock

A MODERN MUSEUM *at Pipestone National Monument houses exhibits on the history of the quarry and its many legends. Courtesy Pipestone National Monument.*

INSCRIPTION ROCK *carries the name of Joseph N. Nicollet and the initials of other members of his exploring party who visited the quarry in 1838.*

so they can get their hoes and axes in the cracks and pry out'' piece after piece.

The quarry to which the Indians took Prescott extends across the prairie for about a mile. The stone occurs in a layer twelve to eighteen inches thick within a deposit of Sioux quartzite. It varies in color from gray to pale and dark red, often having a mottled appearance. Although the pits are now deeper than they were in Prescott's day, many of them are still quite shallow, and today's visitor to certain parts of the monument may easily wonder if he has passed by without noticing them.

Prescott's account of his visit to the quarry was not widely circulated, and it remained for another man to publicize the land of red pipestone. He was George Catlin, noted artist and writer. Catlin spent his life depicting the American Indian, and he heard about the quarry from them. In the summer of 1836

THE ''THREE MAIDENS'' *were regarded by the Indians with awe and respect as the dwelling place of the quarry's guardian spirits.*

he made his way from New York to Minnesota and journeyed up the Minnesota River. The Dakota warned him not to make the trip, but he would not turn back. Although the Indians threatened him, they allowed him to continue unmolested. He sketched the quarry and secured samples of the stone, which on his return were analyzed by a Boston chemist who found it to be a soft indurated clay composed largely of aluminum silicate and iron impurities. The chemist suggested that it be named catlinite in honor of the artist, and so it was.

By sketching the site and collecting some of the legends surrounding it, Catlin did much to make the quarry known. But it was a more scientifically minded traveler, Joseph N. Nicollet, who two years later literally put it on the map. An exacting and ebullient Frenchman, Nicollet spent five days at the quarry in 1838 on an expedition sponsored by the United States government. With Nicollet was another man later destined to leave his mark on the pages of American history — John C. Frémont, the Pathfinder. During their visit, the men carved on a rock the date as well as Nicollet's name and the initials of his five companions — Frémont (who used the initials C. F.), Charles E. Geyer, Joseph Laframboise, J. E. Flandin, and Joseph Renville. Inscription Rock, as it is now known, may still be seen at Pipestone.

Nicollet also called attention to other features still visible at the quarry. He described the "Three Maidens" — three large boulders unlike any other rocks in the region. It is said that the Indians believed these were eggs of the war eagle and that maidens lived beneath the rocks and guarded the quarry. Nicollet noted that the Indians placed offerings of tobacco and food in front of the rocks before venturing to dig. To them, the boulders, which were "erratics" deposited by a glacier and later split by frost action, were objects of veneration and awe.

Near the rocks Nicollet and other visitors observed many petroglyphs, or rock carvings. One tradition says that before daring to quarry each Indian inscribed the figure of a man, turtle, bear, wolf, bison, elk, or crane's foot on the hard surface. Another tells a different story: Before quarrying the Indians who deemed themselves worthy of the privilege bathed in the stream and then walked slowly toward the Three Maidens, where the medicine man placed tobacco and other gifts. The Indians then camped for the night, hoping to learn whether or not their prayers and offerings were acceptable to the spirits beneath the rocks. If they were, in the silence of the night tappings on the rock would be heard or sparks would be seen flying upward. Next morning the Indians would find that the spirit maidens had engraved an answer on the stone. Sometimes the offerings had to be repeated for three days before the Indians could safely begin work on the fourth.

Such preparation rites were observed at the quarry as late as the 1880s. At that time numerous petroglyphs were still in evidence. They were not deeply cut, however, and were later seriously vandalized. A few were rescued from man's destructiveness by C. H. Bennett of Pipestone and are on display at the monument near the Three Maidens.

Still to be seen also is Leaping Rock, a stone column twenty-three feet high, standing alone about seven feet from the nearest ledge. Catlin reported that Indian youths sometimes attempted to leap to this rock, "and those who have successfully done it are allowed to boast of it all their lives." Prescott told the story of a brave who was forced to make the leap in order to gain the maiden he loved. The fur trader noted in some awe that all the Indian could do "was to jump and stand right where he struck"; if he failed he would fall on the jagged rocks below. Frémont, then a young lieutenant, made the leap in 1838 and placed a United States flag atop the rock to mark his success.

All the travelers visiting the quarries spoke of a charming little waterfall in Pipestone Creek. Known today as Winnewissa Falls (a name derived from

SOME *prehistoric rock carvings, on which several Indian legends are based, are now preserved at Pipestone National Monument.*

the Dakota word meaning "envious" or "jealous") it is a scenic spot in the present monument. According to a legend used by Longfellow, the falls were created when the Great Spirit, angered by the warring of his people, called the nations together at Pipestone. Standing on a rock pinnacle, he bade them lay down their arms and live as brothers. As he spoke water gushed from the rocks to form the falls.

Many attempts were made over the years by both Indians and some enlightened white men to protect the quarry from vandalism and from encroaching settlement. In 1884 a railroad was built through the property, and later an Indian school, since abandoned, flourished for years. In 1887 settlers who had illegally built houses and established farms in the area, which was then a Yankton reservation, were evicted by United States troops. At last in 1937 the efforts of a dedicated group of local citizens resulted in the establishment of Pipestone National Monument, the first of Minnesota's two such monuments.

The act establishing the national monument "expressly reserved to Indians of all tribes" the exclusive right to quarry the red stone. Currently more than fifty individuals, most of them Dakota Indians, continue to exercise that right during the summer months. From the rock they fashion pipes, turtles (the Dakota symbol of fertility), and other items that are sold by the Pipestone Indian Shrine Association and the visitors' center operated at the monument by the National Park Service. Pipes of the stone are marketed through dealers nationally and in several foreign countries.

Pipestone National Monument is open daily throughout the year. There is no admission fee. In the handsome museum completely revised exhibits and the Upper Midwest Indian Crafts Center are scheduled to open during the summer of 1972. Behind the building, a "Circle Trail" leads past Leaping Rock, Lake Hiawatha, and other points of historical and botanical interest in the prairie park. Hikers of the trail can also visit with a pipe maker who demonstrates his craft daily except Wednesdays from Memorial Day through Labor Day.

Lac qui Parle Mission

Located in Chippewa [County] Mission State Wayside at the southeastern end of Lac qui Parle Lake. Accessible from Montevideo, eight miles northwest on U.S. highway no. 59, then three miles west on county road no. 13.

A PROTESTANT MISSION established at Lac qui Parle in 1835 to serve the Dakota Indians became the nucleus of one of the earliest and most colorful centers of white civilization in the Minnesota Valley. At this remote settlement the valley's first school and church were founded; the state's first church bell pealed over the Minnesota wilderness; cloth was woven for the first time in Minnesota; and the Bible was first translated into the language of the Dakota for which the missionaries devised a written alphabet. Today a replica of the mission chapel stands on the original site in what is now a neatly kept wayside park.

The founder of the Lac qui Parle Mission was Dr. Thomas S. Williamson, a physician and licensed Presbyterian minister. He was sent to isolated Fort Snelling by the American Board of Commissioners for Foreign Missions in May, 1835, to found a school and church among the Indians. Circumstances led him, however, to seek a place farther from the military post, and a month later he accepted Joseph Renville's invitation to start a mission among the Dakota at his American Fur Company post near the junction of Lac qui Parle Lake and the Minnesota River. On June 23, 1835, Dr. Williamson and his wife, her sister Sarah Poage, and Mr. and Mrs. Alexander Huggins began the two-hundred-mile trip with Renville to his fort on the upper Minnesota River. There on July 9 the five missionaries were greeted by the trader's Indian wife and numerous relatives and were given quarters in a one-room cabin inside the stockade known as Fort Renville.

Renville had been trading among the Dakota at Lac qui Parle since 1826. Two years later he had built a stockaded log house and store to serve the Indians living in villages across the river. Over his wilderness settlement, noted for its hospitality, he ruled "in barbaric splendor quite like an African king." Besides a corps of servants, he maintained a group of braves who acted as his bodyguard, protecting him from any unfriendly visitor. The son of a French trader and a Dakota woman, Renville was highly respected by the Indians. Throughout his long career as a fur trader he wielded great influence over them — a power that often helped, but sometimes hindered, the missionaries' efforts to convert the Dakota to Christianity, teach them to read and write, and help them establish farms. Renville and his wife were the first to join the church which Williamson soon established, and numerous members of the

A REPLICA *of the Lac qui Parle Mission Chapel stands today on its original location. This photograph was taken soon after the chapel was reconstructed in the 1940s.*

THOMAS S. WILLIAMSON, *a physician and missionary to the Dakota Indians from 1835 to 1862, spent much of his life translating the Bible into the Dakota language. This sketch was made by Frank B. Mayer in 1851. Courtesy Newberry Library, Chicago.*

trader's large household led the way for other Indians who accepted Christianity. Until Williamson mastered the difficult Dakota language, Renville opened the services with a prayer in the native tongue and often acted as both interpreter and protector for the missionaries.

Williamson at first held services in Renville's cabin, then in the log houses the missionaries built about a mile from the fort. Not until 1841 was construction of a chapel begun with the help of Dakota women who dug out a place for it on the hillside. These volunteers also assisted in making the adobe bricks used in the building. Later, to protect the sun-baked bricks from the washing rains, three outside walls of the chapel were covered with clapboard and the front wall was plastered and whitewashed. Inside, a ceiling of boards was added and the walls were plastered with lime. The wood used in constructing the church came from the nearby forests.

While the chapel could boast of only the simplest appointments, it did have a bell which is believed to be the first ever used in a Minnesota house of worship. It was purchased in 1846 with funds received from the sale of moccasins donated by the Dakota women. For years it called the Indians to services and to classes, until it finally cracked while being rung on a cold day when temperatures dropped to thirty degrees below zero. Years after the mission closed, this bell was found in a small church in South Dakota and returned to Lac qui Parle, where it is now displayed in the reconstructed chapel.

Shortly after his arrival at Lac qui Parle in 1835, Williamson opened the Minnesota Valley's first school. Classes of women and children were initially instructed in English, but before the year ended, Williamson began to teach the reading of the Dakota language to masculine members of Renville's family and his bodyguard. The missionary learned, however, that it was impossible to keep his pupils in regular attendance, for the hunting season took away great numbers of them for long periods. Discipline, too, was a problem, especially in getting the students to wear what the missionaries considered adequate clothing. Attempting to remedy this, they taught several Indian women to weave sheep's wool and flax threads into material for clothes — the first such cloth woven in Minnesota. But the women soon lost interest, and the project was abandoned.

The missionaries found it difficult to teach in the Dakota language because it lacked symbols for such abstract subjects as arithmetic and religion. Yet they were forced to master the native tongue in order to be effective in their work, for the Indians displayed no desire to learn English. Williamson considered the conquering of the strange-sounding language his most difficult task, even though he was greatly aided in this effort by the arrival in 1836 of Gideon H. Pond and in 1837 of Stephen R. Riggs, both of whom became avid students of Dakota. With his brother Samuel, Gideon Pond had worked among the Indians at Fort Snelling since 1834. Having great natural ability, the brothers learned Dakota and devised an alphabet by which it could be written. They had already prepared a spelling book — printed in the year Gideon moved to Lac qui Parle — which was the first volume published in Dakota.

With the help at times of both Pond brothers, Riggs, and others, Williamson began what was to be the principal work of his life and perhaps the greatest accomplishment of the Lac qui Parle missionaries — the translation of the Scriptures into Dakota. In this task, Renville's assistance was regarded as a necessity. The usual procedure was for one missionary to read a passage to the trader in French; he in turn would translate it into Dakota, and the other missionaries would write it down as he spoke. During the winter of 1837–38 the Gospel of Mark and selected chapters from other books were finished. These were published at Cincinnati in 1839 under Williamson's editorship. In 1842 a Dakota hymnal and a primer, adapted by Riggs from English readers, were printed. Ten years later an impressive *Grammar and Dictionary of the Dakota Language*, edited by Riggs and embodying words collected by all the missionaries, was issued by the Smithsonian Institution. Many years later in 1879 Williamson completed the translation of the Scriptures.

The little mission settlement near "the lake that speaks" prospered until 1846, when Joseph Renville died. Thereafter the Indians' opposition to the missionaries increased, and Williamson left Lac qui Parle to open a church and school at Little Crow's Kaposia village (now South St. Paul). In 1852 he returned to the Minnesota Valley, this time to a spot near the junction of the Minnesota and Yellow Medicine rivers, where he established a new mission named Pajutazee, meaning "yellow medicine."

Lac qui Parle Mission was left in charge of Riggs, who with his wife, Mary, and other personnel continued to labor there until 1854. In March of that year Riggs's home accidentally caught fire and burned to the ground; the family took shelter in the adobe church. In September the missionaries decided to abandon Lac qui Parle for a new location closer to Williamson's station and the new Upper Sioux Agency downriver. There they built the Hazelwood Mission.

After Riggs and his co-workers left, the Lac qui Parle Mission buildings fell into ruin. Stones from some foundations seem to have been used by settlers who later took up claims in the area. No move to preserve the pioneer mission site was made until 1910, when the Congregational Missionary Society of Montevideo and others placed a marker there. In 1931 the state acquired seventeen acres where the mission had stood and established the Chippewa Mission State Historical Wayside, confusingly named for the county in which it is located.

In 1940 an archaeological exploration of the mission and Fort Renville sites was begun by the Works Progress Administration in co-operation with the Chippewa County Historical Society and the Minnesota Historical Society. The investigators located the foundations of the chapel, the sites of houses built for Riggs, Huggins, and a mission farmer named Jonas Pettijohn, and that of Renville's post. Markers now identify the locations of the mission buildings; the general area of Renville's post is indicated by a sign on the roadway about a mile northwest of the mission. Later archaeological studies of Fort Renville, conducted in 1968 by the Minnesota Historical Society under the sponsorship of the Minnesota Resources Commission, re-established the stockade lines and located the sites of three structures — Renville's dwelling, the cabin used by Williamson, and the storehouse. Indications of a bastion at the southeast corner

A PORTION *of the hearthstone used in the cabin of Dr. Thomas S. Williamson at Lac qui Parle marks the site of his log dwelling. It was returned to the park in 1941.*

of the stockade and of a watchtower in the center of the enclosed area also were discovered.

No remains of Williamson's residence at the mission were found, though its approximate site has been determined. It is marked with a sign and a large flat boulder that once served as the hearthstone in the doctor's cabin. On this stone, which weighed over a ton and measured about 8 feet by 4 feet, Williamson placed his cookstove. Later, when the Riggs family occupied an upstairs room, the children's pet cats drank milk from depressions in the rock. The boulder was broken into two parts, and about 1880 the larger portion was recognized by Riggs's son as the old hearthstone. He removed it to Nebraska, but in 1941 it was returned to Lac qui Parle.

In 1941–42 the Chippewa County Historical Society constructed a replica of the mission chapel on its original location. It contains rough wooden benches, a simple wooden altar, and an old-fashioned organ. Although occasional services are held in the small, brown-stained clapboard structure, it serves primarily as a museum for the hundreds of items found when the mission site was excavated. Displays contain bits of china, bone-handled knives, buttons, coins, parts of stovepipes, hinges, locks, and such tools as axes and hoes. Fur trade items, including clay pipes, traps, trading beads, and gunflints, are reminiscent of the mission's close association with Fort Renville. Indian objects — arrowheads, a bone scraper used to prepare hides for tanning, and bits of pipestone — are also on exhibit. The museum is open Sunday afternoons during the summer or by appointment with the manager at Lac qui Parle State Park on the west side of the lake. In the small cemetery situated on the hill behind the chapel stands a marker which reviews the life of Renville. The fur trader's grave, however, is not located in the cemetery.

Traverse des Sioux Treaty Site

Site located in Traverse des Sioux State Park. Accessible from U.S. highway no. 169, two miles north of St. Peter.

ALTHOUGH TRAVERSE DES SIOUX (meaning "crossing of the Sioux") was the scene of one of the most important events in Minnesota history, it is now almost forgotten by travelers passing along the highway that skirts the site. In the summer of 1851, however, the plateau overlooking the Minnesota River was a place of lively activity, for the Dakota had gathered there to meet with emissaries of the United States government which wished to purchase their extensive lands. On July 23, 1851, thirty-five chiefs touched the pen to signify their approval of the treaty that, with a similar agreement signed at Mendota two weeks later (see p. 16), opened to the white man nearly twenty-four million acres of rich land encompassing most of what is now southern Minnesota as well as parts of Iowa and South Dakota. The site is fittingly marked and commemorated in Traverse des Sioux State Park.

The crossing was already well known in Minnesota when the treaty commissioners journeyed there in 1851 to meet the Wahpeton and Sisseton Dakota. For years the Indians had forded the Minnesota River at that point, and fur traders had operated posts off and on at the Traverse since the early 1800s and perhaps before. In the 1820s trader Louis Provençalle conducted a permanent fur station there, and later a small settlement of voyageurs and mixbloods grew up about it. In 1843 Stephen R. Riggs established a mission to the Indians, the first of several operated at Traverse des Sioux.

The crossing gained a permanent place in the annals of Minnesota when it was chosen as the site of the 1851 treaty negotiations. Immigrants pouring into Minnesota after the organization of the territory in 1849 were free to settle only in the small delta of land between the St. Croix and Mississippi rivers which the Dakota and Chippewa had ceded in 1837. All the rest of what is now Minnesota belonged to the Indians. Casting covetous eyes across the Mississippi, settlers urged the federal government to negotiate a treaty that would open the gates to the "Suland," as it was popularly called. Fur traders, too, were interested in such a treaty, for they hoped to satisfy old debts from the money that the Dakota would receive for their lands.

The great drama opened on June 30, 1851, when the steamboat "Excelsior" ascended the Minnesota from Fort Snelling and tied up at Traverse des Sioux. Debarking were Governor Alexander Ramsey and United States commissioner of Indian affairs Luke Lea, who had been appointed as treaty negotiators to represent the government. With them was a large party that included Henry

THE TREATY *of Traverse des Sioux was signed on July 23, 1851, under a bower of leafy branches. First the commissioners signed, then thirty-five chiefs stepped forward to receive gifts and touch the pen used to write their names. This oil painting is by Frank B. Mayer, who attended the treaty negotiations.*

H. Sibley and Richard Chute, representing rival fur companies to which the Dakota were indebted; James M. Goodhue, the colorful editor of Minnesota's first newspaper, the *Minnesota Pioneer,* who with William G. Le Duc would write vivid reports of the proceedings; Frank B. Mayer, a young artist from Baltimore, Maryland, who was to record the treaty scene in his paintings and sketches; and visiting Mdewakanton from Kaposia (now South St. Paul) costumed in festive attire.

Only a few of the Sisseton and Wahpeton whom the white men had come to meet had arrived, and the commissioners pitched tents and prepared to wait. In the days that followed, the Dakota from the Minnesota Valley and the plains to the west slowly gathered at the treaty ground beating their drums and singing their songs. Goodhue described one company of Sisseton "mounted on their horses, and advancing with the noise of two drums, and singing the wildest war song that ever sent the blood curdling over the scalp, marching in line; now they proceed to the marquee of the Commissioners, to present themselves and report their arrival and their miserable starving condition." Much feasting, merriment, games, and dancing passed the time until the commissioners decided a sufficient number of chiefs and headmen were present, although the Dakota from Lake Traverse had not yet appeared.

The lengthy and formal grand councils between the chiefs and the commissioners got under way on July 18 beneath an arbor of green boughs over a framework of young trees. In elaborate speeches the commissioners explained that the Great Father wished to purchase at a fair price the lands that had become useless to the Dakota. The Indians, they said, would also receive other lands of their own where the government would build houses, schools, and farms and would provide medical care and artisans to teach the white man's arts. The Indians, however, were not disposed to quick agreement. Chief Red Iron asked that further negotiations be postponed until the Lake Traverse band arrived, and he left the council when the commissioners flatly refused. The commissioners then averted a mass walkout of the Dakota by cutting off provisions and announcing that they, too, would be leaving in the morning. The move had the desired effect; within two days the commissioners had induced thirty-five chiefs to sign the treaty. Without question the government's representatives had used coercion, flattery, deception, threats, outlandish promises, ridicule, and anger, and they had been greatly assisted in their efforts by traders and mixbloods working behind the scenes.

By this treaty the Sisseton and Wahpeton relinquished all their lands in the territory, except for a small reservation on the upper Minnesota River between Lake Traverse and the mouth of the Yellow Medicine River, for a consideration of $1,665,000. The money was to be divided into a fund of $275,000 to settle their affairs and a second fund earmarked for schools and farms, and the remainder was to be invested at five per cent interest for fifty years. The interest would be paid annually in cash and goods, with special funds for "civilization" programs and education. At the end of fifty years, the principal sum was to be retained by the government.

In June, 1852, the United States Senate finally ratified this treaty and that signed at Mendota, after amending them to remove the designated reservation and give the president authority to select lands outside the ceded territory for the Dakota's new home. Before the amended treaties could be proclaimed, they had to have the Indians' approval, which was once again gained by means of coercion and half-truths.

With the treaties taken care of, there remained one important problem to settle — the payment of the upper Dakota's debts to traders and a settlement for the mixed-blood members of the tribe, most of whom were the children of traders. Serving as the vehicle to accomplish this was the infamous "traders' paper," which the chiefs had signed at Traverse des Sioux. Thinking it was a duplicate of the treaty, the Indian chiefs had put their marks on a paper that later proved to be a list of traders' claims. By signing it, the chiefs promised to satisfy those claims with money received from the treaty. Despite the angry protestations of the upper Dakota that they had been duped, the government declared the paper valid and tried to collect the money late in 1852 by withholding the annuity payment until the Indians agreed to the settlement. Chief Red Iron,

A BRONZE PLAQUE *on a boulder marks the location of the arbor where the 1851 treaty was signed.*

resolute leader of the opposition, stated the Indians' case: "We will receive our annuity but we will sign no papers for anything else. The snow is on the ground and we have been waiting a long time for our moneys. Our hunting season is past. A great many of our people are sick from being hungry. We may die because you will not pay us. We may die, but if we do, we will leave our bones upon the ground, that our Great Father may see where his Dakota children died. We are very poor. We have sold our hunting grounds and the graves of our fathers. We have sold our own graves. We have no place to bury our dead and you will not pay us the money for our lands." The traders' paper, however, was irrevocable and $250,000 was paid directly to the claimants. This bit of sharp dealing is widely cited by historians as one of the causes of the Dakota rebellion in 1862.

Long before the Dakota had moved from the land ceded at Traverse des Sioux, white settlers rushed in to open farms and establish villages. The Traverse des Sioux Land Company quickly platted a townsite near the treaty grounds, and by 1853 the thriving village had some two hundred inhabitants and was the temporary seat of Nicollet County. Three years later there were about seventy buildings, including eleven stores, several taverns, and a steam sawmill. Traverse des Sioux lost its bid for the permanent county seat to nearby St. Peter in 1857, and within a few years the village was largely deserted. Some of the buildings were moved away, leaving scarcely a hint of the town's former activity.

Today the sites of the village of Traverse des Sioux and the arbor where the treaty was signed are within Traverse des Sioux State Park, established in 1963. The treaty site was first acquired by the state in 1906 and was later marked by the Captain Richard Somers Chapter of the Daughters of the American Revolution. The large granite boulder carrying the commemorative plaque supposedly was used for the exchange of gifts during the treaty negotiations. In 1931 the state moved to the site from a nearby farm a log cabin similar to Louis Provençalle's early trading post. At the village site, across the highway, markers locate and describe the steamboat landings, the spring, and eighteen structures that once lined the main street. Admission to the village site is by state park sticker; there is no admission fee to the treaty site. Public picnicking facilities are maintained within the park.

Lower and Upper Sioux Agencies

Lower Sioux Agency located in northeastern Redwood County. Accessible via U.S. highway no. 71, six miles east of Redwood Falls to county road no. 2, then two miles south and east to Lower Sioux Agency Interpretive Center.

Upper Sioux Agency located in eastern Yellow Medicine County. Accessible from state highway no. 67, nine miles north of Echo or eight miles southeast of Granite Falls.

THESE TWO AGENCIES, operated by the United States government from 1854 to 1862, served as administrative centers on the first reservations established for the Dakota (Sioux) Indians by treaties signed in 1851 at Traverse des Sioux and Mendota. During those eight years, the pressures put upon the Dakota by the government, traders, and white settlers mounted and climaxed in the Indians' abortive attempt, known as the Sioux Uprising of 1862, to reclaim their land and their traditional way of life. Like the government's policies of enforced change that provoked them into a war, the Dakota's rebellion was for them a disastrous failure.

The story of the Dakota's existence on the reservations must include a brief description of their earlier life on the land that became Minnesota. In the mid-eighteenth century, these Indians had been forced by the Chippewa from their woodland homes in the Mille Lacs region (see p. 63). By the end of that century, the eastern or Santee Dakota — composed of the Mdewakanton, Wahpekute, Sisseton, and Wahpeton bands — inhabited the southern two-thirds of the state. The Mdewakanton established village sites along the Mississippi River below the mouth of the St. Croix and westward along the Minnesota and Cannon rivers. The Wahpekute, more nomadic, inhabited the region south of the Minnesota Valley, while the Sisseton and Wahpeton elected to live in the upper reaches of that valley and westward on the plains, where they could hunt buffalo. After a hundred and fifty years of infrequent contact with European traders, missionaries, and explorers, the Santee culture remained essentially unchanged except for the adoption of cloth, steel tools, firearms, and horses. Their religious and social traditions were still intact.

This condition began to change in 1805 with the visit of Zebulon M. Pike, initiating the era of American occupation and increased Dakota contact with whites — a process accelerated by the building in the 1820s of Fort Snelling and the arrival of Lawrence Taliaferro as Indian agent closely followed by a swelling stream of settlers. Pike introduced the Dakota to the treaty-making process and negotiated the first of several such agreements that eventually transferred all of the Santee land to white ownership. Taliaferro was charged with

121

carrying out the government's Indian policies: to teach the Indians that the United States government was the sovereign power to which they owed obedience; to protect them from the destructive influence of unscrupulous traders; to stop warfare between tribes; and to begin the difficult transformation of the Indians' way of life into that of the white man.

In 1830 the Dakota signed a treaty that gave them, in return for a land cession, their first annuity payment and provided for agricultural and educational funds — two items with which they would become more familiar. Another treaty, signed in 1837 by twenty-one Mdewakanton chiefs and headmen, provided for the cession of the Indians' land east of the Mississippi River for which the band would receive an annuity payment, another educational fund, money for medicines, agricultural equipment, a physician, farmers, blacksmiths, and "other beneficial objects." A payment of $90,000 was provided to settle the "just debts" of the tribe to the traders. Because the government failed to fulfill its obligations, the treaty of 1837 created more problems than it solved for Taliaferro and the Dakota people.

The decade of the 1840s found the Santee struggling to withstand the on-slaught of change brought by the white man. Most alarming was the disappearance of game animals on which they depended for survival. Suffering the effects of increasingly unsuccessful hunts, the Mdewakanton band, especially, had looked with hope toward the annual arrival of goods and money promised in the treaties. They soon learned that the annuity payments were usually late and provided goods of inferior quality. And the small amount of money they received was quickly absorbed by the traders' debts incurred through a system of high prices and overextended credit. Nearly all the bands had felt the influence of the government's program to "civilize" the Indians, and some individuals had agreed to plant crops in an effort to provide needed foodstuffs. Missionaries, too, were making an impact, but few Dakota were converted to the faith of these sometimes aggressive, condescending men who failed to understand the Indian's own religious traditions or respect his culture. As a direct result of their contact with white men, the Dakota also learned of the hazards of "civilization" — smallpox, cholera, venereal diseases, and alcohol.

The pressures of white settlement increased, and in 1851 the Santee bands reluctantly participated in the treaties of Traverse des Sioux and Mendota (see p. 16, 117). They exchanged all their remaining lands in Minnesota for two reservations and annual payments of goods and money which, they were led to believe, would take care of their needs forever.

From beginning to end, writes Roy W. Meyer in his *History of the Santee Sioux,* the treaties of 1851 were "a thoroughly sordid affair, equal in infamy to anything else in the long history of injustice perpetrated upon the Indians by the authorized representatives of the United States government in the name of that government."

The reservation for the upper Dakota (Wahpeton and Sisseton) comprised a strip of land ten miles wide on each side of the Minnesota River between Lake Traverse and the Yellow Medicine River. It was on this reservation that the Upper Agency was later built. The lower reservation for the Mdewakanton and Wahpekute bands continued downstream about sixty miles to Little Rock Creek; on this reservation the Lower Agency was constructed.

The job of removing the Santee to the reservations and setting up the agencies fell to newly appointed Indian agent Richard G. Murphy. In the summer of 1853 Murphy traveled by steamboat up the Minnesota River to the site that had already been selected for the Lower Agency at the mouth of the Redwood River. There he paid annuities to the upper Dakota, who had come down from their reservation, before returning downriver to find a more suitable agency site some thirteen miles from where Fort Ridgely was being built. The following summer Murphy chose the site for the Upper Agency near the junction of the Minnesota and Yellow Medicine rivers.

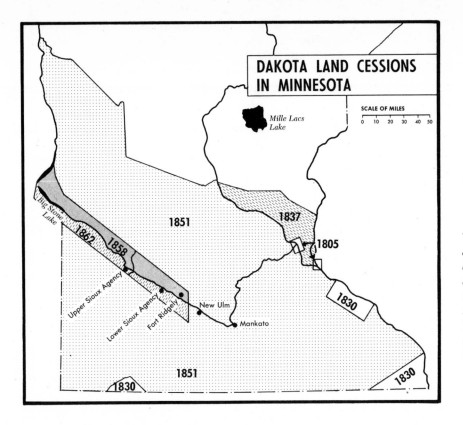

THIS MAP *shows how the land area occupied by the Dakota Indians decreased in size from 1805, the date of the first treaty, until 1858, when they gave up reservation lands on the north side of the Minnesota River. They retained the strip about ten miles wide on the south side of the river until 1862.*

The Lower Agency was to be the residence of the agent and his staff and the place where annuities would be issued to all four bands. The Upper Agency apparently was to serve as a core settlement of government employees around which the Indians would establish farms. (By 1857, however, the upper Dakota received their annuities at the Yellow Medicine Agency. This change in procedure was deemed necessary to protect the lower Indians' gardens and crops from being devoured by the upper bands while they awaited the late payments.)

Getting the Santee to move onto the reservations was "troublesome business" for Murphy, even though most of the upper Dakota found little fault with their reservation, since they already had villages there and a few had begun farming with the help of missionaries at Lac qui Parle and Pajutazee. But the lower Dakota preferred their old homes in the woods to the open prairies of the reservation. Faced with a limited tenancy of five years proclaimed by President Millard Fillmore, they could see little future in planting crops, fencing land, and building houses only to have them taken away. On the other hand, it had been made clear to them that their best hope for survival during the coming winter was to establish themselves on the reserve in order to receive the annuity payments. Most of the Mdewakanton band arrived at the Lower Agency area late in October, 1853. The Wahpekute band was equally slow to enter the reservation, and one group never did leave its haunts near Faribault. As late as 1856 Murphy's "troublesome business" was not finished, and for years afterward small groups of Santee went back to hunt near their former homes, despite the complaints of white settlers who had quickly replaced them on the land.

Construction and farming progressed slowly on the two reservations hampered by lack of funds and equipment, underpaid, incompetent, and disinterested employees, and the reluctance of the Dakota to participate. Not unexpectedly, the government failed to fulfill many of the provisions of the 1851 treaties, especially those concerning the prompt payment of annuities and the expending of special funds for agriculture and schools. The Indians blamed Murphy for shortcomings in the government's system; he in turn warned his superiors, in a report issued shortly before he was removed as agent, that the system should be improved and changed. As Chief Big Eagle put it many years later: "There was great dissatisfaction among the Indians over many things the whites did. . . . the whites were always trying to make the Indians give up their life and live like white men — go to farming, work hard and do as they did — and the Indians did not know how to do that, and did not want to anyway. It seemed too sudden to make such a change. If the Indians had tried to make the whites live like them, the whites would have resisted, and it was the same way with many Indians. The Indians wanted to live as they did before the treaty of Traverse des Sioux — go where they pleased and when they pleased; hunt game wherever they could find it, sell their furs to the traders, and live as they could.''

The list of Dakota grievances included, among others, shortages of food year after year; repeated delay in payment of annuities, which required abandoning fields and hunts while waiting; failure of the government to spend the education fund; no legal recourse for reservation Indians abused by white men, other Dakota, and the Chippewa.

To that list must be added the consequences in 1857 of the killing of more than thirty whites and the kidnaping of four women at Spirit Lake, Iowa, and Jackson, Minnesota, by a renegade band of Wahpekute headed by Inkpaduta. Detachments of soldiers from Forts Snelling and Ridgely failed to capture Inkpaduta and his men. Consequently, the Indian office ordered the reservation Indians to take responsibility for his capture and announced that no annuities

A PLAQUE *bearing the initials of Agent Thomas J. Galbraith and the construction date is still in place in what originally was the front wall of the Lower Agency warehouse.*

THE STONE WAREHOUSE, *built in 1861, is the only original building remaining at the Lower Agency.*

would be paid until the prisoner was brought in. This incredible order served only to force a long and futile man hunt by "volunteers" under Chief Little Crow, and, more important, to heighten the Dakota's disrespect for a government unable to punish a single renegade.

In spite of the refusal of thousands of Dakota to become farmer Indians, enough individuals accepted the white man's ways to encourage the Indian department. In 1856 a small band of Dakota separated from the tribe and formed the Hazelwood Republic whose members agreed to establish and operate individual farms on the upper reservation. A similar organization was founded at the lower reservation with about a dozen families. These farmers received what the traditionalist Indians considered special treatment, giving rise to increased tensions between the two factions. The "cut-hair" or "breeches" Indians were ridiculed and harassed by "blanket" Indians who burned haystacks, killed livestock, stole crops, and tempted the farmers with alcohol. So effective was their campaign that the Hazelwood Republic was forced to disband in 1860.

The government's program to "civilize" the Dakota gained ground from 1858 to 1861 under the administration of agent Joseph R. Brown. Like his predecessors and successors, Brown was a political appointee, but unlike them, he had close and influential associations with the Dakota. A sincere believer in the practicality of breaking up the tribal system through education and agriculture, Brown successfully promoted additional treaties in 1858 to support the government's program. By these treaties the upper and lower Dakota sold off the reservation land on the north side of the Minnesota River. On the remaining reserves, individual farms of eighty acres were to be allotted to each head of an Indian family and every male over the age of twenty-one, provided they adopted the ways of the whites. The disappointing aspect of the treaties for the Dakota involved, as usual, the money they expected to receive. Two years after they were signed, the Senate resolved to pay only thirty cents for land that Brown thought was worth five dollars an acre. The money Congress finally appropriated could not be paid until the familiar traders' papers were settled "in public council," as the treaties stipulated. Although no public council of chiefs was held, the government satisfied the traders' claims, leaving the lower Dakota virtually nothing and the upper Dakota about half the expected amount.

The community comprising the Lower Agency grew by 1860 into a prairie village of over a hundred white and mixblood employees and residents. Although no contemporary description of the settlement is known, it is thought that the agency's buildings were spread out for about a mile along the bluff above the Minnesota River. Additional government structures were maintained at the original agency site seven miles upriver, and the saw and grist mills were located at the falls of the Redwood River nearby.

At the west edge of the settlement stood four traders' stores. Eastward, across the road to New Ulm, were at least fifteen and perhaps more government buildings. Along with various stables, storehouses, a blacksmith shop, cookhouse, schoolhouse, and a boardinghouse, there were living quarters for the physician, interpreter, carpenter, superintendents of schools and farming, and teachers. The agent's house had been put to other use after 1858, when Brown moved to the Upper Agency. The imposing two-story warehouse, built of stone by Indian laborers in 1861, carried the date of construction and the agent's initials on a plaque over its front doors. East of the warehouse the Reverend John P. Williamson, a Presbyterian missionary, built a frame chapel for his small congregation. Nearby the Reverend Samuel D. Hinman, an Episcopal missionary, constructed a little stone church in 1862. From the agency a steeply graded, much-used trail led northeast to the Redwood Ferry then continued eastward to Fort Ridgely.

About 3,200 Dakota lived on the lower reservation. Their major chiefs established villages within a few miles of the agency and lived in the frame two-story

AN INTERPRETIVE CENTER *(above)*
at the Lower Agency houses ex-
hibits like those shown below to
depict the history of the Eastern
Dakota Indians in the state from
1800 to the present.

dwellings provided by the government. Several of these leaders were sympathetic
to the government's program. Little Crow, for example, had agreed to accept
a new brick house in return for his co-operation in recruiting converts to the
farming program. The majority of the lower Dakota, however, continued to
live in scattered villages throughout the reservation. The amount of land under
cultivation increased annually, with 1,357 acres planted to corn, potatoes, turnips,
rutabagas, and wheat in 1862. In August that year, a brickyard to provide
building materials for more Indian homes was in the early stages of construction.

The Upper Agency buildings were erected high on the west bank of the
Yellow Medicine River about a mile from its junction with the Minnesota.
Three miles up the latter river Dr. Thomas S. Williamson had founded Pajutazee
Mission in 1852, and in 1854 the Reverend Stephen R. Riggs built a new
mission at Hazelwood, about three miles beyond Pajutazee. The Wahpeton
band established villages in the lower section of their reservation, and the Sisseton
lived farther upriver near Big Stone and Traverse lakes.

Construction of the Upper Agency buildings utilized the logs and later the
lumber from sparse local timber as well as bricks produced by a plant erected
in 1859. By 1862 the agency had several brick buildings — a large, two-story
warehouse with offices for the agent and the physician; a jail; two employees'
residences of two and a half stories constructed in the manner of today's duplexes;
a two-story manual labor school; a bakehouse and oven; and at least one barn.
To the west of this cluster of buildings, agency employees lived in several
frame dwellings, and beyond them stood the brick plant. About half a mile
from the agency four traders built their stores in the valley of the Yellow Medicine
River, on whose banks were located the agency's saw and grist mills.

Of the estimated 4,500 upper Dakota assigned to the reservation, only about
a hundred families had become farmers living in government-built houses. With
the help of agency employees, they had planted a total of 1,512 acres in 1862.
(Much of the produce from these fields was used to feed some 2,000 Indians,
soldiers, half-breeds, and liberated whites at Camp Release at the end of the
1862 war.)

Brown was replaced in 1861 by Thomas J. Galbraith, another political
appointee whose impatience, arrogance, and stubbornness engendered a less than
cordial response from both Indians and whites. His job was made no easier
by the increased harassment of the Indian families who lived on their own
farms. At the upper reservation the Sisseton and Wahpeton farmers were also
plagued by recurrent raids on their croplands by the Yanktonai bands of Dakota,

who lived north and west of the reservation. The security problem for the farmers was serious enough to warrant military protection in the opinion of the agent, but there simply were not enough soldiers at Fort Ridgely to supply a permanent guard. Crop failures in 1861 aggravated the Indians' unfortunate condition, especially at the upper reservation where over a thousand Sisseton had to be given special allotments of food to keep them alive during the winter. The following spring and summer brought continuing shortages of food, but Galbraith refused to give out provisions from the well-stocked warehouses because the annuity money had not yet arrived, and it was his inflexible procedure to make both distributions at the same time.

In July, 1862, Galbraith bent his rules and reluctantly issued pork and flour at the Lower Agency. Then on July 14 at the Upper Agency he was confronted by four thousand hungry reservation Indians and a thousand Yanktonai demanding provisions. He gave them only a small amount, and on August 4 the Indians decided to take additional food from the warehouse, despite the presence of troops from Fort Ridgely. They had succeeded in carrying out some flour before Lieutenant Timothy J. Sheehan's threats with a howitzer stopped them. The lieutenant then coaxed Galbraith into issuing more provisions on the condition that the Indians return to their homes. Little Crow, who was present at this confrontation, also obtained the agent's promise of additional provisions for his people on the lower reservation, but the promise was never kept. Nor could the Indians obtain more credit from the traders, whose attitude was clearly stated by Andrew J. Myrick: "So far as I am concerned, if they are hungry, let them eat grass."

Shortly before dawn on August 18, 1862, Little Crow was awakened by a party of chiefs and warriors who came to tell him of the murder of settlers at Acton and to discuss an all-out war against the whites. Arguments for an uprising were strong, but Little Crow tried to convince the prowar contingent of the futility of fighting white soldiers as numerous as locusts. Only when his courage was challenged did he agree to lead the Dakota against the whites of the Minnesota Valley and against all "cut-hairs" who refused to take part in the battle. Other lower Dakota chiefs opposed to the war — primarily Wabasha, Taopi, Big Eagle, and Traveling Hail — were forced to join in the hostilities. The first attack was set for dawn.

At sunrise a large number of armed and painted Dakota appeared at the Lower Agency and spread out to surround the trader's stores and other buildings. A prearranged signal launched the attack of gunfire, and the first victims to fall were the traders and their employees. Myrick's body was later found with grass stuffed into his mouth. Thirteen persons were killed at the agency as well as seven others who attempted to flee via the Redwood Ferry to Fort Ridgely. The attackers captured ten prisoners and allowed forty-seven to escape in favor of plundering and burning the buildings.

Across the river at the Redwood Ferry landing, warriors lay in wait for Captain John S. Marsh and some forty-five enlisted men approaching from Fort Ridgely. At least twenty-four soldiers, including the captain, died in the affray that followed. (At the ambush site are two granite markers accessible by foot trail from the Lower Agency. One tells the fate of Marsh and his men. The other honors the brave ferryman who transported so many refugees to safety.) Heartened by the ease with which they had taken the agency and killed the soldiers, the Dakota looked forward to similar victories against Fort Ridgely and New Ulm, the upper valley's largest white settlement.

Rumors of the outbreak reached the Wahpeton living near the Upper Agency by noon, and representatives of the local and visiting bands met in hurried council to discuss their course of action. After a long and heated debate, no clear-cut resolution was reached, and the decision on whether to join the lower Dakota apparently was left to each individual. Christian Indian leaders opposed to the war immediately warned their white friends of imminent danger. Agent

Galbraith was absent, having left the week before to escort to Fort Snelling a group of mixbloods and former agency employees who had volunteered for service in the Civil War. John Other Day gathered sixty-two agency residents and employees in the large brick warehouse, guarded them through the night, and led them to safety as dawn broke on August 19. Chief Akepa, Paul Mazakute-mani (Little Paul), Simon Anawangmani, and others alerted the forty-five whites at the nearby missions of Williamson and Riggs.

Simultaneously with the Indians' organized attacks on the Lower Agency, Fort Ridgely, and New Ulm, small groups of warriors, many of them undisci-plined and independent, fanned through the Minnesota Valley to shoot white farmers, capture or kill women and children, and pillage the settlers' homesteads. The Dakota warrior saw himself, historian William W. Folwell has written, "engaged in war, the most honorable of all pursuits, against men who, as he believed, had robbed him of his country and his freedom, had fooled and cheated him with pretensions of friendship, and who wished to force upon him an alien language and religion." This war was no different, in his mind, from those formerly fought against the Chippewa and the Fox. In reality, however, the Dakota effort was doomed by the more powerful forces of the white men, whose successful defenses of Fort Ridgely and New Ulm turned the tide against the attackers.

Following the crippling defeat of the Dakota at the final battle of Wood Lake on September 23, most of the hostile bands and many of the formerly friendly Indians who feared retribution gathered their families and took refuge on the plains to the west. Those who stayed behind handed over to Colonel Henry H. Sibley at Camp Release 269 captives whom they had protected at Chief Red Iron's village. (The site of Camp Release is marked by a state monument about two miles west of Montevideo on U.S. highway no. 212.) The uprising was over, but the punishment was still to be meted out.

The stupendous job of deciding the guilt of the surrendered and captured Indians was undertaken by a commission of military officers at Camp Release.

THE BRICK *employees' duplex at the Upper Agency, considered the oldest building in Yellow Medicine County, has been restored to its 1862 appearance. The interior will house period furnishings and exhibits describing U.S. Indian policy in the mid-nineteenth century and life at the agency.*

After about 120 cases had been heard, the 2,000 prisoners were marched to the Lower Agency, where the trials resumed in a trader's log kitchen. In all 392 Indians and mixbloods were tried, none of whom had the right to legal counsel to help prove his innocence. Over 300 were sentenced to die for participating in the uprising and were taken under guard to a makeshift camp near Mankato. About 1,700 others — mostly women and children — made a six-day march to a prisoners' camp near Fort Snelling.

Public sentiment demanded immediate death for the "murderous Sioux." But President Abraham Lincoln, after carefully scrutinizing the evidence, pared the list of condemned to thirty-nine Dakota and one more prisoner received a last-minute reprieve. Thirty-eight Indians and mixbloods were hanged on a mass gallows at Mankato on December 26, 1862. The president's leniency was not approved by Minnesotans, who, if they could not see all the Indians dead, insisted that the Dakota be exiled from the state. Early in 1863 Congress took the necessary steps to remove the Dakota (as well as the Winnebago, who were not involved in the war but held rich land coveted by settlers), to reclaim the reservations, to provide payment for damages suffered by whites during the uprising, and to abrogate all treaties with the Dakota. In mid-May some 1,300 Indians were herded onto two river steamers "like so many cattle" and deported to the Crow Creek Reservation on the Missouri River in what is now South Dakota. The Dakota's miserable existence there is another chapter in the shameful record of the government's treatment of American Indians — treatment described by an official in 1869 as "unjust and iniquitous beyond the power of words to express."

Not satisfied that the Indians had been properly punished, the United States Army organized a campaign in 1863 to kill or capture all the hostile Dakota who had escaped to the plains. Later that year, Minnesota authorized the organization of volunteer scouts to track down individual Indians and set a bounty of $25 on each Dakota scalp taken. Civilians, too, were encouraged to kill roving warriors for a payment of $75, later raised to $200 per scalp. A farmer near Hutchinson received a larger reward of $500 for shooting Chief Little Crow on July 3, 1863.

All that was left at the Lower Agency area after the war were the scorched walls of the stone warehouse and part of a trader's residence, the mills, and some Indian homes. By 1866 white farmers had settled on the agency site. August Knueppel purchased the old stone warehouse in 1881 and remodeled it as a residence. This sturdy old structure, measuring 43 feet by 23 feet, with walls varying from 18 inches to 3 feet in thickness, still stands today. Although the interior has been extensively remodeled, the exterior has been little changed and looks much as it did in 1861. Eight small loopholes were enlarged to standard-sized windows; the outside basement entry was replaced by an inside one; a large square window was built into the south wall; and an enclosed porch was added at what is now the back of the house. On the wall above the porch can still be seen the stone plaque bearing Galbraith's initials and the date of construction. The building was purchased by the Minnesota Historical Society in 1967, and it is now the residence of the caretaker at the Lower Agency. IT IS NOT OPEN TO THE PUBLIC, but visitors are welcome to view it from the grounds.

The importance of the agency as it relates to the history of both the Dakota and the white people is emphasized inside the modern interpretive center built by the society in 1970. There exhibits tell the long, proud, and often sad story of the Dakota Indians from about 1800 to the present. The center is open daily from May through October. There is an admission fee. In 1971 the state legislature established the Lower Sioux Agency Historic District, and the site was added to the National Register of Historic Places.

Behind the interpretive center are the graves of Andrew Robertson, who worked at the agencies until his death in 1859, and of some members of the

ARCHAEOLOGISTS *discovered the cistern adjacent to the foundations of the brick warehouse at the Upper Agency. In the background is the barn partially rebuilt by George E. Olds about 1866.*

August Knueppel family. Markers along the road locate the grave of James W. Lynd, a storekeeper killed during the Dakota attack; the stores of the four traders; and the old agency warehouse.

Following the end of hostilities, Galbraith returned to the Upper Agency and found only two Indian houses intact and the rest of the buildings "rendered useless." About three years later, when the first white settlers homesteaded in Yellow Medicine County, the ruins of the government buildings still remained. George E. Olds, who arrived in 1866, filed a claim to the agency site, which included remnants of a brick duplex or boardinghouse, a barn, and the warehouse. He reconstructed the boardinghouse as a residence, rebuilt part of the barn, and razed the warehouse walls. Two other buildings — a second duplex residence and the jail — were rebuilt about 1866 and occupied for a time; both have since disappeared. All that remains of the warehouse is the foundation, and the barn stands as Olds reconstructed it.

In 1963 the legislature authorized acquisition of the Upper Agency site and established a state park. The Minnesota Historical Society, which administers the agency area, conducted extensive archaeological investigations and erected markers locating all but one of the agency's brick buildings and the frame residences in the present picnic area. Major restoration work on the former Olds residence, completed in 1974, has returned it to its 1862 appearance. This site is listed in the National Register of Historic Places as the Upper Sioux Agency Historic District. Admission to the Upper Agency is by state park sticker available at the entrance.

Most members of the upper Dakota bands eventually settled on reservations in North and South Dakota and in Canada; groups of individuals formed offshoot settlements, including one near the old Upper Agency. Fragments of lower Dakota bands that for various reasons had not been exiled remained in their traditional locations after 1863, somehow enduring the hostility of the whites and the poverty resulting from withdrawal of government assistance. Among the villages at Mendota, Shakopee, Faribault, Prairie Island, and Wabasha were many of the Christian Indians who had protected whites during the war and performed services for the military afterward.

Over the ensuing decades, as the government's policies regarding its Indian wards were reshaped, additional Santee returned to Minnesota to live. Intolerable conditions at Crow Creek forced the removal in 1866 of exiled Dakota to the Niobrara River in northeastern Nebraska. A group of Indians left there in 1869 to establish a permanent settlement at Flandreau, South Dakota. Others settled at Morton near the remains of the Lower Agency. In 1970 the Dakota population of the state (outside its urban areas) was estimated at 298 people living on small reservations at the Upper Sioux Community near Granite Falls, the Lower Sioux Community near Morton, Prairie Island near Red Wing, and Prior Lake near Shakopee.

JOSEPH R. BROWN HOUSE — About seven miles downriver from the Upper Sioux Agency, Joseph R. Brown built for his wife and twelve children an imposing three-and-a-half-story house of granite. Construction of the home began in 1861 apparently shortly after Brown was replaced as Indian agent to the Dakota. The mansion was another landmark in his remarkable career in Minnesota, which had begun in 1819 when he arrived as a drummer boy with troops assigned to build Fort Snelling. From 1825, when he left the army, to 1861, the talented Brown had been involved in numerous ventures as fur trader, lumberman, land speculator, founder of cities, legislator, politician, editor, inventor, and Indian agent.

Brown built his house about two hundred yards below the bluff on the north side of the Minnesota River. Granite for the exterior walls came from a nearby quarry and was possibly the first granite to be used in house construction in Minnesota. Bricks for the interior walls came from the brickyard at the

Upper Agency; lime for the mortar was burned in a kiln located about a mile north of the house, and lumber was secured at New Ulm and at the Upper Agency sawmill. The house of nineteen rooms, each finished with lime plaster in various colors, was built into the hillside much as today's homes are constructed with walkout basements. There was an entrance at the second level on the north façade and at the first level on the south side. Long verandas at the second and third levels ran the length of the house on the south wall. Brown also built a stable, had a well dug, and landscaped the grounds. The total cost of this country estate was $9,313.61, according to Brown's records.

Into this elegant prairie home, Mrs. Brown brought her fine furniture, including a grand piano, parlor and cooking stoves (the house had no fireplaces), fancy china and glassware, and wardrobes of clothing and accessories for the family. The large house became popularly known as ''Farther and Gay'' — a pun on the noted Fotheringhay Castle of England's Mary Stuart — and a center of hospitality in sparsely settled southwestern Minnesota.

In mid-August, 1862, Brown was in New York on business concerning his latest invention, a steam wagon, while his Dakota wife and family remained at home on the Minnesota River. Early on August 19, Mrs. Brown was awakened by a mixblood who told her of the Indian attack on the Upper Agency. She immediately put her family into an ox-drawn wagon and, with several neighbors, headed for Fort Ridgely. They had gone only six miles when warriors surrounded the wagon and threatened to kill the party. Mrs. Brown told the Indians in their own language that she was a Sisseton and that the wrath of her relatives would fall upon them if any harm were done to her family. Intimidated, the warriors took the Browns to the home of Chief Little Crow, who treated them with respect. Later they joined their upper Dakota relatives, who cared for them until they were set free at Camp Release.

Brown returned from the East to find his family in captivity and his home ransacked and burned. He joined Sibley's army, took part in the battles at Birch Coulee and Wood Lake, then remained for several years as a commander

THESE RUINS *are all that remain of ''Farther and Gay Castle,'' the huge stone mansion built by Joseph R. Brown in 1861.*

of scouts and a special military agent serving in the Minnesota-Dakota border area. He spent the final years before his death in 1870 at Browns Valley, still active in trading and in the promotion of his steam wagon.

The abandoned Brown property was homesteaded about 1865 by settlers returning to the Minnesota Valley. In 1937 three acres, including the house ruins, were established by the state as a wayside park. The following year the division of state parks began archaeological investigations at the site and uncovered the foundations, walls, and chimney remnants, located the well, and unearthed such artifacts as china, forks, spoons, knives, pieces of a grand piano, sewing machine, stoves, upholstered furniture, and flatirons. It is thought that the site of the stable was obliterated in the process of landscaping the park grounds. With support from the Minnesota Resources Commission, the Minnesota Historical Society undertook additional digging in 1968 which produced more artifacts and located a small granite structure fifty feet north of the house that may have been a root cellar. A plaque erected by the state parks division in 1959 now marks the scenic site located on Renville County road no. 9, eight miles south of Sacred Heart.

 *Fort Ridgely*

Located in Fort Ridgely State Park in the extreme northwestern corner of Nicollet County. Accessible from state highway no. 4, six miles south of Fairfax.

FORT RIDGELY, Minnesota's third military post, was established in 1853 to defend the frontier and watch over the Dakota Indians in the Minnesota Valley. Two years earlier these Indians had ceded their rich southern Minnesota lands to the United States and had agreed to move to new reservations along the upper Minnesota River. Although the ceded tract was not legally opened to settlement until 1854, thousands of white pioneers had already moved onto the land by the summer of 1852. For almost ten years the valley's settlers and the troops garrisoning Fort Ridgely lived in relative peace with their Indian neighbors. Then in 1862 the post was forced to play the role for which it was intended. Twice Fort Ridgely withstood attacks by the rebelling Dakota, who considered it "the door to the valley as far as to St. Paul" and thus a key objective.

The first official proposal to establish a fort in the Minnesota River Valley was made in the summer of 1852 by Henry H. Sibley, Minnesota's territorial delegate to Congress. In a letter to the general in chief of the United States Army, Sibley pointed out the need for military protection of the hundreds of persons who would soon be settling in the valley. Endorsed by congressmen from Iowa and Wisconsin, Sibley's proposal was quickly accepted. Later that year a site for the post was selected just inside the eastern boundary of the Lower Sioux Reservation. It was on a level plateau 150 feet above the valley floor and about three-fourths of a mile north of the river. The location had drawbacks which would make it difficult to defend, for heavily timbered ravines bordered it on all sides except the northwest, where the open prairie extended. It was, however, near supplies of building stone, wood, and water.

In 1853 three companies of the Sixth United States Infantry were assigned to build and garrison the new post. Two companies under the command of Captain James Monroe reached Rock Point, as the site was called, on April 29, 1853. They had traveled from Fort Snelling on the "West Newton," the first steamboat ever to navigate so far up the Minnesota River. On May 20 a third company arrived, headed by Major Samuel Wood, who took over command of the infant post from Captain Monroe. The new fort was probably named for Captain Randolph Ridgely, a hero in the Mexican War, and possibly honors two other officers with the same surname who died in that war.

At first the war department planned to build the fort of stone from a quarry west of the site. But after the soldiers completed two structures — a two-story barracks and a large, one-story commissary — the plans were altered because the available rock proved to be of inferior quality. Thus the rest of the fort was constructed of wood.

When it was completed in 1855, Fort Ridgely consisted of buildings grouped around a parade ground about three hundred feet square. On the south side, facing the river, stood the commodious home of the commandant and the surgeon's quarters. Directly opposite and extending nearly across the north side was the stone barracks with accommodations for four hundred soldiers. Behind it stood a row of log houses used by civilian employees and noncommissioned officers, a hospital, and a small stable. Next to the barracks, along the west side of the parade ground, were the stone commissary and a two-story officers' quarters. The east side of the square had a bakery, a laundry, and additional officers' quarters.

Its builders compounded the problem of defending the fort by scattering numerous buildings beyond the parade area. Both the stables and the two powder magazines, for example, were some distance from the fort proper. To make matters worse, no well was dug, and the stockade and blockhouses called for in the original plan were never built.

From 1853 to 1861 Fort Ridgely was garrisoned by regular United States Army troops. With the outbreak of the Civil War, however, they were replaced by volunteer regiments. The First Minnesota occupied the fort on May 29, 1861, and other Minnesota regiments followed it. Until the summer of 1862, the post served as a training camp for newly enlisted Union soldiers.

That summer, while thousands of Minnesota men fought for the Union in the Civil War, the Dakota Indians of the Minnesota Valley rebelled against the white man in the bloodiest conflict the state has seen. Many factors contributed to the Dakota's disposition to open warfare in 1862 (see p. 121). Briefly, the list would include the 1851 treaties of Traverse des Sioux and Mendota which restricted the Dakota to two reservations along the Minnesota River; the failure of the Great White Father to punish a renegade Wahpekute named Inkpaduta for his massacre of pioneers at Spirit Lake, Iowa, and Jackson, Minnesota, in 1857; a severe crop failure in 1861 that left the Indians near starvation; the delay in the arrival of the government's payment of annuities and foodstuffs in 1862; and a series of other events that destroyed the Indians' respect for the white man and his promises.

The uprising broke on August 17, 1862, with the unplanned murder of several settlers at Acton in Meeker County by four young Dakota from the lower reservation. Fearing the punishment for this action would be severe, chiefs and headmen of the lower bands decided on all-out war to drive the whites from the Minnesota Valley. War parties led by Chief Little Crow first attacked the Lower Agency on August 18. Fort Ridgely's commander, Captain John S. Marsh, responded to reports of the uprising by leading over forty men toward the Lower Agency, thirteen miles upriver. As they neared their destination, however, they were ambushed at the Redwood Ferry. Marsh and more than half his troops never returned to the fort.

Fort Ridgely's role in the war assumed importance from the fact that it was the only military post in southern Minnesota. As Chief Big Eagle said later, the Indians knew that if the post were taken "we would soon have the whole Minnesota Valley." Big Eagle and other chiefs wanted to move against the fort early on August 19, but they were overruled by young warriors who insisted on attacking the second most vital target in the valley, the settlement of New Ulm. It was this decision that undoubtedly saved Fort Ridgely. For that day military reinforcements arrived, enlarging the number of defenders from a handful of soldiers, many of whom were ill, to about 180 able men. Also arriving that day were hundreds of refugees, some of them seriously wounded, whose presence was to greatly complicate the defense of the fort. Lieutenant Timothy

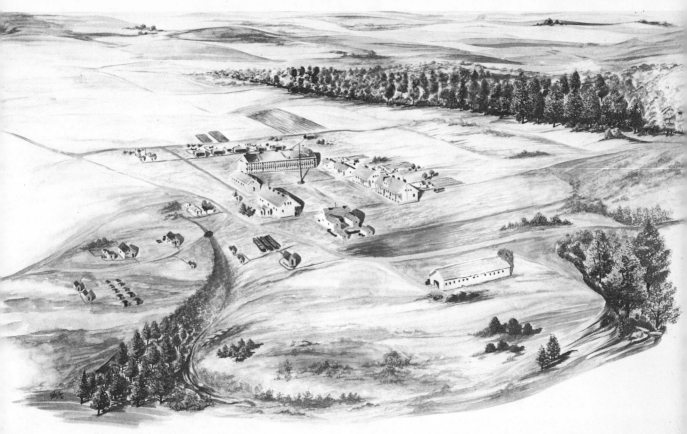

A DRAWING *of Fort Ridgely, based on early descriptions, shows the post and its environs as they appeared in 1862 before the Dakota attack. Drawing by Paul Waller.*

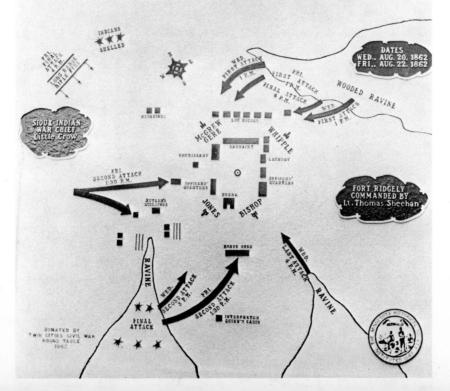

THE TWO BATTLES *of Fort Ridgely are diagramed on this marker in the park. Jones, McGrew, Whipple, and Bishop manned the fort's few cannon at the points indicated.*

J. Sheehan, who took over command of the post on August 19, had one day to plan his defensive strategy.

Having been repulsed by heroic citizen-soldiers defending New Ulm, Little Crow and some four hundred warriors attacked Fort Ridgely early in the afternoon of August 20. The difficulties faced by the outnumbered band of defenders reflected the errors made in planning and building the post: deep ravines on three sides of the post enabled the Indians to advance unseen to within musket range; the wooden buildings quickly caught fire; ammunition had to be brought from the powder magazines some two hundred yards out on the exposed prairie; and water, which had to be carried from a spring below the bluff, was in short supply. Indeed it is doubtful whether Fort Ridgely could have been successfully defended had it not been for the presence of Sergeant John Jones and his gun crew, who expertly manned the few cannon and were able to prevent the Dakota from storming the fort. Overawed by the howitzer shells, the attackers withdrew. They returned two days later with doubled numbers, but once again the well-placed artillery fire proved too much for a spontaneous and undisciplined fighting force. Many historians believe that the successful defenses of Fort Ridgely and New Ulm (which withstood a second attack on August 23) broke the Dakota offensive.

When news of the outbreak reached Governor Alexander Ramsey at St. Paul, he appointed Henry H. Sibley to head an expedition to put down the rebellion. Hastily gathering a small force of fighting men, Sibley left the capital for the Minnesota Valley. At St. Peter they waited for supplies and reinforcements before advancing to Fort Ridgely, lifting the seige of that beleaguered post on August 27. From there Sibley launched an organized military effort to defeat the hostile Dakota and release their prisoners. In its pursuit of the Indians up the Minnesota Valley, Sibley's army suffered a damaging defeat at Birch Coulee, then, some twenty days later, won a decisive victory at Wood Lake. (The site of the Birch Coulee battle is in Birch Coulee State Park in Renville County. Numerous granite monuments outline the action there in 1862. The Wood Lake battlesite is marked by a thirty-foot obelisk in a state-owned monument area about thirteen miles southeast of Granite Falls.)

On September 26, three days after the Wood Lake battle, Sibley entered

A POWDER MAGAZINE, *one of two at the pioneer post, was returned to its original site after many years on a nearby farm.*

THE RESTORED COMMISSARY, *now used as an interpretive center, is the only stone building left at old Fort Ridgely. The foundations of other structures are marked.*

the camp where the white and mixblood captives were being protected by friendly Indians. He then named a military commission to try nearly four hundred Indian and mixblood prisoners, of whom more than three hundred were sentenced to death. This number was later reduced to thirty-eight, and the condemned were hanged at Mankato in December, 1862.

The fighting in Minnesota was over but the toll was heavy. Within thirty-eight days, more than five hundred white settlers had been killed and an unknown number of Dakota — assumed to be many less — had lost their lives; the area of Minnesota bordered by Fort Abercrombie on the north, Lake Shetek on the south, and the Big Woods on the east had been depopulated and ravaged. Surviving settlers flooded St. Paul and other eastern Minnesota towns, where sympathetic citizens cared for them in their sudden destitution.

For three years after the end of hostilities in Minnesota, military brigades combed the Dakota prairies in search of "outlaw" Indians, and in a broad sense, the uprising continued for many years. As the frontier moved westward, other treaties were made, other promises broken, and other Dakota tribes rose in despair against the encroaching white man. Not until 1890 and the bloody battle at Wounded Knee could it be said that the Indian resistance was over.

Fort Ridgely was a key station in supplying Sibley's army as it pursued the Indians up the valley, but once the uprising was over, the glory of the fort quickly faded. During the summers of 1863 and 1864 wagon trains setting out for the western gold fields used the post as a rendezvous, and until the end of the Civil War Union soldiers trained there. From 1865 to 1867 the fort was again garrisoned by regular army troops, but five years later all remaining military property was withdrawn. By 1874 most of the buildings had fallen into disrepair. Within the next few years settlers homesteaded the land and used the fort buildings for various purposes — as a hotel, post office, school, and as a source of construction materials. The commissary was repaired and used for a time as a barn, but gradually the other structures disappeared.

In 1896 the state of Minnesota purchased five acres of the old parade ground and erected on the spot where the fort's flagpole once stood an imposing monument commemorating the Sioux War battles fought there. With the acquisition of additional acreage, the legislature in 1911 established Fort Ridgely Memorial State Park, which has since been further enlarged.

In 1936 an archaeological investigation of the site was begun under the direction of the Minnesota Historical Society with the assistance of the Civilian Conservation Corps. Eight building sites were uncovered, and visitors can now see the marked and exposed foundations. The stone commissary had fallen into partial ruin, but enough of its walls remained so that it could be restored to its original appearance. The only stone building of the old fort to be preserved, it is now an interpretive center where exhibits relating to the post's history may be seen daily from May through September or by reservation in October. Another original building — a log powder magazine — has been repaired and returned to the fort site after years of use on a nearby farm. Through the efforts of the Twin Cities Civil War Round Table the battlefield site was thoroughly marked in 1962. Admission to the historic area, which is administered by the Minnesota Historical Society, requires a state park sticker or daily fee.

In the cemetery immediately southeast of the fort the state has erected three monuments related to the Sioux Uprising. One is dedicated to the memory of Captain John S. Marsh and more than twenty soldiers killed in an ambush at the Redwood Ferry on August 18, 1862. Another recognizes the valor of Mrs. Eliza Muller, wife of Dr. Alfred Muller, the post surgeon. She valiantly cared for the sick and wounded during the siege of Fort Ridgely from August 20 to 27, when an advance section of Sibley's army at last relieved the fort and removed the refugees. The third commemorates the "loyal and efficient services rendered to the State" by the Chippewa Indians during the Sioux War.

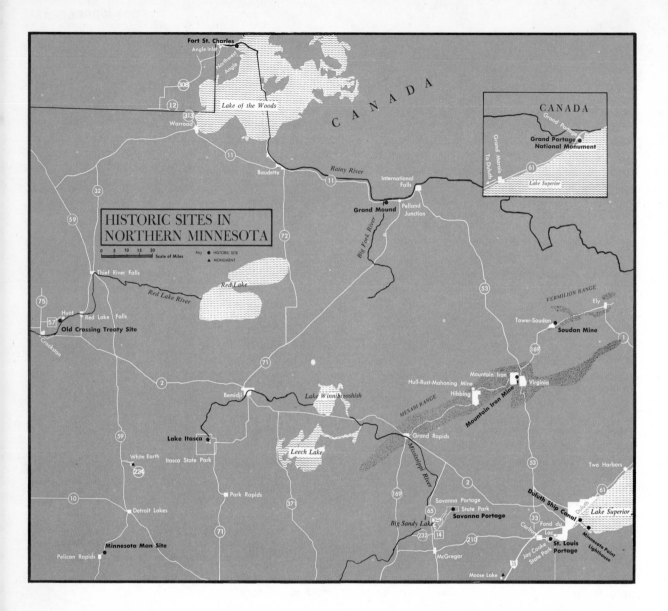

HISTORIC SITES IN
NORTHERN MINNESOTA

Scale of Miles
0 5 10 15 20

Key: ● HISTORIC SITE
△ MONUMENT

Minnesota Man Site

Site located on U.S. highway no. 59, three miles north of Pelican Rapids in northwestern Otter Tail County.

THE FIRST SKELETON in North America to be discovered in geologically dated deposits attributed to the great Ice Age of some eleven thousand years ago was unearthed near Pelican Rapids in 1931. Called "Minnesota Man," the skeleton is actually that of a girl about fifteen years of age. She is believed by some to have drowned in Glacial Lake Pelican, although this theory has been disputed among anthropologists ever since the discovery was made public.

On June 16, 1931, a maintenance crew began digging up the frost-broken surface of the state highway which crossed the lake bed of an extinct body of water known as Glacial Lake Pelican. As the grader blade dug into the earth some ten feet below ground level, it exposed a shiny white clamshell that caught the eye of a crew member. Halting the grader, he continued digging by hand and soon unearthed a human skull, partially crushed by the heavy machine. A broken tool made from an elk antler and a marine-shell pendant were uncovered, and within two hours the men had exhumed an almost complete skeleton. Thinking they had discovered the remains of "an old Indian," they notified Professor Albert E. Jenks, then state archaeologist and head of the anthropology department in the University of Minnesota, who had the skeleton removed to his office.

Because scientists had not seen the skeleton in its original position and location, Jenks had the site of discovery redug. At that time 355 additional bones and artifacts were recovered in sediment concluded to be of late Pleistocene origin.

After an extensive study, Jenks reported that the "measured and observed morphological characters of the skeleton [*especially the lack of reduction of the jaw and the large teeth*] proclaim it to be a primitive type of *Homo sapiens* of an early type of evolving Mongoloid suggesting American aborigines, especially the Eskimo, more than the present Asian Mongoloids."

Jenks's conclusions supported a theory that man had inhabited the North American continent while glaciers still covered part of it, and that he was not a latecomer who made his first appearance after the last glacier retreated. The basis for this belief was the discovery in Folsom, New Mexico, in 1926 of man-made projectile points along with bones of a type of buffalo known to have been extinct for over seven thousand years. Jenks's report lent strength, also, to a conjecture that during the interglacial periods inhabitants of Asia crossed a land bridge to what is now Alaska and eventually migrated south

139

and east to the shores of lakes left by melting glaciers. It was in the soil deposited at the bottom of Glacial Lake Pelican that the skeleton had been found.

Some anthropologists, including Aleš Hrdlička, have attempted to refute Jenks's report, but still the controversy continues. Basically it centers on the question of whether the girl dates from the same time as the deposits in which her bones were found, or whether she lost her life in an accident or was buried by tribesmen in recent prehistoric times. If the lady is as ancient as the glacial deposit of her grave, she may be among North America's oldest known skeletons. The extreme depth of the burial site below the surface tends to support the argument for her early age, according to Minnesota state archaeologist Elden Johnson, since native burial pits are seldom deeply intruded into the earth. On the other hand, unsatisfactory attempts to radiocarbon date the skeleton, while not conclusive, indicated an age that falls between 5000 B.C. and 1000 B.C. In addition, the marine-shell pendant is of a type found in other archaeological sites whose dates correspond with the radiocarbon dating of Minnesota Man. It is Professor Johnson's opinion that "the radiocarbon date is probably correct."

Minnesota Man is owned by the University of Minnesota. The site where the skeleton was found is now marked by a stone monument.

THE SKELETON *of Minnesota Man was found in this road cut in 1931. The marker (at right) stands along U.S. highway no. 59 near Pelican Rapids in Otter Tail County.*

The Grand Mound

Located on the south bank of the Rainy River near its junction with the Big Fork River. Accessible from state highway no. 11, fifteen miles west of International Falls, or four miles west of Pelland Junction.

THE GRAND MOUND is the largest prehistoric burial mound in the upper Midwest. It is one of the fast-disappearing evidences of a prehistoric culture that flourished in Minnesota and Canada sometime between 500 B.C. and 600 A.D. Archaeologically, the Grand Mound and three smaller ones nearby are important as the "type site" for the so-called Laurel culture, a northern forest adaptation of the local Woodland tradition (dating roughly from 1000 B.C. to 1000 A.D.). In laymen's terms this means that the mound group is the site established as the reference to which archaeologists must relate similar finds. Characteristics of the Laurel culture were bone tools and ornaments, the use of native copper, and cannibalistic rites.

The impressive mound dominates a sixty-four-acre tract of virgin deciduous trees long preserved by members of the Fred Smith family, who purchased it in 1889 and sold it to the state in 1970. Its large dimensions — estimated at 136 feet long, 98 feet wide, and about 40 feet high — attracted the area's early settlers and tourists who picnicked and dug for artifacts there.

Although the Grand Mound has never been scientifically examined, two smaller ones in the group have been investigated by University of Minnesota archaeologists. Lloyd A. Wilford dug part of a mound in 1956, but his discoveries did not match the spectacular finds of Albert E. Jenks in 1933. The mound Jenks excavated contained the skeletal remains of about 112 individuals deposited in bundle burials in four successive tiers. Peculiarly, many bones in these secondary burials had been opened to remove the marrow, and the skulls had holes through which the brains had been extracted. Since these operations had been performed immediately after death, it is presumed by archaeologists that the Laurel people were cannibals. Among the most important artifacts unearthed was the only complete pottery vessel of the Laurel culture discovered to date. It is a cooking pot a foot high, more than 11 inches wide, and pointed at the base. Also of interest were bone and antler projectile points, a portion of a bone arm band, and six sharply pointed beaver teeth.

Beneath the mound archaeologists found indications of a habitation site. Remains of fireplaces, ashes, and pottery were also uncovered at various levels, indicating that the mound itself had been used as a living area at different stages in its construction. Primary burials discovered near the surface of the mound are believed to be intrusive interments of a later culture.

141

THE IMPOSING DIMENSIONS *of the Grand Mound are clearly visible in this photograph taken in 1907. Courtesy* Minnesota Archaeologist.

ARTIFACTS *from a mound near the Grand Mound include a cooking pot and bones from bundle burials which helped archaeologists establish characteristics of the Laurel culture. Courtesy University of Minnesota Archaeology Laboratory.*

In 1956 the Grand Mound was named a landmark of national significance in a joint survey conducted by the Minnesota Historical Society and the division of state parks. The Minnesota legislature in 1969 appropriated funds to acquire the site, and the following year it was purchased and placed under the administration of the historical society.

At the turn of the century, there were an estimated ten thousand prehistoric burial mounds existing in the state — a number archaeologists now believe to be conservative. More recent surveys indicate that only a fraction now remain. Some of them are located on state or federally owned land and are, therefore, protected in at least a limited way. Many more mounds are privately owned and face the probability of future obliteration. The purchase and preservation of the Grand Mound represents a renewed effort on the part of the state to save some of Minnesota's prehistoric sites for future generations.

The Grand Mound site has not been developed for public use, although plans are under way to construct an interpretive center which is scheduled for completion in 1976. Until then, access to the site is restricted.

 *Fort St. Charles*

Located on Magnusons Island in Lake of the Woods. Accessible by boat from Angle Inlet, located 72 miles northeast of Warroad via state highway no. 313, Manitoba trunk highway no. 12, provincial road no. 308, and an unnumbered road marked by "Angle Inlet" sign (inquire about road conditions in wet weather). Also accessible by plane or boat from Baudette or Warroad on state highway no. 11.

IN 1731 a vigorous French army officer was dispatched by Marquis Charles de Beauharnois, the governor general of New France, to establish a fur post west of Lake Superior. His full name was Pierre Gaultier de Varennes, Sieur de la Vérendrye, and his remarkable exploits deserve to be better known. Fort St. Charles, which he founded on the Northwest Angle in Lake of the Woods, was occupied longer than any other French outpost on Minnesota soil. From 1732 until 1744 it served as La Vérendrye's headquarters, and it was used by other Frenchmen until the 1750s, the eve of British conquest. From it the French blazed a trail that laid the foundations for the later development of the Northwest under the British. Fort St. Charles has been partially reconstructed by the Minnesota Knights of Columbus.

In sending the enterprising La Vérendrye so far west, the French government had two objectives: to establish a jumping-off place from which to continue the search for the elusive Northwest Passage to the fabled Western Sea; and to set up convenient posts in the rich fur-producing country of the Cree, Monsoni, and Assiniboine Indians. In both objectives, the explorer was partially successful. Although he did not find the Western Sea, one of his sons penetrated farther west than any white man before him. From his Northwest Angle headquarters, La Vérendrye set up a series of posts between Lake Superior and Lake Winnipeg that opened to use the important Grand Portage and Kaministikwia trade routes and enabled the French to compete for furs with the English on Hudson Bay. King Louis XV granted La Vérendrye a monopoly of the fur trade west of Lake Superior to finance his explorations.

To carry out his government's plan, the forty-six-year-old La Vérendrye set out from Montreal in 1731 with three of his four sons, a nephew, a Jesuit priest, and about fifty voyageurs and clerks. Traveling via the Grand Portage route along the present Canadian boundary, La Vérendrye reached Northwest Angle Inlet a year later. There he built Fort St. Charles. (Although the site La Vérendrye selected for his post was at that time on the mainland of the Angle, this is no longer the case. The water level of Lake of the Woods has been raised since La Vérendrye's day, and the fort is now on Magnusons Island, a short distance from the mainland.)

FORT ST. CHARLES, *a French fur trading post used by La Vérendrye in the 1730s and 1740s, has been partially reconstructed. Courtesy Minnesota Knights of Columbus.*

The post consisted of a stockaded area measuring 100 feet by 60 feet, with gates on the north and south sides, four bastions at the corners, and a watchtower. Crowded within a double row of upright wooden stakes twelve to fifteen feet in height were La Vérendrye's dwelling, four houses for his voyageurs, a powder magazine, a storehouse, a chapel, and a house for the missionary. One of the Frenchmen in the party described the post as an enclosure of "a few huts of square logs, calked with earth and covered with bark." Soon after their arrival, the Frenchmen cleared land by burning, and later they planted corn and peas, harvesting ten bushels of peas for one planted. As a result of this attempt to supplement their meager supplies, these explorers may well deserve distinction as Minnesota's first white farmers.

From this rude fortification, the La Vérendryes conducted explorations which carried them into present-day Manitoba and Saskatchewan and southwestward into what is now North and South Dakota. On one of their expeditions in 1742–43, Louis-Joseph, a son of the explorer, journeyed at least as far west as the Black Hills and possibly to the foot of the Rocky Mountains — becoming the first white man to travel so far into the north central part of the continent.

Fort St. Charles also became the depot of La Vérendrye's fur trade empire. As they traveled, the explorer and his men established trading posts to collect the furs so desperately needed to finance their explorations. But the trading operations were beset by difficulties, and when he resigned and emerged from the forests of the Northwest in 1744, La Vérendrye was heavily in debt.

His valiant but vain search for a passage to the Western Sea was also marked by many hardships. His nephew and chief lieutenant, La Jemeraye, died near the mouth of the Roseau River in 1736. Only a few weeks later, La Vérendrye sent his son, Jean-Baptiste, with the missionary Father Jean-Pierre Aulneau and nineteen others eastward for supplies. While camped on a little island in Lake of the Woods "seven leagues" from Fort St. Charles, they were attacked and killed by a Dakota war party. Their decapitated bodies were left on the island, which so far has not been satisfactorily identified.

The sorrowing La Vérendrye had the bodies taken to Fort St. Charles and buried beneath the little chapel, where they were found 172 years later in 1908 by a party of Jesuit fathers from St. Boniface College, Canada. After locating the site of the old French fort, the priests marked it with a wooden cross and excavated the area, finding not only skeletons but also such items as keys, rosary beads, a shoe buckle, and a hunting knife.

In 1951 the Knights of Columbus placed a granite altar on the spot where the original chapel once stood. Additional work was done in 1959, and today the site of Fort St. Charles is marked by a reconstructed stockade of cedar poles with two lookout towers and two gates. Inside, the foundations of the original huts have been marked out, and the four-ton granite altar stands in a chapel made of concrete logs.

THE NORTHWEST ANGLE — The story of the French fort is closely associated with that of the Northwest Angle, a geographic oddity of about 132 square miles separated from the mainland of the United States by Canadian territory and by the waters of Lake of the Woods. Until Alaska was admitted to the

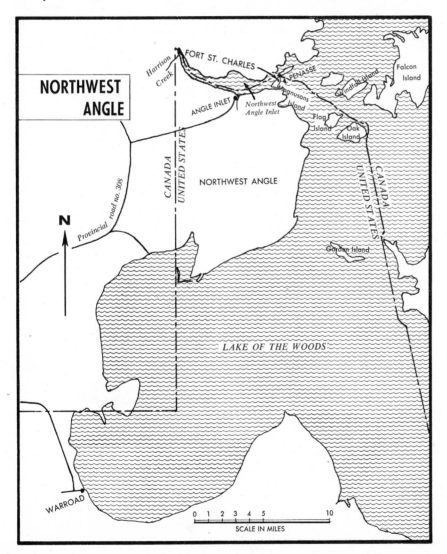

THIS MAP *shows the Northwest Angle and the site of Fort St. Charles on Magnusons Island.*

Union in 1959, the Angle was the northernmost point in the United States.

For this odd projection of land, those venerable founding fathers, Benjamin Franklin, John Jay, and John Adams, were responsible. To end the Revolutionary War they signed in 1783 the Treaty of Paris, which provided that the United States boundary westward from Lake Superior was to follow the line of water communication to Lake of the Woods "and from thence on a due west course to the river Mississippi." This line, of course, proved to be geographically impossible, for the Mississippi's source (which was not discovered until 1832) is south, not west, of Lake of the Woods.

When the northern boundary was later defined as the forty-ninth parallel of latitude, it was found that the line westward from Lake Superior did not meet that drawn eastward from the Pacific. Numerous attempts were made over the years to resolve the problem. After the War of 1812 the so-called Convention of 1818 located the boundary due south from the Northwest Angle to the forty-ninth parallel, leaving a chimneylike projection on the map of Minnesota. The northern boundary of the state was not finally settled, however, until the Webster-Ashburton Treaty of 1842, and the survey which carried out the provisions of this treaty was not completed until 1926.

The Angle was on the route of the famous Dawson Trail between Port Arthur (now Thunder Bay) on Lake Superior and Fort Garry (now Winnipeg) on the Red River. Built and maintained by the Canadian government from 1867 to 1876 to foster immigration to its western lands, the Dawson Trail consisted of forty-five miles of corduroy road at the Lake Superior end and about ninety miles of roadway between the Red River and Lake of the Woods. In between the route traversed over three hundred miles of waterway broken by nine portages. Westward traveling immigrants passed by the site of Fort St. Charles as they completed the trek by water. They then picked up the Dawson road at what is now Harrison Creek, located about four miles northwest of Angle Inlet.

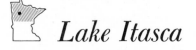 *Lake Itasca*

Located in Itasca State Park. Accessible from U.S. highway no. 71, twenty-one miles north of Park Rapids or thirty-two miles southwest of Bemidji.

AT LAKE ITASCA, on the north edge of Itasca State Park, the Mississippi River has its beginning in a small stream bubbling over a few smooth rocks. As the rivulet leaves Lake Itasca to begin its more than 2,300-mile journey to the Gulf of Mexico, it is small enough to jump across.* More than a million persons visit this spot annually. In so doing they are following in the footsteps of the explorers of four nations who long sought the source of North America's greatest waterway.

Although the Spanish explorer, Hernando de Soto, discovered the lower reaches of the Mississippi in 1541, more than a hundred years passed before its upper waters were seen by Europeans. Radisson and Groseilliers, two French traders, may have reached the upper Mississippi in the 1650s, but we cannot be certain where they went. Credit for discovering the upper river is generally given to Jacques Marquette, a Jesuit priest, and his companion, Louis Jolliet, who glided onto the broad Mississippi at the mouth of the Wisconsin River in 1673. Other Frenchmen — La Salle, Father Louis Hennepin, Du Luth, and Le Sueur — also traveled the upper Mississippi, but for three centuries after its discovery the true source of the Father of Waters remained a mystery.

Many men searched for the river's head, and at least seven claimed the honor of discovering it. The first of these was David Thompson, a British fur trader in the employment of the North West Company, who explored the upper Mississippi in 1798 and named Turtle Lake in Beltrami County as its source. He was followed by another trader, William V. Morrison, who said that he first visited the region in 1803–04. Morrison may well have reached Lake Itasca in his rambles, but his claim to having discovered it remains unproved, since his journals were lost in a canoe accident.

Then came Zebulon M. Pike, an American army officer. He declared in 1806 that he had found the "main source of the Mississippi" at Leech Lake and the river's "upper source" at Red Cedar (now Cass) Lake. Some fifteen years later Governor Lewis Cass of Michigan announced that he had found the headwaters when he reached the northern Minnesota lake that now bears

*Although the marker at the river's source indicates that the Mississippi is 2,552 miles long, changes in the river's channel since the sign was erected have cut the figure to an estimated 2,330 miles in 1972.

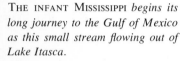

THE INFANT MISSISSIPPI *begins its long journey to the Gulf of Mexico as this small stream flowing out of Lake Itasca.*

LAKE ITASCA *was named the true source of the Mississippi River in 1832 by Henry R. Schoolcraft, one of many explorers from several nations who searched for the headwaters of the great river.*

his name, but he was challenged in 1823 by an Italian explorer, Giacomo C. Beltrami — one of the most picturesque men to engage in the search.

A political exile from Venice, Beltrami arrived in America in 1823 and immediately set out to discover the Mississippi's true starting point. He hitchhiked as far as Pembina (North Dakota) with an expedition headed by Major Stephen H. Long. There the uncongenial Italian left the party (to Long's great relief), secured an interpreter and two Indian guides, and set out on his own. His companions soon deserted him, leaving Beltrami alone in the wilderness with a canoe full of provisions protected from the elements by a ludicrous red umbrella — an ornament the Indians eyed with suspicion.

Unable to paddle the canoe by himself, Beltrami dragged it up the Red Lake River until he was able at last to hire a Chippewa guide. The explorer ended his search twelve miles north of Bemidji at a lake he christened Julia to perpetuate the name of a deceased lady friend. He returned to civilization and proclaimed to the world in grandiose terms that he had found the Mississippi's northernmost source in Lake Julia. Today a marker points out Beltrami's camping place on the lake's east shore.

It remained, however, for an American to be acclaimed the discoverer of the true source of the country's greatest river. That honor is accorded by historians to scholarly Henry Rowe Schoolcraft, Indian agent, author, and geologist. Schoolcraft first visited the upper river as a member of Governor Cass's exploring party in 1820. Although the governor was satisfied that he had found the source of the Mississippi in Cass Lake, Schoolcraft did not agree. He believed that it lay farther to the southwest, and he privately resolved to return some day and find it. His opportunity came twelve years later when, as Indian agent to the Lake Superior Chippewa at Sault Ste. Marie, Michigan, he asked for and received permission to head an expedition to establish peace among the

THE STORY *of the search for the Mississippi's source is told in this museum located on the north shore of Lake Itasca.*

tribes, look after the Indian trade, and gather statistics on the western part of his vast territory.

Schoolcraft set out from Sault Ste. Marie on June 7, 1832. In his party were Lieutenant James Allen, who commanded the small military escort; Dr. Douglass Houghton, who was to vaccinate as many Indians as possible against smallpox; and the Reverend William T. Boutwell, who was to survey the pos- sibilities of establishing missions among the Indians. They were under orders to "proceed to the country upon the heads of the Mississippi, and visit as many of the Indians . . . as circumstances will permit." No mention was made of Schoolcraft's personal goal, which was to reach the true source of the great river.

When the party arrived at Cass Lake, Schoolcraft engaged as his guide a Chippewa named Ozawindib, or Yellow Head, and made a side trip to the Mississippi's headwaters with sixteen men in five light canoes. On July 13 Yellow Head led them up "the last elevation," said Schoolcraft, and they "got the first glimpse of the glittering nymph we had been pursuing. . . . At a depression of perhaps a hundred feet below, cradled among the hills, the lake spread out . . . presenting a scene of no common picturesqueness and rural beauty."

Apparently Schoolcraft was so certain he would find the ultimate source of the river that he had a name for it all prepared. Boutwell later wrote that while the party was crossing Lake Superior, Schoolcraft said that he would like to give the birthplace of the Mississippi a name "that will be . . . expressive of the *head* or *true source*." He asked Boutwell, "Can you give me any word in Latin or Greek that will convey the idea?" The minister replied, "The nearest I can come to it is *Verum Caput,* or, if you prefer the noun *Veritas*." Schoolcraft took the last two syllables of *veritas,* meaning truth, and the first syllable of *caput*, meaning head, and announced, "I have got the thing . . . Itasca."

The explorer had time to make only a hasty survey of the lake, for he could not delay work on the stated objectives of his expedition. Thus he spent only two hours at Itasca, raised the American flag on the island which today bears

ANCIENT BURIAL MOUNDS *within Itasca State Park were found near a Dakota village site believed to have been inhabited before 1700.*

his name, and set out on the return journey. In his report to the Indian office, Schoolcraft described his discovery of the Mississippi's true source in two brief sentences omitting all details.

Not until four years after Schoolcraft's discovery did the world receive any detailed information on Lake Itasca. In 1836 Joseph N. Nicollet, a distinguished French scientist, carefully surveyed and mapped the entire Itasca basin, fixing the latitude, longitude, and altitude of the region. In his valuable study the modest Nicollet acknowledged the work of Schoolcraft on which, he said, he had "merely enlarged." Yet to Nicollet must go the credit for being the first to map reliably the area surrounding the source of the Mississippi.

The last man to claim credit for the discovery of the Mississippi's source was Willard Glazier, who insisted he found it at Elk Lake, south of Lake Itasca, in 1881. In a contrived publicity campaign Glazier produced a book using false maps and plagiarizing entire passages from Schoolcraft's narrative of fifty years earlier. His claims were soon discredited by James H. Baker in a special report to the Minnesota Historical Society in 1887. Two years later the society authorized a comprehensive survey under the skillful direction of Jacob V. Brower, who proved conclusively that Glazier was a fraud.

Because of his dedicated interest in Lake Itasca, his valuable studies, and his persistent recommendations that the area be preserved, Brower was named the first commissioner of Itasca State Park when it was established in 1891. He devoted the last fourteen years of his life to acquiring land for the park and enhancing its beauty. It is now one of the state's largest parks, consisting of more than thirty-two thousand acres of heavily wooded terrain and encompassing Lake Itasca and over a hundred other lakes as well as magnificent stands of red pine. Brower's contributions to the park are memorialized in a marker placed near the entrance to Brower Inn, located near the headwaters.

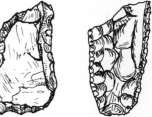

SOME SEVEN THOUSAND years ago aboriginal hunters ambushed bison as they forded a stream at this site on the south shore of Lake Itasca. Below are sketched three stone knives that are among artifacts found there.

   Visitors to Itasca State Park will find comfortable, modern accommodations and campgrounds, as well as extensive recreational facilities. Activities include fishing, hiking, swimming, boating, and nature tours. At the headwaters a museum features exhibits on local plant and animal life and on the settlement of northern Minnesota. Additional displays in the recently constructed visitors' center recount the discovery of the Mississippi River's source.

   Prehistoric occupation of the region is indicated at two sites — one near the museum where centuries-old burial mounds are visible, and the other located at the opposite end of the lake where Nicollet Creek flows in from Elk Lake. At the latter location, archaeologists discovered a bison kill site or camp which was occupied from seven thousand to eight thousand years ago by aboriginal hunters, who waited to ambush bison as they forded the stream during the fall migration. Investigators of the site found many stone artifacts and bones, including the skeleton of a dog — the earliest evidence of that animal to be discovered in Minnesota.

   Admission to Itasca State Park requires a park sticker available at the entrances.

Grand Portage

Located in Grand Portage National Monument on the north shore of Lake Superior. Accessible from U.S. highway no. 61.

GRAND PORTAGE NATIONAL MONUMENT situated near the tip of Minnesota's Arrowhead Country encompasses one of North America's most important fur trade sites. The strategic location of Grand Portage between Lake Superior and the interconnected waterways along the present Minnesota-Ontario border guaranteed it an important place in history, for it guarded one of the two best natural routes to the northern interior of the continent (the other being Hudson Bay). Because of its geographical advantages, Grand Portage was selected as the headquarters of the North West Company, a powerful British fur trading firm. In the late 1700s the North West Company controlled from Grand Portage an empire that reached from the Atlantic to the Pacific. Today the national monument, which includes the sites of the North West Company's posts on Grand Portage Bay and at Fort Charlotte as well as the nine-mile portage trail that bypasses the formidable falls of the lower Pigeon River, lies within the Grand Portage Indian Reservation.

Although there are no records, it is likely that the portage trail was known and used by the Indians long before the coming of white men. Grand Portage, meaning "the great carrying place," was so named by French explorers who ventured into the Lake Superior area in the 1600s. Du Luth may have been the first white man to see it when he coasted along the lake shore in 1679. A map of 1688 shows the Pigeon River, and the Grand Portage route along the present international boundary was mentioned as early as 1722. A daring Frenchman, Pierre de la Vérendrye, was the first man to leave a record of his visit to Grand Portage. Members of his party crossed the trail in 1731. La Vérendrye's countrymen held sway over Grand Portage until the close of the French and Indian War in 1763, when control passed to Great Britain.

It was under the British flag that Grand Portage had its greatest days. During this period, it was occupied first by independent traders, who by 1768 had cleared ground for a meeting place at the Lake Superior end of the portage trail. Within a decade the dominant occupant was the North West Company, which in its most prosperous years employed more than two thousand people and traded goods for furs with northern Indian tribes from coast to coast. Just when the nucleus of this company was formed is not clear. With resumption of the trade in 1765, after a two-year hiatus caused by the Indian wars, came increasingly bitter, sometimes bloody competition. Aggressive traders, determined to ease the hostilities, joined together in a series of co-operative agreements, most of them short-lived. It is likely that several Montreal traders involved in the original North West Company had formed such a loose combine at least as early as 1775, and it is a matter of record that after repeated shifting of partners a stable company was organized in 1779. From that time until 1803, the outpost called Grand Portage was the headquarters of the fabled North West Company's far-flung empire.

The firm's activities gave rise to a unique way of life on the waterways of the Northwest and produced a picturesque and dedicated band of traders (or "pedlars," as they were called) and voyageurs or canoemen who helped explore and map northern North America. These hardy men traveled fantastic distances in their frail birch-bark canoes, for the company's business took them from Montreal to the remote Athabasca region of Canada — a distance of some three thousand miles. Alexander Mackenzie, a partner in the company for whom the Mackenzie River is named, was the first white man to cross the continent north of Mexico; another Nor'Wester, David Thompson, discovered and mapped the first practicable route across the Canadian Rockies.

The company's annual meeting was held at Grand Portage, and to it each summer came the firm's partners from Montreal and traders from its fur posts far to the west. At that time accounts were tallied, the men paid, and their assignments for the next year decided. There, too, the orders for the supplies necessary to keep the company's network operating were compiled, and canoes needed in the trade were made and mended. Long before Minnesota was settled, Grand Portage was the scene of much feasting and merriment each July, when as many as a thousand people gathered for the annual rendezvous at the company's headquarters.

One of the few known descriptions of the busy Grand Portage post during its heyday was penned by John Macdonell, a North West Company trader, in 1793. Although his spelling is odd, he paints a vivid word picture. "All the buildings within the Fort," Macdonell wrote, "are sixteen in number made with cedar and white spruce fir split with whip saws after being suquared, the Roofs are couvered with shingles of Cedar and Pine, most of their posts, Doors, and windows, are painted with spanish brown. Six of these buildings are Store Houses for the company's Merchandize and Furs &c. The rest are dwelling houses shops compting house and Mess House — they have also a warf or kay for their vessel to unload and Load at."

Macdonell also gives us a glimpse of life at Grand Portage during the annual rendezvous. He writes that the "North Men" (those who wintered in the wilderness west of Lake Superior) "while here live in tents of different sizes pitched at random, the people of each post having a camp by themselves and through their camp passes the road of the portage." The camp of the North Men, he says, was separated from that of the "Pork eaters" (the canoemen who plied between Montreal and Grand Portage) by a brook which can still be seen flowing through the grounds of the national monument. As for the stockade, "the Gates are shut alyways after sunset, and the Bourgeois and clerks Lodge in houses within the pallisades, where there are two Sentries keeping a look out all night chiefly for fear of accident by fire."

Supplies for the North West Company's inland posts were brought by canoe from Montreal to Grand Portage by early July. Fifteen days and a hundred men were usually needed to transport the trade goods up the Grand Portage Trail to Fort Charlotte, the company's depot on the Pigeon River. Then the furs brought to Fort Charlotte by the wintering brigades were carried down the trail to the Grand Portage stockade for shipment to Montreal and the markets of the world.

Over the rugged nine-mile path, the voyageurs toted tons of furs, as well as beads, blankets, guns, powder and shot, kettles, knives, mirrors, cloth, tobacco, thread, rum, and even tomahawks to be taken westward in exchange

GRAND PORTAGE NATIONAL MONU-
MENT, *pictured here in 1971 when
the great hall was being reconstructed, was the site of the British
North West Company's headquarters for over thirty years before 1803.
At that time it was the busiest fur
trading center on the continent.*

for the Indians' furs. Each voyageur was required to carry a total of eight
packs over the portage. If more had to be transported, the men were allowed
a Spanish dollar for each extra pack. It was not unusual for a voyageur to
take two ninety-pound packs over and bring back two more, covering the eighteen
miles in six hours. The tremendous labor involved in getting goods and furs
over this trail can be better appreciated when one realizes that the portage
is generally uphill from Lake Superior to the Pigeon River, rising in elevation
from 600 feet at the lake to 1,360 feet at Fort Charlotte. It traverses some
of the roughest land in Minnesota, and it was cleverly laid out to make the
most of any advantages the difficult terrain offered.

So valuable was the Grand Portage route as a life line of the early fur trade
that its eastern terminal may have been the destination of the first military
voyage made across Lake Superior under the British flag. In May, 1762, a
detachment of Robert Rogers' Rangers is thought to have escorted traders from
Mackinac (Michigan) to Grand Portage, guarding the canoeloads of goods against
plunder by those Indians whose loyalties remained with the French.

It is certain that remote Grand Portage has the distinction of being the only
place in Minnesota where troops were stationed during the Revolutionary War.
Despite the events occurring in the colonies, British traders continued to make
the annual voyage to Grand Portage, but they took the precaution of requesting
military escorts for their protection. One of these detachments was led by Lieutenant Thomas Bennett of His Majesty's Eighth Regiment of Foot, who with
five soldiers was dispatched to the portage in May, 1778. This little band was
to settle "Jarring & disputes" among rival traders and between voyageurs and
traders, impress the Indians with a display of British power, secure the loyalty
of doubtful traders, and prevent them from sending supplies to George Rogers
Clark and his Americans in the Illinois country.

During their short stay, Bennett and his men were also to have "the Canoe
men . . . erect a small fort," which was half finished when the troops left
in August, 1778. To aid them in their construction work, the soldiers were
equipped with two saws, an adz, a spade, two shovels, an auger, one ax,
and a "clawed hammer." The fort, however, was erected at the "great Company's" expense and its voyageurs supplied both the timbers and the labor.

Reorganizing frequently and absorbing rival firms like the XY Company in 1804 (which also had a post north of the brook on Grand Portage Bay), the North West Company increased in scope and importance until about 1814. The British traders were dismayed to learn that under the terms of the treaty of 1783, which closed the Revolutionary War, Grand Portage had become the property of the United States. Since the trade of the area amounted in normal years to about £150,000 sterling, the Nor'Westers were understandably reluctant to turn over their posts to the Americans. Not until a United States customs collector appeared at Grand Portage in 1800 and threatened to levy a duty on its goods did the company make plans to move its headquarters to British soil.

In 1803 it removed to Fort William, a new post at the mouth of the Kaministik-wia River within present-day Thunder Bay, Ontario. From that time on, the firm encountered increasing competition from the Hudson's Bay Company, which finally absorbed it in 1821. That date marks the end of an era and the disappearance from the historical scene of the fabulous band of Nor'Westers, who conquered half a continent and built a commercial empire the like of which North America had never seen. It also marks the disintegration of the company's Grand Portage fort, of which "scarce a vestige" could be seen among the rank grass and red clover in 1822.

Although the greatest days of Grand Portage were over, the American Fur Company of John Jacob Astor and independent traders continued to operate a fur post and fishing enterprise there until the 1840s. Probably about 1816 the portage was improved and oxcarts were used on it. Later, parts of the trail were used by logging companies, but gradually it almost disappeared beneath encroaching underbrush.

The portage was cleared in 1946–48 by American and Canadian Boy Scouts. From that time to the present, it has been used intermittently by hardy canoeists bent on retracing this famous voyageur route. The Grand Portage Trail was and still is an international road. Under the terms of the Webster-Ashburton Treaty of 1842 use of the trail remains free and open to this day to citizens of both the United States and Great Britain, although users are required to report to the nearest customs office.

Steps to preserve Grand Portage were first taken in the 1930s. In 1931 local supporters of the historic fur trade site built a 365-foot dock on the spot where remains of an old wharf were visible under the water. (This reconstruction

THE GATEHOUSE *at the entrance to the Grand Portage stockade was reconstructed on its original site.*

THE NINE-MILE *Grand Portage trail, connecting Lake Superior and the Pigeon River, is now within Grand Portage National Monument.*

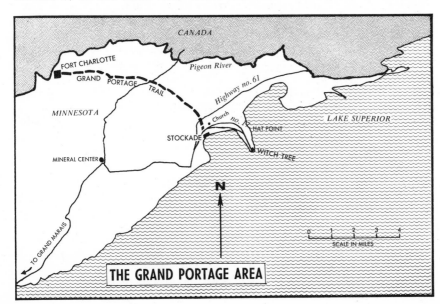

was destroyed by a storm in 1951 and has been rebuilt.) From 1936 to 1940 Grand Portage was the scene of archaeological investigations conducted by the Minnesota Historical Society and the United States Indian Service. At that time field crews located the outlines of the old stockade and uncovered a number of pointed cedar pickets, the foundations of the main building or great hall, the remains of at least one gate of unusual design, several fireplaces, a well, indications of fourteen other structures, and some five hundred identifiable artifacts. Based on these discoveries, the stockade and the great hall were reconstructed in 1938–40; in 1969 lightning struck the great hall and it burned to the ground.

Grand Portage was designated a national historic site in 1951. Nine years later Congress established Grand Portage National Monument, placing it under the management of the National Park Service. In 1961 the park service resumed archaeological study of the fort under the direction of Alan R. Woolworth, chief archaeologist of the Minnesota Historical Society. For four seasons crews dug both inside and outside the stockade. Results of the work included definition of the stockade lines; discovery of possible building sites outside the palisades; and re-examination of structures indicated by earlier digging in the 1930s. In 1964–65 the stockade and gatehouse were rebuilt and a historically inaccurate blockhouse, erected earlier, was removed. Following the 1969 fire, Woolworth headed another archaeological dig for the National Park Service. His discoveries during the summer of 1970 shed new light on the old fur trade depot. Redigging the foundation area of the great hall, workers found that a long porch had been attached to the front of the building. Another major discovery was the remains of a structure located behind the great hall and determined to be a kitchen — so identified by an elevated fireplace and a stone-lined cooler. A sizable collection of artifacts helped date the kitchen to the period from about 1785 to 1803. Other evidence indicated that the fort had twice been enlarged by extending the stockade to enclose additional parcels of land, resulting in three distinct areas within the depot.

The present reconstruction of the great hall was built in 1970–71. Extensive research by National Park Service personnel, combined with results of the archaeological studies, led to changes in the design of that building as well as in the relocation of the gatehouse erected in 1964. Since no sufficiently precise descriptions of the furnishings in the great hall are known, its interior restoration, to be completed in 1972, will be based largely on numerous early accounts of the good life enjoyed by wealthy Montreal traders at Fort William. As additional knowledge of Grand Portage is gained through continued investigation, the park service hopes that more of the old fort's buildings can eventually be reconstructed. Long-range plans propose development of the site as a living museum, where the atmosphere and activities of the fur trade era can be recreated for visitors.

Grand Portage National Monument is open to the public throughout the year. In the summer months National Park Service personnel are on duty to provide information. There are no regular tours of the site, but special arrangements for groups may be made with the superintendent at the monument headquarters in Grand Marais. There is no admission fee.

OUR LADY OF THE ROSARY CATHOLIC CHURCH, in the Chippewa village north of the stockade, has a long and interesting history. It has been called the "oldest Catholic parish in Minnesota." The first missionary known to have visited Grand Portage was Father Charles Mesaiger, a member of La Vérendrye's party in 1731. A century later the well-known Catholic missionaries Frederic Baraga and Francis X. Pierz arrived to minister to the Chippewa. Father Pierz dedicated the first Catholic chapel of cedar bark and deerskin in 1838, and in it he also opened a mission school. In 1851 a log chapel was erected. It

THE WITCH TREE *on Hat Point leans over Lake Superior as it has for more than three centuries. This gnarled old cedar, sometimes called Minnesota's oldest living landmark, was thought by early Indians to possess an evil spirit.*

was replaced in 1865 by the present church of tamarack logs held together with wooden pegs. The structure has since been covered with siding and the interior modernized. The original logs can be seen, however, in the attic of the church. Until recent years the small cemetery in front of the church contained both pagan and Christian burials, including a number of typical Chippewa wooden grave houses.

THE WITCH TREE, located on Hat Point east of the stockade, is probably Minnesota's oldest living landmark. This gnarled and twisted cedar, battered by the storms of centuries, was growing out of the lichen-covered rock when La Vérendrye passed that way in 1731. Legend has it that the Indians believed the tree was possessed of an evil spirit in the form of a big, brown, hawklike bird that caused many of their canoes to be wrecked on the rocks of Hat Point. It is said that the Indians attempted to appease the evil spirit by placing gifts of tobacco and vermillion on the rocks at the foot of the tree. The white man with his guns is thought to have frightened the evil bird away.

During the great days of the fur trade at Grand Portage, the big canoes from Montreal often paused above Hat Point, and the voyageurs washed and put on their best clothes for a grand dash across the bay. They would swing around the Witch Tree and paddle swiftly over the water singing one of their lively songs.

The Witch Tree can be reached by taking Cook County road no. 17 two and one-half miles east from the stockade. It stands on private property, and permission to visit the tree should be requested at the residence near the end of the road. From there a footpath to the left winds approximately three blocks through a spruce forest to emerge at the lake shore near the picturesque tree.

OUR LADY OF THE ROSARY CHURCH *in the Chippewa village of Grand Portage was built in 1865 of tamarack logs which have since been covered with a protective siding.*

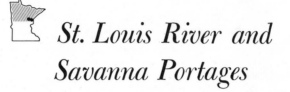

St. Louis River and Savanna Portages

The Grand Portage of the St. Louis River is located within Jay Cooke State Park near Duluth. Accessible from state highway no. 210. The Savanna Portage is located within Savanna Portage State Park in Aitkin County. Accessible from McGregor north on state highway no. 65 for seven miles, east on county road no. 14 for 5.5 miles, bear right on county road no. 36 for 4.5 miles to the park entrance.

THE STREAMS AND LAKES threading the map of Minnesota were the highways of the fur trade, the area's first big business. Of the many fur trade routes in northern Minnesota one of the most important was the complex of lakes and streams connecting the Great Lakes and the Mississippi River. The route began at the mouth of the St. Louis River on Lake Superior near present-day Duluth and ended at Big Sandy Lake and the Mississippi, some seventy miles to the west in what is now Aitkin County. Traders going between these two major points often followed several smaller streams and negotiated two famous portages — the Grand Portage of the St. Louis River and the Savanna Portage farther west. Both portages have been partially re-established by the Minnesota division of state parks and recreation.

When the French explorer Du Luth traversed at least a portion of the route in 1679, the two portages had already been used by the Indians for many years. Within the next century the trails to Sandy Lake became a major invasion route of the Chippewa against the Dakota. The portages did not become important to the fur trade, however, until after 1783. At that time the region was technically the property of the United States, but traders of the British North West Company continued to hold sway for another three decades. Not until after the War of 1812 and the expulsion of British traders from the United States did the American Fur Company take over, operating posts at each end of the route until the 1840s. Thus the history of this significant water highway was written by both British and American fur traders who struggled over its arduous portages collecting furs for more than fifty years.

Because the route connected the Mississippi trading region with the supply and shipping conduit of the Great Lakes, it was logical that both Britain and the United States should establish important fur-collecting depots at each end of it. At the Lake Superior end, the North West Company maintained a post on Rices Point (the wide sand bar which, with Minnesota Point, forms what is now Duluth harbor) at least as early as 1784 and built a new and larger depot within present-day Superior, Wisconsin, in 1793. Called Fort St. Louis, the latter served for years as the headquarters of the company's Fond du Lac department and as a chief distributing and collecting center. About 1816 John Jacob Astor's American Fur Company constructed a trading post in what is now Fond du Lac, a suburb of Duluth. This important post in the company's trading area functioned until the mid-1840s.

At the western end of the route the situation was similar. From 1794 until 1816 the North West Company operated a departmental headquarters post located on Brown's Point on the northwestern shore of Big Sandy Lake. After the War of 1812 the American Fur Company took over that post, maintaining it until shortly after 1820. Sometime during the next ten years, the company built a new station at the mouth of the Sandy River on the east bank of the Mississippi and occupied it until the 1840s.

All the furs, trading goods, and supplies that passed between the posts on Lake Superior and those at Sandy Lake had to be carried over the two long and difficult portages — the Grand Portage of the St. Louis, seven miles in length, and Savanna Portage, which was six miles long. From Lake Superior laden canoes began their journey to the Mississippi. The first mile and a half up the St. Louis River was easy; then any extra passengers had to get out and walk three-quarters of a mile over Woman's Portage, at the end of which they met the paddlers who had laboriously worked their canoes upriver to that point. There the bark crafts had to be unloaded and carried with their contents across the Grand Portage of the St. Louis.

The trail is described in the journal of Lieutenant James Allen, a member of Henry R. Schoolcraft's expedition in 1832. It "commenced by ascending a hill 100 feet high," he wrote. "No pains have ever been bestowed to make a road up it; and the ascent is by means of little imperfect steps, just large enough for the toes, that wind up the hill without any regularity as to direction or relative position." The voyageurs measured portages in pauses, or "poses," indicating the distance a carrier toted his two ninety-pound packs before setting them down and returning for another load. The lengthy Grand Portage of the

THE FOAMING RAPIDS *and falls of the St. Louis River made the seven-mile Grand Portage necessary in the days of the fur trade.*

St. Louis had nineteen pauses — the first being at the top of the ascent described by Allen.

From the second pause at Roche Galet (Shingle Rock), wrote Allen, the trail continued over "a little, narrow, crooked path, with bushes crowding it on either side, winding round trees, through marshes, over ridges, and across ravines, and presenting all the irregularities and inconveniences of a rude trail through difficult woods. There has been little or no cutting to clear it out, and all the bridging consists of a few small poles, laid in the length of the path, which serve rather to annoy than to assist the passenger. No idea can be formed of the difficulty of this portage without witnessing it," Allen went on. "The men, with heavy loads, are sometimes forced to wade through a swamp of half a mile, full of roots and bushes, and over their knees in mire at every step. And where the road is dry, it is generally over a hill, or across a gulley, the steep banks of which are worse to pass than the swamps."

A party of traders with an average load trudged up and down hills and through watery marshes for at least three days before reaching the portage's end near the southern tip of Maple Island. From there loaded canoes could manage to fight the rapids upriver to Fortress Island, while the passengers made another portage. On the west riverbank, opposite the island, began the most painful part of the trip up the St. Louis — the aptly named Knife Portage where sharp slate rocks cut the voyageurs' moccasins and bruised their feet at every step. This mile and a half of torture ended above Knife Falls, at present-day Cloquet, where the canoes once more were launched for the trip to the mouth of the East Savanna River at Floodwood.

Near the junction of the two rivers stands a marker indicating that here the voyageurs turned away from the St. Louis River and began the second leg of their journey to the Mississippi River. Traders could also continue up the St. Louis River, eventually reaching the Vermilion Lake area and connecting with the well-traveled Grand Portage canoe route.

About twenty miles upstream from its mouth, the East Savanna River became a shallow, unnavigable stream. There, on the edge of a tamarack swamp, the travelers set out for the West Savanna River over the six-mile Savanna Portage, generally considered "the worst carrying place in the Northwest."

A CLEARED PORTION *of the St. Louis River Portage trail is marked along state highway no. 210 in Jay Cooke State Park.*

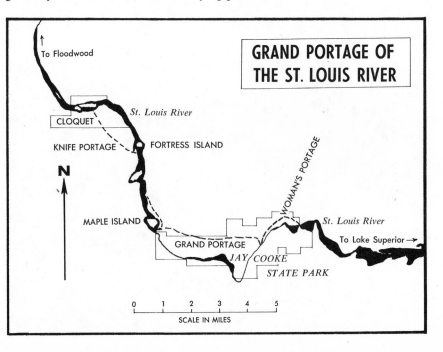

GRAND PORTAGE OF THE ST. LOUIS RIVER

To Floodwood

St. Louis River

CLOQUET

KNIFE PORTAGE

FORTRESS ISLAND

WOMAN'S PORTAGE

N

MAPLE ISLAND

St. Louis River

To Lake Superior →

GRAND PORTAGE

JAY COOKE STATE PARK

0 1 2 3 4 5

SCALE IN MILES

THIS MAP *shows the Grand Portage of the St. Louis River, an important fur trade route that was also used by the Indians at least three hundred years ago.*

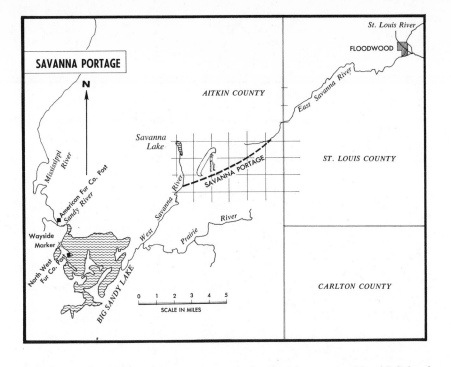

SAVANNA PORTAGE, *shown on this map, was a key link in the early fur trade route between Lake Superior and the Mississippi.*

    The Reverend William T. Boutwell, a missionary who traversed it with School-craft's party in 1832, left a typical comment on the notorious trail: "To describe the difficulties of this portage, would puzzle a Scott, or a Knickerbocker, even," he wrote. "Neither language nor pencil can paint them. After making about half a pose, our baggage was landed on a wharf made of poles. A dyke was then made, and our canoes brought up through mud and water knee deep . . . one [*man*] at the bow and another at the stern, the latter pushing and the former drawing in mud and water to their middle. . . . The musketoes came in hordes and threatened to carry away a man alive, our [or] devour him ere they could get him away. . . . The mud, for the greater part of the way will average ankle deep, and from that, upwards . . . a perfect quag-mire. Our men look like renegades, covered with mud from head to foot, some have lost one leg of the pantaloons, others both." Boutwell's colorful description applied mainly to the eastern third of the portage, a stretch of about two miles. The remaining four miles were dry by comparison.
    Some measures to ease the hardship of the men traversing the swamp were taken as early as 1798, when David Thompson, the North West Company's famous cartographer, described the portage. "Heavy Canoes cannot be carried over but at great risque both to the Men and Canoes," he wrote, "and the Company have Canoes at each end." Still the packs had to be toted through the swamp, and to avoid getting precious furs wet and sinking waist-deep into the mud, a slippery walkway was formed "by means of a few sticks laid length-ways." Later, North West Company men built a platform across the extent of the bog. (Remnants of the pole walkway were noted in 1833 and again in 1969, when an archaeologist uncovered a sixteen-foot section of logs that had been laid layer upon layer as they sank below the surface.) Along the remainder of the portage, the travelers made the most of every natural advantage in the hilly terrain. It required five days, on the average, to portage over the thirteen pauses of this fatiguing trail. At its western end, the canoes were again loaded for the relatively easy paddle down the West Savanna and Prairie rivers and into Big Sandy Lake.
    Until about 1840 this lake was the center of a trading area that included

REMNANTS *of a walkway made of poles, laid by voyageurs to take them through "the worst carrying place in the Northwest," were discovered by archaeologists in 1969.*

THE SIX-MILE *Savanna Portage trail terminates in a bog at the edge of the East Savanna River. From this point, eastward-traveling traders could go by canoe to the St. Louis River near present-day Floodwood.*

much of central Minnesota and the Mississippi Valley almost as far south as the Twin Cities. After the Sandy Lake post on Brown's Point was abandoned by the American Fur Company, it was occupied for a short time by independent traders. Then it gradually fell into decay. In later years the Chippewa took over the clearing for gardens, graves, and a camping ground, and about 1900 the land was cultivated as a farm. It is now a resort area.

A marker, erected in a wayside park on state highway no. 65 about two miles north of its junction with county road no. 14, locates the site of the trading post. From this park one can see three historic spots — the North West post site; the Prairie River leading to Savanna Portage; and the outlet into Sandy River where the American Fur Company post was built. A second marker describing the American Fur Company site, which is on private property, is located at the Sandy Lake Dam northeast of the Libby store.

With the demise of the fur trade and the advent of wagon roads, use of the famous old canoe and portage route quickly declined. By the end of the nineteenth century only a few persons could trace the trails, which had begun to be obliterated by fallen trees and heavy undergrowth.

Today, the Grand Portage of the St. Louis is marked and partly preserved in Jay Cooke State Park (a state park sticker, available at the entrance, is required for admission). The marker is located on state highway no. 210 about four miles northeast of the campground, or about eight hundred yards west of the boundary between St. Louis and Carlton counties. From the marker, the modern-day voyageur can follow the trail for a portion of its length, but much of the portage lies on privately owned property and is inaccessible. Changes in the river bed have flooded the original starting point of the Grand Portage and covered the well-known Roche Galet. One can still visualize the steep climb up to the first pause, however, and imagine how the voyageurs struggled to boost their heavy packs and canoes to the top.

Savanna Portage is more easily accessible and is marked by guideposts and flags along its full length. Within Savanna Portage State Park about three-fourths of a mile from the entrance, a marker indicates the beginning of the trail at its western end (parking facilities are available here). For some four miles eastward the portage trail follows as far as possible the ridges of land, affording striking vistas of deep ravines and open valleys. Along this section, the trail passes through wooded areas, which, because of differences in the soil, vary from stands of aspen, maple, basswood, and birch to stretches of spruce, tamarack, and cedar. Leaving the forested hills, the trail emerges onto a more level plain of brush and tall wild grasses. For the last mile and a half, the portage follows a pole catwalk laid by park employees through the bog to the eastern end at the East Savanna River. There are eight rest stops along the way and rest room facilities at the midway point. Hikers can follow the same route back or select from a number of other trails that branch off along the portage. A helpful map is available at the park entrance, where visitors are requested to check in before beginning the six-mile walk.

Savanna Portage State Park, established in 1961, includes nearly 15,000 acres of rolling, forested terrain. Picnicking, camping, and swimming facilities are maintained. Admittance is by state park sticker available at the entrance.

Old Crossing Treaty Site

Site located in Old Crossing Treaty State Wayside on the north bank of the Red Lake River a short distance southwest of the village of Huot on state aid road no. 17. Accessible from Crookston via U.S. highway no. 75 three miles north to state aid road no. 57, then about nine miles east.

IN THIS SCENIC PARK on the Red Lake River, the United States and the Chippewa Indians in 1863 signed a treaty which paved the way for white settlement of the fertile Red River Valley. Under its terms the Red Lake and Pembina bands of Chippewa conveyed to the United States 9,750,000 acres of land in northwestern Minnesota and northeastern North Dakota, a vast domain that was to become the country's breadbasket.

The so-called Old Crossing of the Red Lake River was selected as the treaty site because of its convenient location on one of the rough but well-defined Red River oxcart trails that meandered across pioneer Minnesota. The choice of this site was appropriate, for it was in part the existence of the Red River trails which made the treaty necessary.

Over these trails, which were the state's first important roads, a flourishing trade had developed between St. Paul, the state capital, and the Canadian settlements on the Red River. Beginning in the 1840s, creaking trains of ox-drawn, two-wheeled, wooden carts transported valuable furs and pemmican to St. Paul and returned to the northern settlements laden with groceries, tobacco, dry goods, and other articles.

The caravans passed through the lands of the Red Lake and Pembina bands of Chippewa, who from time to time raided the trains for provisions and threatened to close their country to the passage of the carts as well as to the steamboat traffic that developed on the Red River after 1859. Earlier efforts in 1851 and 1862 to conclude a treaty with these Chippewa had failed for various reasons. By 1863 Minnesotans were demanding that Congress either purchase the lands or acquire a right of way through them.

In the summer of 1863 Senator Alexander Ramsey was instructed to buy from the Indians a strip of land that would ensure safe passage to the oxcart trains. Accordingly in September, 1863, he set out from St. Paul with more than five hundred mules, horses, and beef cattle, and some ninety supply wagons, for the government planned to feast the Indians while the negotiations were going on. Ramsey's party, which also included three companies of mounted soldiers, reached Old Crossing via the trail that stretched between St. Cloud and Fort Abercrombie on the Red River. From there the travelers followed the river to a spot near present-day Georgetown, and then cut inland, arriving at the Red Lake crossing on September 21.

Treaty negotiations got under way at a grand council held beside the stream on September 23. More than 1,600 Chippewa and mixbloods and about 250 whites were gathered near what is now Old Crossing Wayside. A few logs placed on the ground in front of Ramsey's tent formed seats for the chiefs. Finding the Chippewa unwilling to sell the white man a right of way through their lands, Ramsey then negotiated for the purchase of all the lands claimed by these Indians.

Twelve days were spent in speechmaking, horse racing, and feasting on government supplies before the Old Crossing Treaty was signed on October 2. By it the United States gained possession of all or part of the present Minnesota counties of Roseau, Kittson, Marshall, Pennington, Red Lake, Polk, Norman, and Mahnomen, and a comparable tract in what is now North Dakota extending from the Canadian boundary south to the Sheyenne River. In exchange the Chippewa were to receive from the United States government $20,000 annually for twenty years, reservations, and other considerations.

Ramsey returned to St. Paul much pleased with his bargain. But the matter

THIS BRONZE STATUE *of a Chippewa Indian by sculptor Carl C. Mose was commissioned with federal funds to mark the site in Old Crossing Wayside where a treaty was signed.*

was not to be settled so easily. When the treaty was submitted to the Senate later that year, various amendments were offered which would have reduced the amount of cash the chiefs were to receive. The Indians refused to accept the changes, and in 1864 the principal Chippewa chiefs were taken to the nation's capital to adjust the differences. As a result, supplementary articles were worked out which differed somewhat from those negotiated at Old Crossing. The Senate then ratified the new articles and the Old Crossing Treaty, and President Abraham Lincoln proclaimed them in 1864.

The oxcart crossing and at least a part of the treaty grounds are included in this attractive, wooded state wayside of over a hundred acres. The site was selected in 1914 by committees of citizens from Crookston and Red Lake Falls. About 1931 a small portion of the present park was presented to the state of Minnesota by the commissioners of Red Lake County. Additional land was acquired in 1947.

To memorialize the historic conference, a handsome monument by sculptor Carl C. Mose was erected in 1933 with funds appropriated by Congress. It consists of a bronze, standing figure over six feet in height, representing a Chippewa in simple regalia. His left hand holds a peace pipe, and his right is extended in a gesture of friendship. His presence is intended as a reminder of the words of Article I of the Old Crossing Treaty: "The peace and friendship now existing between the United States and the Red Lake and Pembina bands of Chippewa Indians shall be perpetual." On a large boulder nearby, a plaque outlines (with some inaccuracies) the significant events of 1863.

A footpath circles through the park to a small marker on the oxcart trail. Although erosion has changed the riverbanks, the old ford used by the oxcart caravan can still be discerned. Near the trail stands a giant cottonwood more than six feet in diameter. This ancient tree is said to have served as an early postal station. Beneath its branches, a small box was fastened in which letters were left by occasional traders and passers-by to be picked up by drivers of the cart trains. The wayside offers picnicking and camping facilities to twentieth-century travelers.

A HUGE COTTONWOOD TREE, *over six feet in diameter, was used as a postal station by early settlers in the Old Crossing area. This photograph was taken in 1955. Courtesy* Minneapolis Star and Tribune.

Duluth Ship Canal

Fine views of the harbor may be obtained from Interstate highway no. 35 and Skyline Boulevard in Duluth. Canal Park and Minnesota Point may be reached via Lake Avenue.

DULUTH is a city built on a dream — a dream of a harbor teeming with steamships and stevedores handling the trade of the world. In 1857 Duluth was little more than a collection of shanties hugging the rocky, wind-beaten shore of Lake Superior. To its far-sighted citizens, however, it was much more, for all that was needed to make it a great inland port was an entrance into the harbor. The construction of the Duluth Ship Canal in 1871 provided that entrance, and the city began to fulfill its dream. The modern ship canal may be seen from Canal Park.

The story of the canal is one of determination, disappointment, and complicated legal maneuvers. It begins in 1857, the year Duluthians organized the Minnesota Point Ship Canal Company as a step toward transforming Superior Bay into "the largest, most easily accessible and safest harbor on the great chain of lakes." The plan was to build an entry at the north end of the bay, instead of depending on the natural entry at the tip of Minnesota Point, which opened on a tortuous, crooked route to the mainland. Before anything could be accomplished, however, the depression of 1857 hit Duluth, leaving it for some years an almost deserted village.

The idea of the canal did not fade completely during those trying years. By 1865, when the empty buildings of Duluth once more were filled with people, plans for harbor improvements again took shape. At first it was thought a harbor formed by extensive breakwaters outside the bay would suffice, but the violent northeasters soon proved the breakwaters' protection inadequate. Besides, Duluthians felt that, sheltered or not, such a harbor would be too small to accommodate the increased commerce stemming from the Lake Superior and Mississippi Railroad which was soon to reach Duluth from St. Paul. Thus, in 1870, the city council decided to build the long-awaited canal across Minnesota Point.

Reactions to the decision were immediate. The railroad company agreed that a canal would be in the common interest, but citizens of Superior, situated near the natural entry in Wisconsin, quickly voiced their opposition. Such a canal, they argued, would divert the current of the St. Louis River from its normal flow into Lake Superior and thereby ruin the natural entrance to Superior's harbor. It was an argument that would be heard, with others, for the following six years, during which time the Wisconsinites attempted to stop work on the project by legal action.

DULUTH HARBOR *has been one of the world's leading ports since 1959. Ships from many countries enter the harbor through the canal beneath the Aerial Bridge (center background in this photograph) and handle millions of tons of cargo each year. Photograph by Basgen Photography, Duluth; courtesy of the Seaway Port Authority of Duluth.*

Digging of the cut across Minnesota Point began in the fall of 1870 under threat of an injunction sought by citizens of Superior. Work ceased during the winter, but late in April, 1871, the steam dredger was again put into action. The job was almost done on April 29 when the dredger was stalled by a solidly frozen stratum of gravel near the lake shore. Still fearing that an injunction might stop the work, the people of Duluth determined to finish it themselves.

"Some of our citizens," said the *Duluth Minnesotian* of May 6, "being determined to mingle the waters of the Bay and Lake, before the week expired, at once turned in with shovels and picks and drills and powder (two kegs) to aid the machine; and being thus assisted, the dredge was finally enabled, at one o'clock P.M., to break through a passage of about fifteen feet wide and two or three feet in depth."

So enthusiastic were the crowds at seeing the first feeble trickle of water across the point that one excited man, waving his hat wildly, almost jumped into the icy water. During the night the pressure and warmth of the water flowing from the bay into the lake deepened the canal by several feet. The following day the first boat — a little steam tug called the "Frank C. Fero" — chugged its way through the canal and out into the rough waters of Lake Superior.

While the steam dredger continued to enlarge the canal, Superior interests worked for an injunction to stop its progress. After a delay, the court heard the case and ruled that since federal appropriations had financed improvements in Superior's harbor, the canal should not be built. The judge added, however, that if a dike were placed between Rices and Minnesota points to avoid disturbing the harbor waters, the injunction would be dissolved. Before the city of Duluth could begin building the dike, the writ of injunction was served, even though the canal was already in use. Ten days later, when the city promised to complete the dike before December 1, 1871, the injunction was dissolved. During the entire litigation, no work was lost on the canal project.

Refusing to give in, the state of Wisconsin on June 20, 1872, three months after the dike was finished, filed a bill of equity against the canal promoters to prevent the building of any obstruction in Superior Bay, which Wisconsin considered a public waterway. The bill was dismissed by the circuit court and later by the United States Supreme Court.

An initial glimmer of agreement between the two factions began to shine faintly in 1873. Urged by officials of the Northern Pacific Railroad Company, which had become interested in the increased rail traffic promised by an improved harbor, a committee from Duluth met with Wisconsin's governor and the president of the railroad to settle the controversy. As a result of the conference the canal was placed under federal control; Superior received railroad service and dredging of its harbor; and the dike was removed. In addition, a congressional appropriation, obtained by joint effort, was divided for improvements in both harbors.

The final litigation over the canal occurred in 1874. In a bill of complaint the state of Wisconsin asked that Duluth and the Northern Pacific Railroad (which had taken over the canal's construction) be forever restrained from maintaining the canal, and that the opening be filled in. This time the tables were turned, and the judge ruled that since the canal was now controlled and maintained by the federal government, the court could not order it to be destroyed. Wisconsin had lost its case.

Throughout the years improvements have been made in the ship canal. Around the turn of the century new concrete piers were built; the grounds near it were landscaped; and a lighthouse was placed at the lake end of the south pier. In 1972 the canal was 300 feet wide and 1,734 feet long. Living up to its promise, Duluth harbor for many years ranked second only to New York in the annual tonnage it handled. It is still among the eight leading ports of the

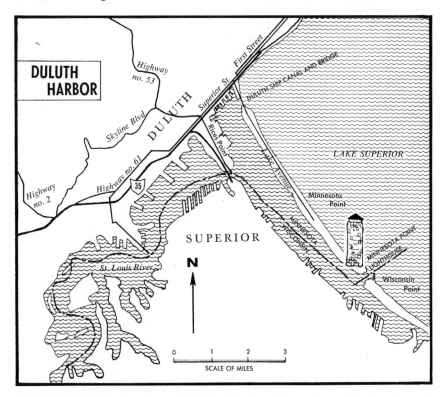

LOCATED *on this map of Duluth Harbor are Rices Point, Minnesota Point, the old lighthouse tower, and the Duluth Ship Canal.*

United States and is considered the world's largest bulk traffic port. Since the opening of the St. Lawrence Seaway in 1959, ocean vessels flying the flags of more than thirty nations have passed through the canal.

The Aerial Bridge, spanning the harbor entrance at Canal Park, has been a tourist attraction since its construction in 1905. It was built to transfer pedestrians and traffic to and from Minnesota Point more safely and faster than the footbridge and ferryboats that preceded it. Patterned after a bridge at Rouen, France, it was originally built with a suspended car that traveled from one end of the structure to the other at a normal speed of four miles an hour. In 1930 the movable platform was replaced with the present lift span of 386 feet. Electrically operated, it can be raised 138 feet above the water level in 55 seconds.

Plans to construct a visitors' center and marine museum were being developed in 1972 by the United States Army Corps of Engineers. The two-story structure will be located in Canal Park; it will house public rest areas on the ground floor and a museum on the second level. Exhibits relating to Duluth's historic associations with navigation and shipping are being planned in close co-operation with a citizens advisory committee. The center will also contain an observation platform and public information area.

MINNESOTA POINT LIGHTHOUSE — The ruins of a brick tower, all that is left of a lighthouse that guided ships into Superior harbor from 1858 to 1878, stand on the eastern tip of Duluth's Minnesota Point. In its heyday, the lighthouse, with its French-made lenses, was considered the finest on the Great Lakes. During foggy weather ship captains watched for its strong beacon and listened for the warning sound of the tin horn, which the lighthouse keeper and his wife took turns blowing.

After the ever-shifting channel into Superior Bay was permanently fixed in 1878, the Minnesota Point Lighthouse was dismantled and its lenses were installed in the new one located a quarter mile away on the west pierhead of the entry. The small keeper's house, which like the lighthouse was built of Cleveland brick, also was removed, and the tower soon fell into disrepair. It was doomed to destruction until the United States Coast and Geodetic Survey found that the base contains a marker indicating it is the zero point, or beginning, of the surveys of Lake Superior. Now only two thirds of its original height, the isolated tower is preserved as a landmark.

The lighthouse ruins are accessible by foot from the end of the Lake Avenue bus line, a hike of about two miles. They may also be viewed from Interstate highway no. 35, from the end of Wisconsin Point in Superior, or by boat from Duluth harbor.

MINNESOTA POINT LIGHTHOUSE, *now a ruin, was built in 1858 to guide ships into Superior Harbor.*

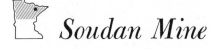 *Soudan Mine*

Located in Tower Soudan State Park, .5 mile north of Soudan or two miles northeast of Tower on state highways nos. 1 and 169, on the Vermilion Iron Range.

THE OPENING of the Soudan Mine on the Vermilion Range has been called "one of the great commercial events" of the nineteenth century. The first iron ore mined in Minnesota was shipped from the Breitung pit of this mine on July 31, 1884, beginning the development of Minnesota's rich iron ore deposits. Although it soon became an underground operation, the Soudan at first was mined from seven open pits. The mine, which operated from 1884 until 1962, is the oldest and deepest in the state. Its shaft extends to a depth of 2,400 feet, with drifts or tunnels running about a mile to the east and west of the shaft. At its peak production in the 1890s, the Soudan employed 1,800 men, and in 1897 it shipped a record 592,196 long tons of high-grade ore. With nearly a thousand acres of land on Vermilion Lake, the mine was given to the state of Minnesota by the Oliver Iron Mining Division of the United States Steel Corporation in 1963. Now open to the public, the famed mine provides visitors with an experience unique among the state's historic sites.

Although specimens of iron ore were reported in Minnesota as early as 1850, the first important survey of the iron region was made by Henry H. Eames, state geologist, in 1865. But Eames found gold as well as iron ore on the Vermilion Range, and his report, published in 1866, touched off the Vermilion gold rush. In the excitement the iron ore deposits he described were largely overlooked. The gold of the Vermilion proved unprofitable, however, and nine years later George C. Stone, an energetic promoter from Duluth, brought Minnesota iron to the attention of Charlemagne Tower, a wealthy Pennsylvania industrialist. Tower sent Professor Albert H. Chester to Minnesota in 1875 to explore and report on his findings. After visiting the eastern Mesabi Range as well as the Vermilion, Chester wrote a report favoring the Vermilion. The good professor had seen only the lean ores on the eastern tip of the mighty Mesabi, and thus missed his opportunity to gain enduring fame as the discoverer of the rich ores that lay farther west on that large range.

After receiving Chester's report, Tower did not act immediately, but five years later he employed Stone to buy land on the Vermilion. In 1882 he incorporated the Minnesota Iron Company and transferred to it the more than twenty thousand acres of land Stone had acquired for him in northeastern Minnesota. In 1883 Tower also gained control of the Duluth and Iron Range Railroad, which at the time existed in name only. The following year his company sent to the Vermilion from Michigan more than a hundred experienced Cornish

THIS IS THE HEADFRAME *of the Soudan Mine on the Vermilion Iron Range from which the first iron ore mined in Minnesota was sent by rail to Two Harbors in 1884.*

and Swedish miners with their wives and children. They occupied company-built houses near the mine site at Soudan, while at nearby Tower, a new town named for the Pennsylvania millionaire who founded it, businesses soon sprang up to serve the fast-growing population.

To ship the ore, Charlemagne Tower began in 1883 to build the Duluth and Iron Range Railroad, linking the mine with Two Harbors on Lake Superior. Its tracks climbed the rugged hills bordering the lake, traversed swamps in which logs had been placed, and crossed bridges built by hand. Barely twenty miles of track were laid in 1883 by contractors who worked late into December after the ground froze so hard that ice had to be chopped from the roadbed. During the next year a total of 1,400 men worked twenty-four hours a day to complete the road by the August 1 deadline called for in the contract. In July, 1884, when the track reached the sixty-fifth mile and was within sight of the Vermilion Range, the seventy-four-year-old Tower had more than a million dollars invested in the venture.

While the last few feet of track were being laid on the morning of July 31, jubilant miners and citizens of Tower gathered to load the wooden ore cars by hand and with wheelbarrows. Whistles blew and great clouds of steam billowed from the stack of Engine no. 8. Chippewa Indians from the nearby Vermilion Lake Reservation joined the celebration. At four o'clock in the afternoon, the first trainload of ore began its run over the new track to Two Harbors. Stopping frequently to take on water from streams and ponds along the way, the train crawled cautiously down the steep slopes, reaching the lake at 11:00 P.M. that night — one hour before the deadline set by the contract. Early the next morning Tower's son telegraphed his father that the first train had arrived safely and that 220 tons of ore were stored in the new dock on the shore of Lake Superior.

Two large samples of ore from Minnesota's first shipment may be seen in front of the Carnegie Library in Two Harbors. These blocks of iron ore, weighing seven hundred pounds each, were presented to the city by Thomas Owens,

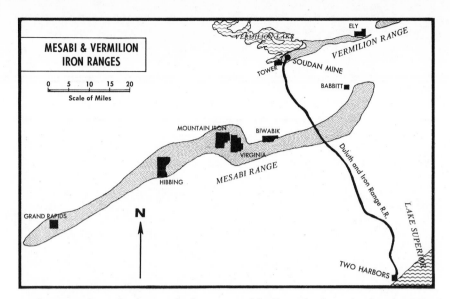

THE ROUTE *of the Duluth and Iron Range Railroad, built by Charlemagne Tower from Lake Superior to the Soudan Mine in 1883–84, is shown on this map.*

engineer on the train that made the memorable first trip from the Soudan Mine to Two Harbors in 1884.

Charlemagne Tower's first wooden dock was located on the site of the modern steel and concrete ore docks that may be seen from Paul Van Hoven Park on the lake shore at Two Harbors. In the park, too, is the "Three Spot," the first locomotive shipped to Minnesota by Tower's company in 1883. A wood-burning engine, it was used in the construction of the Duluth and Iron Range Railroad. Beside it stand a wooden ore car and caboose, and nearby are a wagon and a four-seated sleigh used in 1883 to transport men and supplies between Duluth and Two Harbors. In the former depot building, the Lake County Historical Society maintains a museum with exhibits on mining, logging, and the settlement of the area.

Throughout its history, the Soudan Mine shipped ore every year except one, a record for the Lake Superior ranges. In 1887 Tower sold the Minnesota Iron Company and the railroad to a syndicate, thereby realizing a substantial profit on his three-million-dollar investment. When the United States Steel Corporation was formed in 1901, the Soudan came under the control of its Oliver Iron Mining Division.

Under the administration of the division of state parks and recreation, the

THE "THREE SPOT," *a locomotive used in the construction of the Duluth and Iron Range Railroad, is preserved at Two Harbors.*

mine was opened to the public in July, 1965. It has since been designated a National Historic Landmark. Visitors can take a self-guided surface tour to see the open pits, ninety-foot headframe, enginehouse, crusher building, and drillshop. At the visitors' center, which formerly was a locker room where the miners showered and changed clothes, hour-long guided tours of the underground mine begin. A three-minute ride in the electrically operated skip or elevator takes visitors down 2,341 feet to the twenty-seventh level of the mine. Former miners, who have received special training, act as guides and explain complex mining operations. A small, three-car train takes passengers the length of the 3,000-foot tunnel, along which can be seen a miners' lunchroom, powder and fuse room, unmined ore, and such machines as an exploration drill and a loader, both seemingly ready for action. At the end of the tunnel a circular stairway rises to the Montana stope, the scene of final mining operations in the Soudan when it closed in 1962.

Unlike most underground mines, the Soudan requires no supporting timbers along tunnels or stopes because the walls are of solid rock. Temperatures in the mine average 52 degrees the year around, and visitors are reminded to dress adequately for the underground visit. They are also requested to wear the hard hats provided.

Tours of the mine are given daily in the summer months and by reservation only from mid-September until late in May. Tour fees are charged. Group tours are available by reservation. Admission to Tower Soudan State Park requires a vehicle permit (necessary for visits to the mine), which may be purchased at the entrance. A picnic area and hiking trails are maintained in the park; camping facilities are available at nearby Bear Head Lake State Park.

MORE THAN *two thousand feet underground, this train stands loaded with iron ore taken from Soudan Mine. On a similar train, visitors ride through a long tunnel to view the scene of final mining activity.*

Mountain Iron Mine

Viewpoint located in the village of Mountain Iron at the end of Biwabik Avenue north of U.S. highway no. 169 on the Mesabi Iron Range.

THE DISCOVERY of the Mountain Iron Mine on the Mesabi Range in 1890 set in motion a series of events that was to revolutionize the steel industry, make Minnesota the largest producer of iron ore in the nation, and enable the United States to become the world's largest manufacturer of steel. Stretching diagonally across northeastern Minnesota, the Mesabi (a Chippewa word meaning "giant") was the largest iron ore deposit the world had ever known. From the Mountain Iron Mine's first shipment in 1892 until 1961, this giant range supplied over two billion gross tons of iron ore for the nation's steel furnaces — more than half the iron ore mined in the United States during those years. The first mine to ship ore from the Mesabi was for a time an underground operation before being worked as an open pit; it is now abandoned and filled with water.

Although there is some evidence that the Indians knew of the existence of iron on the Mesabi, the first published record of its occurrence was made by geologist J. G. Norwood in 1850. Sixteen years later Henry H. Eames, the Minnesota state geologist who was looking for gold, reported that he had observed iron ore outcrops on the Mesabi. But Eames also declared that he had found gold, and his announcement touched off the rush to the supposed gold fields near Vermilion Lake in the late 1860s. The magic lure of gold drew hundreds of adventurers into northern Minnesota. In their haste to find the valuable metal, men tramped over parts of both the Mesabi and the Vermilion ranges without suspecting the treasure of iron that lay beneath their feet.

Several of them, however, were more observant. Christian Wieland, a pioneer settler of Beaver Bay on the north shore of Lake Superior who was Eames's guide, noted the occurrence of iron near present-day Babbitt and brought it to the attention of Michigan mining men. A group living in the Michigan town of Ontonagon formed a syndicate and sent Peter Mitchell, an experienced mining man, to the Mesabi to explore for them. In 1871 Mitchell put down the first known test pit on the Mesabi Range. He believed that he had found a mountain of rich iron ore, but in reality he had discovered taconite, a lean ore that was not to be utilized for almost a century. Mitchell's first test pit is fittingly commemorated today by a marker composed of a twenty-eight-ton piece of taconite which stands in the village of Babbitt.

Another disappointed gold seeker was Lewis H. Merritt, who returned to his home in Duluth with a sample of iron ore. Although Lewis did nothing

175

OPERATIONS *at the Mountain Iron Mine were photographed in 1890. The "X" at lower right marks the spot where Captain Nichols discovered iron ore for the Merritts.*

to follow up his find, he told his sons about it. Four of them — Leonidas J., Alfred R., Cassius C., and Lewis J. — grew into strapping young men who became experienced timber cruisers and landlookers. As they trudged over the hills of northern Minnesota, the Merritt brothers remembered their father's words and watched for indications of ore. Four of their nephews — Bert U., Wilbur J., John E., and Alva L. — joined in the search.

For sixteen years the Merritts continued their explorations, and at last in 1890 — six years after the Vermilion Range had been opened — they made the first important discovery on the mighty Mesabi. Spurred to greater activity by the interest others were showing in the area, the Merritts hired J. A. Nichols, a mining captain, to explore for them. On November 16, 1890, Nichols found the ore deposit that was developed into the now-famous Mountain Iron Mine, the first on what proved to be the largest of the state's three iron ranges. (The third and smallest range — the Cuyuna — was discovered later; its first ore was shipped in 1911.)

When he was an old man, Leonidas Merritt described for a committee of the United States Congress how the Mountain Iron Mine was discovered. "I remember," he said, "that Alfred and I went up there one day . . . and we had spent then $20,000 on the Mountain Iron . . . and we had a miner in there [*Nichols*] . . . who was a good miner. . . . He was an honest, straightforward man, and we went up there and we said: 'Here, now, we have worked long enough up on this rim, let us go down in this basin and sink a pit,' and we took him down with us to show him where, according to the theory which we had evolved, the ore ought to be, if it was anywhere. . . . He went down with us, and we said: 'Sink a pit here.' If we had gotten mad and kicked the ground right where we stood we would have thrown out 64-per-cent ore, if we had kicked it hard enough to kick off the pine needles. But, of course . . . we did not have any idea that this ore could possibly be found, if found at all, except at considerable depth. We were influenced, of course,

THE MOUNTAIN IRON MINE, *aban-doned in 1956 after sixty-four years of production, is now flooded.*

more or less, by the traditions of the miners generally, you know. He [*Nichols*] said that he had something of a reputation as a mining man, which he had, and that he did not propose to be called with the rest of us, farmers. They used to call us farmers and lumber jacks and all that sort of thing, in derision. . . . Well, we told him to put his men down there . . . and we would send up men that did not have any reputations as miners. . . . The next day after we got to town he came down with about a bushel of ore. . . . He did not dig where we dug. He compromised with us and went about halfway up the hill and got ore in 14 feet.''

The Merritt brothers went on to discover other rich mines, including the Biwabik. Elated, they attempted to develop these properties and to raise capital to construct a railroad from the mines to Lake Superior. In 1891 they and other Minnesotans incorporated the Duluth, Missabe, and Northern Railway Company. The following year this firm laid some forty-five miles of track from the Mountain Iron Mine to present-day Brookston near Duluth. From there the ore was to travel to Superior, Wisconsin, over the tracks of another railroad, the Duluth and Winnipeg. On October 17, 1892, the first trainload of Mesabi ore — 4,245 tons — was loaded at the Mountain Iron Mine and shipped in wooden ore cars over the Merritts' railroad.

For many years the Merritts had been laughed at for their faith in the Mesabi. When they did find ore there, it was unlike any other ore body then known, for it occurred in shallow deposits near the surface. It could not be mined by the underground methods usual at that time, but could simply be scooped up from open pits. Moreover, the structure of the ore was unlike that of the older iron ranges. Although it was very rich, it was soft and powdery and at first steelmakers did not know quite what to do with it. When they put it into their furnaces, which were designed for harder, rocklike ores, it sometimes exploded, wrecking the furnaces.

While steelmakers experimented with the new ore, the Merritts in 1893 attempted to extend their railroad into Duluth and to build ore docks on the lake shore there. In so doing they overextended themselves in the midst of a great depression and lost both the railroad and their ore properties to John D. Rockefeller. That financier gained control of the Lake Superior Consolidated Iron Mines Company, which included the Mountain Iron Mine, poured the huge sums of money required into the development of the Mesabi Range and the railroad, and in 1901 exchanged the stock of the Consolidated Iron Mines for roughly eighty million dollars' worth of stock in the newly formed combine known as the United States Steel Corporation.

The Oliver Iron Mining Division of United States Steel operated the Mountain Iron Mine until 1956, when it was closed down. During the years from 1892 until 1956 this first mine on the Mesabi shipped over forty-eight million gross tons of iron ore. In 1969 the mine was designated a National Historic Landmark by the United States Department of the Interior. Today a bronze tablet commemorating the first shipment of Mesabi ore is located in front of the high school building in Mountain Iron. Not far away in the yard of the Mountain Iron Public Library stands a ten-foot statue of Leonidas Merritt in miner's garb. Unveiled in 1940, the statue is the work of sculptor Robert N. Crump.

While the Mountain Iron Mine was the first to be developed on the Mesabi, it was far from the largest and most productive of the many mines later operated there. That distinction is reserved for the combination of mines known as the Hull-Rust-Mahoning Open Pit, which is also a National Historic Landmark. (To reach the Hull-Rust, go north on Third Avenue East in Hibbing to the observation platform. Attendants who explain the mine area are on duty daily in the summer.) Although it is known as "the largest iron ore mine in the world," the Hull-Rust-Mahoning is not one mine but a combination of more than nine open pits operating from what appears to the uninitiated observer to be a single hole in the ground. It has been called "Minnesota's Grand Canyon." More material has been removed from it than was necessary in the construction of the Panama Canal. The area of the present mine was explored by W. C. Agnew in 1893–94 and operations began in 1895. Since its opening in 1895 six hundred million gross tons — or about a fourth of all the ore shipped from the Mesabi Range — have come from this pit. It is now nearly 4 miles long, 2 miles wide, and 534 feet deep at one point. When President Calvin Coolidge visited the mine in August, 1928, he is said to have remarked with his usual economy of words, "That's a pretty big hole."

LEONIDAS J. MERRITT *is portrayed in a ten-foot statue by Robert N. Crump unveiled in 1940 at the town of Mountain Iron.*

Minnesota State Monuments

STATE MONUMENTS officially established by the Minnesota legislature are found in the following areas:

BECKER COUNTY, in Calvary Catholic Cemetery, a mile south of White Earth. A monument honoring Chippewa Chief White Cloud (1828–1898) was erected on June 14, 1909.

BROWN COUNTY. (1) A twenty-four-foot shaft on Center Street in New Ulm was dedicated on August 22, 1891, to commemorate the two Sioux Uprising battles fought there. (2) A monument on county road no. 11 near Essig was dedicated in 1929 in memory of over fifty Milford Township settlers who died in the uprising. (3) A fifty-foot granite monument dedicated in 1902 and a marker dedicated in 1964 designate the grave near the railroad station in Sleepy Eye of Chief Sleepy Eyes, Sisseton Dakota leader from 1824 until his death about 1860, whose principal village was located nearby.

CARLTON COUNTY, in Riverside Cemetery at Moose Lake. A granite shaft twenty-seven feet high was dedicated on October 12, 1929, in memory of 183 victims of a disastrous forest fire that swept the Moose Lake area on October 12, 1918.

GOODHUE COUNTY, in Cannon Falls City Cemetery. An impressive granite shaft bearing a statue of William Colvill honors the colonel who led the First Minnesota Regiment in the Civil War battle of Gettysburg in 1863. The monument was unveiled by Mrs. Calvin Coolidge on July 29, 1928.

JACKSON COUNTY, in Ashley Park at Jackson. State funds were provided in 1909 to erect a granite shaft naming nineteen pioneer settlers who were killed here by the Dakota in 1857 and 1862.

KANDIYOHI COUNTY. (1) A granite shaft erected in 1891 in Lebanon Swedish Cemetery, New London, marks the mass grave of thirteen members of the Anders P. Lundborg and Anders P. Broberg families who were killed by the Dakota on August 20, 1862. (2) A red granite monument dedicated on July 21, 1907, marks the grave of Sioux Uprising heroine Guri Endreson Rosseland (1813–1881) in Vikor Lutheran Cemetery north of Willmar.

LAC QUI PARLE COUNTY, in a state-owned wayside park west of Montevideo. The fifty-foot granite shaft, dedicated on July 4, 1894, marks Camp Release, where the Indians surrendered and released their 269 captives at the close of the Sioux Uprising on September 26, 1862.

MEEKER COUNTY. (1) A granite shaft at Acton, southwest of Grove City, marks the

THE SITE OF CAMP RELEASE *near Montevideo is marked by this monument standing in Minnesota's oldest state park, established in 1889.*

site of the Howard Baker cabin, where the Sioux Uprising began on August 17, 1862. (2) A monument in Ness Lutheran Cemetery, southwest of Litchfield, was dedicated on September 13, 1878, to mark the mass grave of the first five settlers killed at the Baker cabin.

MURRAY COUNTY, in Lake Shetek State Park. A granite monument twenty-five feet high was dedicated August 3, 1925, "to the memory of those who were slain" by the Dakota near here on August 20, 1862.

NICOLLET COUNTY, in Fort Ridgely State Park. A granite shaft fifty-two feet high was dedicated on August 20, 1896, to commemorate the heroism of the fort's defenders during its seven-day seige in August, 1862. Nearby Fort Ridgely Cemetery contains three more state monuments: (1) in memory of Captain John S. Marsh and twenty-five men killed by the Dakota at Redwood Ferry in 1862, erected on November 24, 1873; (2) in recognition of the loyalty of Chief Mouzoomaunee and the Chippewa Indians during the Sioux Uprising, unveiled August 20, 1914; (3) in memory of Mrs. Eliza Muller, wife of the post surgeon at Fort Ridgely, for her valor in caring for wounded refugees and soldiers during the seige of the fort, erected in 1877.

PINE COUNTY. (1) A thirty-two-foot granite shaft in Brook Park Cemetery was dedicated on October 1, 1915, to mark the two trenches that are the graves of twenty-three Brook Park Township residents who perished in the forest fire on September 1, 1894. (2) A fifty-two-foot granite monument dedicated on September 1, 1900, marks the mass graves in Hinckley Memorial Cemetery of 248 victims of the fire.

RENVILLE COUNTY. (1) A fifty-two-foot granite shaft overlooking highway no. 19 at Morton was dedicated in 1894 to the memory "of those gallant soldiers and citizens" who fought in the Sioux Uprising battle of Birch Coulee on September 2, 1862. (2) Close to the Birch Coulee monument at Morton a granite shaft was erected in 1899 "to commemorate the brave, faithful, and humane conduct of the loyal Indians who saved the lives of white people" during the 1862 conflict. (3) A granite monument on county road no. 15 northwest of North Redwood was dedicated on August 18, 1915, to honor six members of the Johann Schwandt family who were killed by the Dakota on August 18, 1862. (4) The 1971 Minnesota legislature voted to authorize the erection of a Dakota Indian Monument near Morton and appropriated $1,000 for the purpose. (Not yet erected in 1972.)

SIBLEY COUNTY. A granite shaft, dedicated on September 27, 1910, marks the grave of Joseph R. Brown (1805–1870) in Brown's Cemetery at Henderson.

TRAVERSE COUNTY. A bronze tablet placed in Sam Brown Memorial State Wayside, Browns Valley, honors Samuel Brown (1845–1925), the "Paul Revere of the Northwestern frontier" for his valiant ride of April 19, 1866, to warn settlers in Dakota of a suspected Indian raid.

YELLOW MEDICINE COUNTY, in Wood Lake State Wayside southeast of Granite Falls. In 1910 a granite shaft was erected to the memory of seven soldiers who died in the Sioux Uprising battle at this site on September 23, 1862.

Selected Bibliography

The Alexander Ramsey House. [St. Paul: Minnesota Historical Society, 1970.] Pamphlet.

Baker, James H. "The Sources of the Mississippi," in Minnesota Historical Society *Collections.* St. Paul: Minnesota Historical Society, 1894, vol. 6, pp. 1–28.

Bleed, Peter. *The Archaeology of Petaga Point: The Preceramic Component.* St. Paul: Minnesota Historical Society, 1969.

Blegen, Theodore C. "Fort St. Charles and the Northwest Angle," in *Minnesota History,* 18:231–248 (September, 1937).

——— *Minnesota: A History of the State.* [Minneapolis]: University of Minnesota Press, [1963].

——— ed. "The Unfinished Autobiography of Henry Hastings Sibley," in *Minnesota History,* 8:352–359 (December, 1927).

Bridges, Hal. *Iron Millionaire: Life of Charlemagne Tower.* Philadelphia: University of Pennsylvania Press, 1952.

Brower, Jacob V. *Memoirs of Explorations in the Basin of the Mississippi: Kathio.* Vol. 4. St. Paul: [H. L. Collins Company], 1901.

———and D[avid] I. Bushnell. *Memoirs of Explorations in the Basin of the Mississippi: Mille Lac.* Vol. 3. St. Paul: [H. L. Collins Company], 1900.

Brown, Dee A. *Bury My Heart at Wounded Knee: An Indian History of the American West.* New York: Holt, Rinehart and Winston, [1971], pp. 37–65.

Buck, Solon J. "The Story of the Grand Portage," in *Minnesota History,* 5:14–27 (February, 1923).

Burpee, Lawrence J. *The Search for the Western Sea: The Story of the Exploration of North-Western America.* 2 vols. Revised edition, Toronto: The Macmillan Company of Canada, Ltd., 1935.

Carley, Kenneth. *The Sioux Uprising of 1862.* St. Paul: Minnesota Historical Society, 1961.

Carver, Jonathan. *Travels Through the Interior Parts of North America in the Years 1766, 1767, and 1768.* London: The Author, 1778. Reprint edition, Minneapolis: Ross and Haines, 1956.

Clapesattle, Helen B. *The Doctors Mayo.* Minneapolis: The University of Minnesota Press, [1941].

Coddington, Donn M. *Historic Preservation in Minnesota.* [St. Paul]: Minnesota Historical Society, 1971. Report Number 1, 1969–73.

Davidson, Gordon C. *The North West Company.* Berkeley: University of California Press, 1918.

Davis, E[dward] W. *Pioneering With Taconite*. St. Paul: Minnesota Historical Society, 1964.

Davis, John W. *A History of the Pipestone Reservation and Quarry in Minnesota*. [Boulder: The University of Colorado], 1934. Duplicated typescript.

Dean, William B. "A History of the Capitol Buildings of Minnesota. With Some Account of the Struggles for their Location," in Minnesota Historical Society *Collections*. St. Paul: Minnesota Historical Society, 1908, vol. 12, pp. 1–42.

De Kruif, Paul. *Seven Iron Men*. New York: Harcourt, Brace and Company, [1929].

Dobie, John G. *The Itasca Story*. Minneapolis: Ross and Haines, 1959.

Duluth News-Tribune. "Iron for Tomorrow," supplement, August 16, 1953.

Duncan, Kenneth. "The Soudan Mine and Minnesota Iron Co.," in *Skillings' Mining Review* (Duluth), vol. 56, no. 44 (November 4, 1967).

Dunn, James Taylor. *Marine on St. Croix: From Lumber Village to Summer Haven, 1838–1968*. Marine on St. Croix, Minn.: Marine Historical Society, 1968.

_____ *The St. Croix: Midwest Border River*. New York: Holt, Rinehart and Winston, [1965].

Engebretson, Betty L. "The House that Mr. Stevens Built," in *Gopher Historian*, vol. 20, no. 3, pp. 1–7 (Spring, 1966).

Folsom, W[illiam] H.C. *Fifty Years in the Northwest*. [St. Paul]: Pioneer Press Company, 1888.

Folwell, William Watts. *A History of Minnesota*. 4 vols. St. Paul: Minnesota Historical Society, 1921–30. Revised editions, 1956–69.

Gates, Charles M., ed. *Five Fur Traders of the Northwest: Being the Narrative of Peter Pond and the Diaries of John Macdonell, Archibald N. McLeod, Hugh Faries, and Thomas Connor*. [Minneapolis]: Minnesota Society of the Colonial Dames of America, The University of Minnesota Press, 1933. Reprint edition, St. Paul: Minnesota Historical Society, 1965.

_____ "The Lac qui Parle Indian Mission," in *Minnesota History*, 16:133–151 (June, 1935).

Gilman, Rhoda R. and Patricia Smith. "Oliver Hudson Kelley, Minnesota Pioneer, 1849–1868," in *Minnesota History*, 40:330–338 (Fall, 1967).

_____ and June D. Holmquist, eds. *Selections from "Minnesota History": A Fiftieth Anniversary Anthology*. St. Paul: Minnesota Historical Society, 1965.

Glover, Richard G., ed. *David Thompson's Narrative, 1784–1812*. Toronto: Champlain Society, 1962.

Grant, Campbell. *Rock Art of the American Indian*. New York: Crowell, 1967.

Greer, Clifford. *Twelve Poses West: A History of the McGregor Lakes Region and Savanna Portage State Park*. McGregor, Minn.: O. L. Johnson, 1967.

Haines, Lynn and Dora B. *The Lindberghs*. New York: The Vanguard Press, [1931].

Hansen, Marcus L. *Old Fort Snelling, 1819–1858*. Reprint edition, Minneapolis: Ross and Haines, 1958.

Hart, Irving H. "The Old Savanna Portage," in *Minnesota History*, 8:117–139 (June, 1927).

Haugland, John C. "Alexander Ramsey and the Birth of Party Politics in Minnesota," in *Minnesota History*, 39:37–48 (Summer, 1964).

_____ "Politics, Patronage, and Ramsey's Rise to Power, 1861–63," in *Minnesota History*, 37:324–334 (December, 1961).

Hawkinson, Ella. "The Old Crossing Chippewa Treaty and Its Sequel," in *Minnesota History*, 15:282–300 (September, 1934).

Heilbron, Bertha L. *The Thirty-second State: A Pictorial History of Minnesota*. St. Paul: Minnesota Historical Society, 1958. Revised edition, 1966.

Holbert, Sue E. and June D. Holmquist. *A History Tour of 50 Twin City Landmarks*. St. Paul: Minnesota Historical Society, 1966.

Holmquist, June D., Sue E. Holbert, and Dorothy D. Perry, comps. *History Along the Highways: An Official Guide to Minnesota State Markers and Monuments*. St. Paul: Minnesota Historical Society, 1967, and *Supplement*, 1972.

Hughes, Thomas. *Indian Chiefs of Southern Minnesota*. Mankato, Minn.: Free Press Company, [1927].

_____ *Old Traverse des Sioux*. St. Peter, Minn.: Herald Publishing Company, 1929.

Jacobsen, Christina H. *The Burbank-Livingston-Griggs House: Historic Treasure on Summit Avenue*. [St. Paul: Minnesota Historical Society, 1970.] Pamphlet.

Jenks, Albert E. "Minnesota's Browns Valley Man and Associated Burial Artifacts," in American Anthropological Association *Memoirs* (Menasha, Wis.), no. 49, 1937.

_____ *Pleistocene Man in Minnesota: A Fossil Homo Sapiens*. Minneapolis: The University of Minnesota Press, 1936.

_____ "Recent Discoveries in Minnesota Pre-history," in *Minnesota History*, 16:1–21 (March, 1935).

Johnson, Elden. *Prehistoric Peoples of Minnesota*. St. Paul: Minnesota Historical Society, [1969].

Jones, Evan. *Citadel in the Wilderness: The Story of Fort Snelling and the Old Northwest Frontier*. New York: Coward-McCann, 1966.

_____ *The Minnesota: Forgotten River*. New York: Holt, Rinehart and Winston, [1962].

Kane, Lucile M. *The Waterfall That Built a City: The Falls of St. Anthony in Minneapolis*. St. Paul: Minnesota Historical Society, 1966.

Kelley, Oliver H. *Origin and Progress of the Order of the Patrons of Husbandry in the United States: A History from 1866 to 1873*. Philadelphia: J. A. Wangenseller, 1875.

Kellogg, Louise Phelps. "Fort Beauharnois," in *Minnesota History*, 8:232–246 (September, 1927).

Koeper, H[oward] F. *Historic St. Paul Buildings*. St. Paul: St. Paul City Planning Board, 1964. Reprint edition, 1967.

Larson, Bruce L. "Lindbergh's Return to Minnesota, 1927," in *Minnesota History*, 42:141–152 (Winter, 1970).

League of Women Voters of Minnesota. *Indians in Minnesota*. [St. Paul: League of Women Voters of Minnesota, 1971.]

Le Duc, William G. *Minnesota Year Book*, 1851–1853. St. Paul: The Author, [1851–53].

Lindbergh, Charles A. *Boyhood on the Upper Mississippi: A Reminiscent Letter*. St. Paul: Minnesota Historical Society, 1972.

_____ *The Spirit of St. Louis*. New York: Scribner, 1953.

_____ *We*. New York, London: G. P. Putnam's Sons, 1927.

Lindeman, Carla G. and David W. Nystuen. *The Joseph R. Brown House: Final Report on Archaeological Excavations*. St. Paul: Minnesota Historical Society, 1969.

Longyear, Edmund J. *Mesabi Pioneer: Reminiscences of Edmund J. Longyear*. St. Paul: Minnesota Historical Society, 1951.

Macdonald, Dora Mary. *This Is Duluth*. Duluth: [Duluth Board of Education], 1950.

Mackenzie, Alexander. *Voyages from Montreal on the River St. Laurence through the Continent of North America to the Frozen and Pacific Oceans in the Years 1789 and 1793 with a Preliminary Account of the Rise, Progress, and Present State of the Fur Trade of that Country*. London: T. Cadell, Jun. and W. Davies [etc.], 1801.

McNulty, Rev. Ambrose. "The Chapel of St. Paul, and the Beginnings of the Catholic Church in Minnesota," in Minnesota Historical Society *Collections*. St. Paul: Minnesota Historical Society, 1905, vol. 10, pt. 1, pp. 233–245.

Mayer-Oakes, William J., ed. *Life, Land and Water: Proceedings of the 1966 Conference on Environmental Studies of the Glacial Lake Agassiz Region*. Winnipeg: University of Manitoba Press, 1967. Reprint edition, 1969.

Mayo, Charles W. *The Story of My Family and My Career*. Garden City, N.Y.: Doubleday, 1968.

Meyer, Roy W. *History of the Santee Sioux: United States Indian Policy on Trial*. Lincoln: University of Nebraska Press, [1967].

Minnesota Historical Society. *Chippewa and Dakota Indians: A Subject Catalog of Books, Pamphlets, Periodical Articles, and Manuscripts in the Minnesota Historical Society*. Reprint edition, St. Paul: Minnesota Historical Society, 1970.

Minnesota History. Vol. 38, no. 3 (September, 1962). Special Sioux War issue.

Morse, Eric W. *Canoe Routes of the Voyageurs: The Geography and Logistics of the Canadian Fur Trade*. [Ottawa]: Royal Canadian Geographical Society, [1962].

_____ *Fur Trade Canoe Routes of Canada/Then and Now*. [Ottawa: Queen's Printer, 1969.]

Nevins, Allan. *John D. Rockefeller: The Heroic Age of American Enterprise*. 2 vols. New York: C. Scribner's Sons, 1940.

Nute, Grace Lee, ed. "A Description of Northern Minnesota By a Fur-Trader in 1807," in *Minnesota History*, 5:28–39 (February, 1923).

_____ *Rainy River Country: A Brief History of the Region Bordering Minnesota and Ontario*. St. Paul: Minnesota Historical Society, 1950. Reprint edition, 1969.

_____ *The Voyageur*. New York, London: D. Appleton and Company, 1931. Reprint edition, St. Paul: Minnesota Historical Society, 1955.

_____ *The Voyageur's Highway, Minnesota's Border Lake Land*. St. Paul: Minnesota Historical Society, 1941. Reprint edition, 1970.

Nydahl, Theodore L. "The Pipestone Quarry and the Indians," in *Minnesota History*, 31:193–208 (December, 1950).

Nystuen, David W. and Carla G. Lindeman. *The Excavation of Fort Renville: An Archaeological Report*. St. Paul: Minnesota Historical Society, 1969.

Poatgieter, A. Hermina and James Taylor Dunn, eds. *Gopher Reader: Minnesota's Story in Words and Pictures — Selections from the* Gopher Historian. St. Paul: Minnesota Historical Society and Minnesota Statehood Centennial Commission, 1958. Reprint edition, 1966.

Potter, Alan H. "Minnesota's Most Famous Spot: Minnehaha Falls," in *Gopher Historian*, vol. 19, no. 3, pp. 8–13 (Spring, 1965).

Prucha, F[rancis] Paul. "Fort Ripley: The Post and the Military Reservation," in *Minnesota History*, 28:205–224 (September, 1947).

Riggs, Stephen R. "In Memory of Rev. Thos. S. Williamson, M.D.," in Minnesota Historical Society *Collections*. St. Paul: Minnesota Historical Society, 1880, vol. 3, pp. 372–385.

_____ *Mary and I. Forty Years With the Sioux*. Chicago: W. G. Holmes, [1880]. Reprint edition, Boston: Congregational Sunday School and Publishing Society, [1887].

Schoolcraft, Henry R. *Narrative Journal of Travels through the Northwestern Regions of the United States; Extending from Detroit through the Great Chain of American Lakes, to the Sources of the Mississippi River*. Albany: E. and E. Hosford, 1821. Reprint edition, Mentor L. Williams, ed., [East Lansing]: Michigan State College Press, 1953.

_____ *Summary Narrative of an Exploratory Expedition to the Sources of the Mississippi River, in 1820; and Resumed and Completed, by the Discovery of its Origin in Itasca Lake, in 1832*. Philadelphia: Lippincott, Grambo, and Company, 1855.

Schorer, Mark. *Sinclair Lewis, An American Life*. New York: McGraw-Hill, [1961].

Sibley, Henry H. "Memoir of Jean Baptiste Faribault," in Minnesota Historical Society *Collections*. St. Paul: Minnesota Historical Society, 1880, vol. 3, pp. 168–179.

Snow, Dean R. "Petroglyphs of Southern Minnesota," in *Minnesota Archaeologist* (Minneapolis), 24:102–128 (October, 1962).

Stipe, Claude E. *Eastern Dakota Acculturation: The Role of Agents of Culture Change.* [Minneapolis: University of Minnesota], 1968. Duplicated typescript.

Thompson, Erwin N. *Grand Portage: A History of the Sites, People, and Fur Trade.* Washington: U.S. Office of Archeology and Historic Preservation, Division of History, 1969.

Torbert, Donald A. *Significant Architecture in the History of Minneapolis.* Minneapolis: [Minneapolis Urban Design Study], 1969.

United States Supreme Court. *The State of Wisconsin vs. The City of Duluth and the Northern Pacific Railroad Company: Answer of Defendant, City of Duluth.* St. Paul: Ramaley and Cunningham, Printers, [1872]. Title on cover: *Duluth Harbor Case 1872.*

Warren, William W. "History of the Ojibways, Based Upon Traditions and Oral Statements," in Minnesota Historical Society *Collections.* St. Paul: Minnesota Historical Society, 1855, vol. 5, pp. 21–394. Reprinted as *History of the Ojibway Nation*, Minneapolis: Ross and Haines, 1957.

West, Nathaniel. *The Ancestry, Life, and Times of Hon. Henry Hastings Sibley, LL.D.* St. Paul: Pioneer Press Publishing Company, 1889.

The Western Architect (Minneapolis). Vol. 4, no. 10 (October, 1905). Special number on the Minnesota State Capitol Building.

Upham, Warren. *Minnesota Geographic Names: Their Origin and Historic Significance.* Minnesota Historical Society *Collections.* St. Paul: Minnesota Historical Society, 1920, vol. 17. Reprint edition, St. Paul: Minnesota Historical Society, 1969; includes supplementary material.

Wilford, Lloyd A., Elden Johnson, and Joan Vicinus. *Burial Mounds of Central Minnesota.* St. Paul: Minnesota Historical Society, 1969.

Willand, Jon. *Lac qui Parle and the Dakota Mission.* Madison, Minn.: Lac qui Parle County Historical Society, [1964]. Duplicated typescript.

Williams, J. Fletcher. "Henry Hastings Sibley, A Memoir," in Minnesota Historical Society *Collections.* St. Paul: Minnesota Historical Society, 1894, vol. 6, pp. 257–310.

Winchell, Newton H. *The Aborigines in Minnesota: A Report Based on the Collections of Jacob V. Brower, and on the Field Surveys and Notes of Alfred J. Hill and Theodore H. Lewis.* St. Paul: Minnesota Historical Society, 1911.

Ziebarth, Marilyn and Alan Ominsky. *Fort Snelling, Anchor Post of the Northwest.* [St. Paul]: Minnesota Historical Society, 1970.

Index

Fort St. Charles

Grand Mound

Old Crossing Treaty Site

Soudan Mine ★

Mountain Iron Mine ★

Lake Itasca

Duluth Ship Canal
Minnesota Point Lighthouse ☆

Savanna Portage ★

St. Louis Portage ★

Minnesota Man ★

Old Crow Wing ☆

Mille Lacs Indian Museum ★

Fort Ripley ★

Connor's Fur Post ★

Lindbergh House ★

Sinclair Lewis Boyhood Home ★

Folsom House ★

Browns Valley Man ★

Kelley Farm ★

Marine on St. Croix ★

Lac qui Parle Mission ★

Gideon Markers

Stillwater ★

Upper Sioux Agency ★

J. R. Brown House ☆

Grimm Farm ★

TWIN CITIES SITES ★

Fort Beauharnois ★

Lower Sioux Agency ★

Fort Ridgely ★

Traverse des Sioux ★

Mayo House ★

Pipestone National Monument ★

Jeffers Petroglyphs ★

Mayo Clinic ★
Mayowood